SHAKESPEARE'S ACCENTS

Voices and accents are increasingly perceived as central markers of identity in Shakespearean performance. This book presents a history of the reception of Shakespeare on the English stage with a focus on the vocal dimensions of theatrical performance. The chapters identify key moments when English accents have caused controversy, if not public outrage. Sonia Massai examines the cultural connotations associated with different accents and how accents have catalysed concerns about national, regional and social identities that are (re) constituted in and through Shakespearean performance. She argues that theatre makers and reformers, elocutionists and historical linguists, as well as directors, actors and producers, have all had a major impact on how accents have evolved and changed on the Shakespearean stage over the last four hundred years. This fascinating book offers a rich historical survey alongside close performance analysis.

SONIA MASSAI is Professor of Shakespeare Studies at King's College London and has published widely on the history of the transmission of Shakespeare on the stage and on the page. Her publications include *World-Wide Shakespeares: Local Appropriations in Film and Performance* (2005), *Shakespeare and the Rise of the Editor* (Cambridge University Press, 2007), *Shakespeare and Textual Studies* (Cambridge University Press, 2015), *Ivo van Hove: from Shakespeare to David Bowie* (2018), and critical editions of John Ford's *'Tis Pity She's a Whore* (2011) and *The Paratexts in English Printed Drama to 1642* (Cambridge University Press, 2014).

SHAKESPEARE'S ACCENTS

Voicing Identity in Performance

SONIA MASSAI

King's College London

CAMBRIDGE
UNIVERSITY PRESS

CAMBRIDGE
UNIVERSITY PRESS

University Printing House, Cambridge CB2 8BS, United Kingdom

One Liberty Plaza, 20th Floor, New York, NY 10006, USA

477 Williamstown Road, Port Melbourne, VIC 3207, Australia

314–321, 3rd Floor, Plot 3, Splendor Forum, Jasola District Centre, New Delhi – 110025, India

79 Anson Road, #06–04/06, Singapore 079906

Cambridge University Press is part of the University of Cambridge.

It furthers the University's mission by disseminating knowledge in the pursuit of education, learning, and research at the highest international levels of excellence.

www.cambridge.org
Information on this title: www.cambridge.org/9781108429627
DOI: 10.1017/9781108571739

First published 2020

Printed in the United Kingdom by TJ International Ltd, Padstow Cornwall

A catalogue record for this publication is available from the British Library.

ISBN 978-1-108-42962-7 Hardback

To Denton Chikura, Tonderai Munyevu and Arne Pohlmeier,
sine qua non.

Contents

Illustrations

Acknowledgements

Two Gents Productions have been the main source of inspiration for this book. I first met Denton Chikura, Tonderai Munyevu and Arne Pohlmeier in 2008. Their very first production, *Vakomana Vaviri ve Zimbabwe*, or 'what happens when Shakespeare's *The Two Gentlemen of Verona* meets South African township theatre', quite literally blew me away. I had not until then, and I have not since then, come across theatre artists who work as creatively and joyfully with Shakespeare. They infuse Shakespeare's language with Zimbabwean sonorities, with snippets of Shona, with humour, improvisation, and, of course, with Zimbabwean accents. By 2008, I had already started to teach and write about 'Global Shakespeare', but watching them, and listening to them, alerted me to the acoustic richness of Shakespeare's language, when Shakespeare's language is not delivered in English Standard Pronunciation. 'What is in an accent?' – this book attempts to answer this question by telling the story of a very exciting journey of discovery, which starts in the present, thanks to the innovative work of companies like Two Gents Productions.

Sarah Stanton, former commissioning editor at Cambridge University Press, did not only support my decision to extend my journey by stepping back in time, but advised on structure and asked searching questions about the methodological challenges faced by scholars interested in voices that were long gone before Thomas Edison invented the phonograph in 1877. Other scholars invested in acoustic archaeology had paved the way, of course, and I found their work helpful and inspiring. Among them, I am particularly indebted to Gina Bloom, Wes Folkerth and Bruce R. Smith. The anonymous readers who supported the publication of this book also made hugely generous suggestions: it was one of the two readers who, for example, recommended that the book should travel back in time, from the present to Shakespeare's own time, rather than vice versa. I agreed instantly that allowing living voices to be heard first would help me establish how we got to speak and hear Shakespeare the way we do now.

Other colleagues with an expertise in the different areas covered by this book have helped along the way. Eric Rasmussen, who advised as dramaturg on the Original Pronunciation production of *Hamlet* directed by Rob Gardner for the Nevada Repertory Company at the University of Nevada, talked me through how he first proposed this project to David and Ben Crystal, how the actors were voice coached, and how audiences responded to Original Pronunciation. Jonathan Hope kindly discussed the finer points of his work on early modern socio-historical linguistics with me, and Susan Bennett has continued to inspire my curiosity in audiences, past and present, and how 'culturally constituted horizons of expectations' affect how voices are heard and decoded.

I am also hugely grateful to my wonderful research assistants. Rowena Hawkins was awarded a King's College London Undergraduate Research Fellowship in 2015, which allowed her to help me do archival research at the Shakespeare Birthplace Trust, in Stratford-upon-Avon, and the LIFT Archive held in the Special Collections at the University Library at Goldsmiths, University of London. Miranda Fay Thomas also worked as my research assistant in 2015, when she helped me identify non-standard accents in productions staged at the National Theatre, by patiently trawling through the records held at the National Theatre Archive. Romola Nuttall assisted with indexing, providing much welcome support in the final stages of production.

Last, but not least, my thanks to Emily Hockley, who kindly adopted this project when Sarah Stanton retired from the Press; to Tim Mason, Carrie Parkinson and Natasha Burton, Editorial Assistants for Literature at Cambridge; to my copy-editor, Barbara Wilson, to Sarah Lambert, Content Manager at the Press, and to Ishwarya Mathavan, Project Manager at SPi Content Solutions; to the curators in the Listening Services at the British Library, in the Manuscript Collections at the University Library in Cambridge, and the librarians at Christ Church College, Oxford; to the BBC and the estates of Bernard Miles and Mary Hope Allen, namely Ben Frow and Julia Hope-Manheim, for kindly supporting my request to access and reproduce photographic and archival materials included in this book; to Hugh Quarshie, Lucian Msamati and the Royal Shakespeare Company, and to Ludovic des Cognets, for granting permission to reproduce the production photos on the front and back cover of the book.

Abbreviations and Conventions

Quotations from Shakespeare's works are referenced to *The Arden Shakespeare: Complete Works*, Revised Edition, ed. by Richard Proudfoot, Ann Thompson and David Scott Kastan (London: Bloomsbury, 2011).

Quotations from Shakespeare and other early modern texts in Chapter 4 are from the earliest printed or manuscript editions listed in the Bibliography. The early modern spelling in these editions preserves the morphological and phonetic features associated with the dialects and variations, which I discuss in detail in this chapter. Speech headings are expanded and original lineation is preserved only when the quoted extracts are in verse. The earliest printed editions are identified by date of publication and STC or WING numbers, and quotations from these editions are located by signatures and line numbers.

The following abbreviations have been used throughout the book, including its footnotes, preliminaries and bibliography:

Anon.	Anonymous
BAME	Black, Asian and Minority Ethnic
BBC	British Broadcasting Corporation
Bite	Barbican International Theatre Events
CWS	The Complete Works Season (2006–2007)
ed.	Editor
EDD	*The English Dialect Dictionary*, compiled by Joseph Wright (1898)
eds.	Editors
G2G	The Globe to Globe 2012 Festival
l.	line
ll.	lines
NSE	Non-Standard English
NT	The Royal National Theatre, London
ODNB	*The Oxford Dictionary of National Biography*

OED	*The Oxford English Dictionary*
OP	Original Pronunciation
RP	Received Pronunciation
RSC	The Royal Shakespeare Company
STC	The Short-Title Catalogue
StP	Standard Pronunciation
TLN	Through Line Number, based on Charlton Hinman's *The Norton Facsimile: The First Folio of Shakespeare* (New York: Norton, 1968)
Trans.	Translator
TwoGents	Two Gentlemen Productions
Vol.	Volume
Vols.	Volumes
WING	Donald Wing, ed., *Short-Title Catalogue of Books Printed in England, Scotland, Ireland, Wales, and British America and of English Books Printed in other Countries: 1641–1700*, 3 vols (New York: Columbia University Press, 1945–51)
WSF	The World Shakespeare Festival (2012)

Introduction

English accents are powerful markers of national and social identity. The standard of what constitutes an accurate or a desirable accent of course changes over time, despite the tendency among speakers to assume that their attitudes to accents are natural, innate and ultimately ahistorical. However, the connotations of accents, that is how accents define speakers, are as powerful today as they have been ever since the word 'accent' acquired its current meaning as 'a way of pronouncing a language that is distinctive to a country, area, social class, or individual' (*OED, n.* 7a).[1] The earliest examples quoted in the *OED* are predictably from Shakespeare, although cutting remarks about uncouth English accents date as far back as Chaucer.[2] 'Your accent is something finer than you could purchase in so removed a dwelling' (3.2.334–5),[3] says Orlando to Rosalind in *As You Like It*, implying that a rural accent is not as clear or as sophisticated as a courtly one. National accents are similarly the subject of humorous mockery in Shakespeare: in *The Reign of King Edward III*, a play now partly attributed to Shakespeare, the king reports how the Countess of Salisbury, besieged by the Scots, imitated their 'broad' speech as an act of defiance (2.195) and as a way of showing her natural superiority over her 'barbarous' enemies (2.201).[4] 'Broad' was derogatory then as it is today, while 'barbarous' is used in its original, etymological sense of '"not Latin nor Greek" and therefore "pertaining to those outside the Roman empire" …, hence "uncivilized and uncultured"'(*OED, adj* 1–3).

Accents are especially significant in relation to Shakespeare, because of the role that Shakespeare has played as England's 'National Poet' in the establishment of a Standard English pronunciation (henceforth StP) since

---

[1] For other meanings of the word 'accent' in the early modern period, see, for example, Hope 2010: 99–105.
[2] Aleyn and John have a Northeastern inflection in 'The Reeve's Tale'.
[3] All quotations from Shakespeare's works, unless otherwise specified, are from Proudfoot et al., 2011.
[4] Quotations from *The Reign of King Edward III* are from Proudfoot and Bennett, 2017.

the mid-eighteenth century. Efforts to standardize English pronunciation went hand in hand with the rise of English as the language of Empire.[5] What is less well known is the recurrent alignment between those who championed a revival of Shakespeare on stage and those who advocated the need for a 'supra-regional standard' of pronunciation for all (Mugglestone 2007: 13). A good example is Thomas Sheridan (1719?–1788), the father of Richard Sheridan and the author of *A General Dictionary of the English Language* (1780), one of the earliest dictionaries of English Standard pronunciation. Sheridan also ensured the regular programming of Shakespeare's plays while he was stage manager at the Smock Alley Theatre in Dublin between the mid-1740s and the mid-1750s.[6] The accent most readily associated with correctness and distinction in England since then, and later known as Received Pronunciation (henceforth RP), has recently started to decline, acquiring negative connotations of snobbishness and elitism.[7] However, the use of anything but an educated, Southern accent is still problematic when deployed on the Shakespearean stage.

In 2011, in an otherwise generous review of Roxana Silbert's production of *Measure for Measure* for the Royal Shakespeare Company (henceforth RSC), Ian Shuttleworth, for example, critiqued Jodie McNee's Isabella for sounding 'impassioned (and Liverpudlian)' and for 'lack[ing] much of either the religious or the sexual magnetism required' by the role (2011a). It is remarkable that, as recently as 2011, Shuttleworth regarded McNee's *accent* as an inappropriate vehicle to convey the psychological,

---

[5] Representative of such efforts is James Buchanan's 1766 pamphlet 'An Essay towards Establishing a Standard for an Elegant and Uniform Pronunciation of the English Language *throughout the British Dominions*, and Practised by the Most Learned and Polite Speakers' (my emphasis). As late as 1917, in his preface to Daniel Jones's *English Pronouncing Dictionary*, linguist and educationist Walter Ripman stressed how, 'when a language is spread as widely over the world as ours is, a generally recognized form of speech is not less desirable than a common literary language' (v).

[6] While Sheridan was stage manager at the Smock Alley Theatre, 43 out of the 145 productions staged during the 1749–50 season were Shakespeare's plays (Sheldon 1967: 153). Writing about 'the intimate connection between ... the move towards the orthoepical doctrine and prescription that marks lexicography after Dr Johnson ... and the theatre', Peter Holland gives further examples of mid-eighteenth century orthoepists who were connected to the revival of Shakespeare on stage, including William Kenrick, who had written *Falstaff's Wedding* (1766), a sequel to *2 Henry IV*, and aspired to edit Shakespeare, as suggested by his 1765 critique of Johnson's edition (*A Review*), and John Walker (1732–1807), who had acted at Drury Lane before he started a school of elocution and published his *Critical Pronouncing Dictionary and Expositor of the English Language* in 1791 (2007: 253–6).

[7] By the 1970s, RP was negatively associated with privilege, arrogance and social exclusivity (see, for example, Gimson 1970). By the turn of the century, Nikolas Coupland noted that it was 'no longer permitted in British Society to be seen to discriminate against someone on the basis of their accent' (quoted in Trudgill 2002: 176). By the same token, 'some of the strongest sanctions [were] exercised against people who [were] perceived as being "posh" and "snobbish"' (Trudgill 2002: 176).

personal and ethical qualities associated with Isabella's character. More generally, though, and despite a lingering prejudice against marked voices in Shakespearean performance, a veritable sea change is taking place, both on mainstream and fringe, national and regional stages, where non-standard accents are starting to inform casting and directorial decisions. As Chapter 1 shows, accents are now increasingly being used, along with other crucial markers of social identity, like race and gender, in order to activate a different interpretation of the fictive worlds of the plays and to challenge a traditional alignment of Shakespeare with cultural elitism.

However, while a considerable amount of attention has been paid to the benefits and challenges of unconventional race and gender casting,[8] there has been no sustained attempt to gauge the impact of marked voices on the production and reception of Shakespeare in performance. The topic is therefore ripe for further exploration and this study, which offers the first book-length critical analysis of the use and connotations of accents in Shakespearean performance over the last four hundred years, builds on the growing interest in the voice in several disciplines, ranging from philosophy to sociolinguists, from historical phonology to theatre and performance studies.

§

The 'performative turn' that took place within the humanities in the second half of the twentieth century directed attention towards the 'felt experience of the voice',[9] which began to be understood not as a mere carrier or vehicle, but as a central constituent element of speech. Though focusing primarily on the singing voice, Roland Barthes wrote about the voice as having its own 'grain', which is produced by the material body as it speaks its own mother tongue (1982 [1977]: 182). By writing about 'the body of the voice' (1982 [1977]: 188), Barthes shifted critical interest from the semantic to the vocalic qualities of speech. More recent philosophers of the voice have continued to highlight the role of the material attributes of the voice – including intonation, pitch, rhythm and accent – in determining how speech is produced, heard and decoded. Giorgio Agamben has, for example, drawn attention to 'that which one necessarily says without

---

[8] See, for example, Thompson (2006) and Bulman (2008).

[9] I borrow this suggestive phrase from Katie Adkison's 'Singularity and Bare Voice: The Politics of Vocal Representation in *Coriolanus*', a paper discussed as part of the 'Locating (And Dislocating) Voices in Shakespeare' seminar, led by Bruce R. Smith at the Shakespeare Association of America conference in Los Angeles in March 2018.

knowing', that is to how the interplay between the vocalic and the semantic produces signification (1991: 89). Similarly inspiring and suggestive is Adriana Cavarero's insistence that we consider not only the material qualities of the voice, but also its sociability, by establishing how those qualities are heard and decoded by other speakers. In order for a voice to register as such, as opposed to mere noise, an embodied speaker needs to connect with an embodied listener, making the production and reception of the spoken word intrinsically relational and inevitably political activities. In other words, when considering speech, we need to be mindful not only of what is being said, but also by whom, how and under what circumstances. Cavarero's main focus on vocality, that is 'the whole of the activities and values that belong to the voice as such, independently of language' (2005: 12), makes her work less directly relevant to my own interest in how accent affects the production and reception of (Shakespearean) meaning on stage. Cavarero also stops short of considering how unique speakers and listeners 'appear to each other in the first place' (Burgess and Murray 2006: 169), that is how context informs how speech is produced, heard and decoded. Conversely, I aim specifically to reconstruct the historical contexts within which marked voices have been deployed on the Shakespearean stage and how these contexts have affected the way in which these voices have been interpreted over time.

Theatre studies have started to respond to the need to historicize the auditory dimensions of speech. In his book on *Dramatic Theories of Voice in the Twentieth Century*, Andrew Kimbrough takes as his starting point the assumption that '[t]here is more to language than what meets the eye, so to speak', and celebrates the fact that 'various disciplines in the twentieth century went to the ear and the body to prove it' (2010: 12):

> The tradition of western philosophy generally has been less concerned with individuals and the circumstances of their embodiment than with universals, the abstract, and at times, the metaphysical. A concrete and individual voice, replete with gender, ethnicity, age, and dialect, has little room within this frame. Therefore, . . . when the unique, resonant, and particular human voice surfaces and makes itself heard, it unhinges the scaffolding upon which visualist philosophy is secured. (2010: 7)

Kimbrough then proceeds to identify and discuss twentieth-century experimental theatre directors and theorists, including Antonin Artaud, Jerzy Grotowski, Peter Brook, and Richard Schechner, and avant-garde performers and collectives, such as Robert Wilson, Richard Foreman,

Karen Finley, Laurie Anderson and the Wooster Group, who promoted the 'aesthetic presentation of the human voice'. His analysis of the work of these artists shows how 'ideality', including 'our regard of ourselves' or 'the contents of thought', is made present 'in performance through vocalization' (2010: 260, 22). Kimbrough however regrets that an adequate level of theorization and historicization has not as yet matched such a rich range of practices:

> Until recently, theatre scholarship focused almost exclusively on the visual artifact: the body, the mise-en-scène, and the dramatic text. A handful of articles on the voice serve as exceptions, but the exceptions tend to suffer because, as a discipline, we have yet to create a critical language adequate to address the voice. (2010: 2)

To sum up, at least according to Kimbrough, scholarship is currently lagging behind theatrical practices, which effectively foreground the material, vocal and aesthetic qualities of the voice and their impact on the modulation of (fictive) identities.

This blind spot in contemporary theatre studies does not seem to have affected work specifically focused on the place of the voice on the early modern stage, which has in fact proved to be a particularly exciting and fast-developing area of research interest. In *The Acoustic World of Early Modern England*, Bruce R. Smith has, for example, reconstructed 'a world view centered on sound', by highlighting how 'one of the ways in which early modern subjects achieved selfhood [was] through speech' (1999: 165). When dealing with 'the auditory field of the play', Smith privileges the impact of the position of the actors and how their voices projected and resonated within the physical space defined by the architecture of an early modern amphitheatre, or indoor theatre:

> Instead of characters, we might more accurately talk about the "persons" of the play. Not only is "person" the term used by early modern witnesses themselves; it also captures the double sense of person as a body (the actor's) and a voice (. . . from per-sonare, "to sound through"). (1999: 280)

Despite the lack of sound recordings from the period, Smith shows that an archaeological recovery of sound, though based on written archival sources, is not only possible but that it can help us understand how the act of voicing and hearing constituted speakers and listeners into socially and historically defined 'acoustic communities' (1999: 166). Smith draws attention to a fascinating range of 'dialects, varieties, registers, and codes' . . . as well as 'means of communication' beyond 'phonemic speech . . . includ[ing] singing, whistling, drumming, horn calling' and, ultimately, 'whatever sound-making keeps the community in aural contact with one another' (1999: 43). Smith however does not consider national, regional or class accents and how they may have impacted on the delivery and decoding of Shakespeare's plays as originally performed on the early modern stage.

Similarly interested in how listeners of Shakespeare as performed on the early modern stage constituted and re-constituted themselves into interpretative communities is Wes Folkerth's book, *The Sound of Shakespeare*. Particularly useful is Folkerth's insight according to which sound is 'closely linked to ideas about identity and the representation of identity in the period . . . [b]ecause [it] was thought to communicate and commingle with the spiritual essences of people and objects' (2002: 56). Although invested in establishing how the soundscape of a Shakespearean play 'would have been received by people who heard and understood [it] in specific contexts, with early modern ears' (2002: 9), Folkerth, like Smith, overlooks accents as a determinant of early modern subjectivites. Also groundbreaking in terms of its stated commitment to the 'historicization of the voice' is Gina Bloom's *Voice in Motion: Staging Gender, Shaping Sound*, where she establishes how the voice, as opposed to the logocentric quality of regulated speech, was believed to possess a specific type of volatile and unruly agency and to have a powerful, physical impact on the listeners. Once again, though, Bloom focuses on exploring the gender implications of early modern philosophies of the voice, but she does not address the use of dialect or accents in early modern drama, because neither dialect nor accent is directly relevant to her gender-focused approach.

And yet accents need to be carefully considered to understand how sound constituted early modern speakers and listeners, because they functioned as prime markers of early modern (dramatic) subjectivities, as the extracts discussed in the next section suggest. Accents, as much as the other material features of the early modern voices addressed by theatre historians so far, need to be studied in the specific cultural, historical and linguistic contexts in which they were originally spoken, heard and decoded. While historical phonetics has made the most significant contribution to date to our understanding of early modern spoken English, it has also highlighted important methodological challenges. The next section therefore goes on to show how powerfully connotative English accents were on the early modern stage and how I have approached the methodological challenges associated with an historically informed analysis of voices that have long gone, leaving 'not a rack behind'.

§

In Brome's *The English Moor* (1659, WING B4872), Mandeville Quicksands teases Phillis Winloss, saying 'O th'art a Norfolk woman (cry thee mercy) / Where Maids are Mothers, and Mothers are Maids' (C6, 23–4). These punning lines suggest that Brome's audience would have recognized 'modder' as a regional variant associated with East Anglia, meaning 'a girl or young woman' or 'a girl just growing into womanhood'.[10] The pun is particularly funny and salacious in the context of this short exchange because Phillis introduces herself to Quicksands as 'a Mother that do lack a service'; but Quicksands initially fails to decode her regional use of the word 'mother/modder' and promptly rejects her: 'You have said enough. I'le entertain no Mothers. / A good Maid servant, knew I where to find one' (C6, 17–18). Seemingly outraged, Phillis retorts: 'He is a knave, and like your worship, that / Dares say I am no Maid' (C6, 19–20).

What makes this exchange even funnier, of course, is the fact that Phillis is not a maid and that she not from Norfolk! Phillis is in fact the spirited and resourceful daughter of Winloss, a gentleman who, having lost all his money in lawsuits brought against him by two other gentlemen, Meanwell and Rashley, has been forced to leave the country to seek his fortune overseas. Left to fend for herself, Phillis ends up winning back the gallant Nathaniel Baneless, who has seduced and abandoned her, mostly through her ability to look and sound other than who she is: at key moments in the play she dons disguises and modulates her voice, most notably when she imitates the Norfolk regional variation at the core of this exchange with Quicksands and when she adopts a 'blackface' dialect to personate a Moor in 4.4.[11] Arguably her 'blackface' speech amounts to little more than a crude stage dialect, even in a play which is rightly celebrated for presenting interestingly 'inconsistent discourses about race' (Steggle 2004: 128), and at a time 'when London supported a growing and, for the moment, increasingly tolerated black community' (Steggle, 'Introduction'). But her sophisticated grasp of a regional accent is remarkable and her ability to imitate it helps her protect her identity and get a job: after initially spurning Phillis, Quicksands is attracted by the 'wholesomeness' of her

---

[10] 'modder, n. α. Etymology: Of uncertain origin; Etymon: mother *n.1*; origin uncertain; perhaps originally a variant of mother (*OED, n.1*); see also *EDD*: 'modder, Yks. [Yorkshire] Glo. [Gloucestershire] Hrt. [Hertfordshire] eAn. [East Anglia] Wil. [Wiltshire]; also mauther w.Yks. [West Yorkshire], e.An. Ess. [Essex] Wil.; morther Suf. [Suffolk]; and in forms maadhur Ess.; modder Cmb. [Cambridgeshire] Nr. [Norfolk] Suf. Ess.; modhdher e.An.; modher Cmb. Nrf. Suf. Ess.; motha Glo'.

[11] Examples of Phillis's blackface dialect include 'But howa can ita be donea' and 'I will doa my besta' (E4, 9; 13).

regionally inflected speech and mimics it in the aside that concludes this exchange: 'This innocent countrey Mother takes me. / Her looks speak Wholesomness' (C6v, 21–2).

The bawdy quality of the 'mawther (modder)/mother' regional pun is heightened by further wordplay triggered by Phillis's association with Norfolk and East Anglia more generally.

QUICKSANDS	But where about in *Norfolk* wert thou bred?
PHILLIS	At *Thripperstown* Sir, near the City of *Norwich*.
QUICKSANDS	Where they live much by spinning with the Rocks?
PHILLIS	Thripping, they call it, Sir.

(C6, 33–6)

Thripperstown is a fictional location that serves a dual purpose here. On a purely linguistic level, it allows Phillis to pun on the meaning of 'thripping' as 'spinning' (*OED*, v.3) and as the jerking of thumb and fingers, as they pull on the yarn (*OED*, v.2), with its obvious sexual undertones.[12] On a more contextual level, it reminds the audience of the thriving spinning industry in East Anglia, which, as Matthew Steggle has pointed out, 'creat[ed] the exports . . . enabl[ed] by imports from Africa'. The regional accent used by Phillis, along with references to the local economy of the region, allows Brome to hint at the origin of the slaving trade, a concern which, still according to Steggle, is central to the play as whole ('Introduction'). Regional variation is therefore a key dramatic feature in this exchange and the sustained punning linked to it depends entirely on the assumption that early modern audiences would recognize it and that they would be alert to its connotations, which are not generically rustic but specifically associated with a region and its local economy.

This example shows that regional dialect and phonetic variation were used on the early modern stage to achieve specific and nuanced dramatic effects. As Manfred Görlach has put it, if it is true that 'the loss of regional features in the writing of "provincials" was so rapid in the fifteenth century that no consistent dialect, or even regional characteristics that would allow attribution to a particular place, are normally found in written evidence', the sporadic use of dialect is all the more significant, because 'whenever a sixteenth- to eighteenth-century writer chose to use [it], this . . . [was] due to a conscious decision to aim for a special effect' (1999: 506). By and

---

[12] The same pun is used later in the play in 4.5, when Arnold says of Quicksands's illegitimate and mentally disabled child, Timsy, that 'he has learn'd to thrip among the Mothers; / But . . . to do more harm than good by't', because 'by his cunning at the Rock, / And twirling of his spindle on the Thrip-skins, / He has fetch'd up the bellies of sixteen / Of his Thrip-sisters' (E5, 12–13; 17–20).

large, though, historical linguists and phoneticians have tended to disagree about the significance and social connotations attached to English accents as used by early modern writers. Paula Blank has for example argued that, generally speaking, '[early modern] authors borrow accents, briefly, to serve their turn' and that the regionally or class inflected voices reproduced in their work were constructs that 'had, finally, nothing to do with the "people" at all' (1996: 99). Writing more specifically about the early modern stage, Jonathan Hope has similarly argued that accents were 'non-realist symbols of identity' (2010: 112). However, what the Brome extract above shows is that, although the connotations of stage accents may not have mapped precisely on how accents were used and heard off stage, they signified in highly specific, local ways that were recognizable both within the fictive world of the play and among members of its original audience.

Also worth stressing is how this diversity of views stems first and foremost from practical methodological challenges that apply more generally to the study of early modern voices, both on and off stage. As Susan Fitzmaurice and Jeremy Smith explain,

> [s]tudents of the history of English pronunciation have a major problem ...: for the most part, they have to approach their subject indirectly. Until the end of the nineteenth century, there are no recordings of speech, and for that reason scholars depend on comments of contemporaries (often frustratingly vague) on the analysis of spelling or verse or on reconstruction, and none of these resources is problem-free. We have evidence, but interpreting that evidence is a challenging enterprise. (2012: 33)

Even so, the phonetic spelling used in early modern manuscripts and printed texts[13] and the writings by early modern spelling reformers, who lamented the widening gap between written and spoken English,[14] provide enough evidence to establish that early modern English was characterized by great acoustic diversity. As Hope has pointed out, 'current spoken English retains at least as much variation as would have been found in early modern spoken English'. Besides, as Hope goes on to remind us, acoustic diversity in the early modern period was also amplified by the Great Vowel Shift, which 'increased the variety of possible pronunciations'

---

[13] By phonetic spelling, phoneticians mean a type of spelling that, at a time when orthography had not become fully standardized, reflected pronunciation rather than a conventionally sanctioned written form.

[14] Among them, the most prominent were Thomas Smith (1513–1577), Jon Hart (c. 1501–1574), William Bullokar (c. 1531–1609), Richard Mulcaster (1531/2–1611), George Puttenham (1529–1590/91), Robert Cawdrey (1537/8?–d. in or after 1604) and Alexander Gill (1565–1635).

at a time when changing sounds 'did not all move together, and . . . did not move at the same time for all speakers' (1999: 251).

The extent to which acoustic diversity defined speakers in terms of their nationality, social status and class, on and off the early modern stage, remains, however, a moot question. As the extracts from Brome above show, accents could be used to great dramatic effect. But the frequency with which accents were used on the early modern stage is harder to establish, because, unlike other literary forms, the oral dimension of drama was mostly lost, as plays were transmitted from performance into print. Also challenging is deciding how early modern listeners heard and decoded national, regional and class accents. What did it mean for an early modern English speaker to sound like a Northerner or a Scot; or, even more to the point, what did it mean for an early modern actor (or the fictive character an early modern actor personated) to sound like a Northerner or a Scot on the Shakespearean stage? How did the English spoken by the educated and uneducated inhabitants of the Capital measure up against the regional dialects and accents associated with rural elites or the English spoken by their servants or local labourers? And how did early modern audiences react to these regional and class accents, when they were used on the Shakespearean stage?

While discussing the methodological challenges involved in answering these questions, Hope sounds an important cautionary note about the risk of imposing our own parameters of acoustic decorum onto a period that predated the emergence of a non-regional standard associated with well-educated, elite speakers. He therefore takes his distance from other recent scholars, who have detected an emergent standard associated with London and the Court in Shakespeare's time. As Hope puts it, '[t]here [was] no sense of a fine-grained social order associated with regional dialects, nor of an upper / lower class split' (2008: 219–220). Other scholars however believe that broad, if not fine-grained, associations of national, regional and class variations with varying levels of prestige (or lack therefore) cannot easily be discounted. Among them, Charles Laurence Barber, for example, queried Börje Holmberg's view that social accents had no role to play in Shakespeare's England, by pointing out how difficult it is to explain away references by sixteenth- and seventeenth-century authors to 'vulgar pronunciations' (1986: 178 [288]).[15]

---

[15] Even Barber, though, cautions us from assuming that regional accents would automatically be negatively connotated as uncouth and lower status, as it would become the case after the rise of StP in the eighteenth century (see Barber 1997). Among the scholars who detect the emergence of a prestige accent in Shakespeare's time, see, for example, Dobson 1968 and Fox 2000.

A survey of scholarly research into early modern accents to date shows that the same diversity of views about the relative frequency and significance of early modern accents can also be detected among earlier historical linguists, starting from the rise of a scholarly interest in earlier forms of English pronunciation in the mid-nineteenth century. This long-standing diversity of views clearly stems from the problematic nature of the available evidence, as explained above. However, it would also seem to originate from how scholars feel about the desirability of StP versus regional and class variations in their own time. While reviewing the work of their early modern spelling reformers, nineteenth- and early to mid-twentieth-century phoneticians detected standards of pronunciations that seem suspiciously close to their own.

Among them, Alexander John Ellis (1814–1890) and Helge Kökeritz (1902–1964) aligned Shakespeare, both as originally pronounced on the early modern stage and as they thought Shakespeare should be performed in their own time, with the speech of the educated elites. Ellis, for example, posited that 'in Shakspere's [sic] time ... dramatic authors and actors rather affected the newest [phonetic] habits of the court'. He also believed that 'modern utterance' only marginally affected the sound of Shakespeare's language when read aloud or performed, because, 'although archaic enough in structure', it was 'familiar ... from the constant habit of reading his plays' (1869–89 3: 918, 984). The link Ellis detected between the phonetic habits of the Elizabethan and Jacobean court and the way in which Shakespeare was still being read and performed in his own time in turn persuaded him that StP was still best suited for the delivery of Shakespeare's lines on the contemporary stage. Even Ellis, who had written the first extensive study in English historical phonology, his five-volume *On Early English Pronunciation* (1869–1889), devising a sophisticated notation system that predated the International Phonetic Alphabet (IPA), and who had founded the English Dialect Society in 1973 (MacMahon), showed no tolerance towards the idea that there was a place for phonetic variation on the nineteenth-century Shakespearean stage. Like eighteenth-century orthoepists, who had championed the emergence of a national standard and the revival of Shakespeare in performance, Ellis also believed that the standard for a correct pronunciation of English should be determined by 'the norm unconsciously followed by persons who, by rank or education, ha[d] most right to establish the custom of speech' (1869–89 2: 624). Ellis went as far as to argue that StP was crucial to the well-being not only of the working classes, whose living conditions could be improved by raising levels of linguistic competence, but of the nation as a whole:

> Is ... standard pronunciation desirable? The linguist and philologist may perhaps sigh over this unnatural and inorganic orthoepic treatment of language. For one, the present writer could not suppress a feeling of regret. But the well-being of our race points in another direction. Recognizing the extreme importance of facilitating intercourse between man and man, we should feel not double, and allow no sentimental regrets to interfere with the establishment of something approaching to a general system of pronouncing, by means of a general system of indicating our pronunciation in writing. (1869–89 2: 630)

The linguist and the philologist in Ellis, who was interested in historical and regional variations, bowed to the orthoepist's imperative to enforce a standard of pronunciation determined by rank and education, in order to ensure the well-being of a nation, whose language extended across class and regional divisions, as well as national borders throughout the Empire.

The prevailing alignment of Shakespeare with StP continued to affect the work of historical phoneticians as late as the mid-1950s. Helge Kökeritz, for example, in his *Shakespeare's Pronunciation* (1953), confidently stated that, 'though there is no record of the existence of a stage pronunciation at the time, we can hardly be wrong in assuming that the actors endeavoured to conform to some kind of standard pronunciation and that this was the colloquial type of speech used in polite circles' (4). Roughly three decades later, Kökeritz was criticized by Fausto Cercignani, in his *Shakespeare's Works and Elizabethan Pronunciation* (1981), for over-relying on internal evidence, that is phonetic spelling and rhyming patterns, and for overlooking key external evidence, including the work of early modern spelling reformers. Cercignani argued instead that the English spoken by Shakespeare and his contemporaries departed more radically from modern English than previously assumed, and that different connotations attached to its spoken variations.

Other twentieth-century scholars have argued that standards of pronunciation have changed dramatically since Shakespeare's time and that early modern accents carried different connotations from modern ones, both on and off the stage. These scholars believe that early modern accents and their connotations need to be studied and understood in their own right. However, even scholars who are interested in reconstructing early modern pronunciation, or, as it has become more widely known, early modern original pronunciation (henceforth OP), disagree about the reasons why OP has intrinsic interest value for scholars and theatre practitioners alike.

Some scholars regard OP as lending authenticity to the delivery of Shakespeare's lines on stage and institutional authority to the discipline of historical phonology more generally. Daniel Jones, for example, pioneered Shakespeare in OP in the early twentieth century. However, he did so strictly within academic circles and in order to garner support for his plans to establish a centre for (historical) phonology at University College London. Conversely, Jones the orthoepist, somewhat like Ellis, had very strict views about the need for speakers to acquire and use StP. In the preface to his book *The Pronunciation of English* (1909), Jones explained that he was addressing 'students and teachers, and more especially ... students in training-colleges and teachers whose aim is to correct cockneyisms or other undesirable pronunciations in their scholars' (quoted in Crowley 1988: 165). Jones was invited to join the BBC Advisory Committee on Spoken English in 1926, which was set up to ensure that, only four years after its foundation, national radio would contribute not only to instruct his listener through mass entertainment, but also to reinforce a standard of speech across the nation. For Jones, OP was a scholarly pursuit aimed at furthering the cause of historical phonology within a strictly academic context. As with Ellis, his agenda as a philologist and historical phonologist was quite different from his views about the desirability of StP.

Conversely, other scholars regard OP as having great potential entertainment value for theatre practitioners committed to developing new audiences for Shakespeare. These scholars also tend to have more progressive ideas about the place of regional and class variations in Modern English. David Crystal, for example, who has produced Shakespeare in OP since the early 2000s, has often stressed how OP makes Shakespeare sound more accessible to modern audiences, because 'OP is a sound that often reminds English speakers of the accent of their home'. According to Crystal, OP is 'a more universal sound than we are perhaps used to hearing Shakespeare spoken in. It is an Everyman sound, well suited to writing that was written for everyone' (2012).

All in all, the enduring diversity of views about how Shakespeare and his contemporaries sounded and how their voices were heard and decoded at the time would seem to be the product both of methodological challenges inherent to the study of historical phonology and of ingrained assumptions about the desirability of StP, both on and off the Shakespearean stage. Rather than attempting to adjudicate the *generic* significance of any given accent as used in Shakespearean performance over the last four hundred years, this book explores and exposes the social and cultural biases that

have informed those ingrained assumptions about what sounded acceptable and what sounded unacceptable at key moments in the history of the
reception of Shakespeare on stage. The four chapters in this book focus on
four specific time periods, when accents took on urgently political and
fiercely *local* connotations, and when controversy prompted speakers to
verbalize assumptions that were normally left unspoken. Comments,
reports and reviews that harp, often polemically, on how actors speak
Shakespeare's lines, make it possible to establish the *local* qualities of
specific accents within the fictive worlds of the plays and of their target
audiences. In turn, a close analysis of the controversy caused by marked
voices on the Shakespearean stage provides a rich point of entry into an
alternative stage history that focuses on acoustics (rather than visual or
textual) elements of theatrical performance.

Readjusting the field of enquiry from an assessment of the *generic*, to a
reassessment of the *local*, connotations attached to inflected voices in
Shakespearean performance is also in keeping with a more current understanding of the history of English 'not [as] a march toward "standard
southern British English" but rather [as] . . . something more dynamic, . . .
as the history of "a population of variants moving through time"'(Roger
Lass, in Fitzmaurice and Smith 2012: 32). Accents can now be more
productively understood not as *static* markers of identity but as *dynamic*
'acts of identity', that is as a speaker's conscious selection of specific
acoustic variants from a wider pool of other available variants.[16] As this
book shows, the selection of specific accents in specific productions of
Shakespeare at four key moments in the history of its reception on the
English stage has played a central role in the dynamic fashioning and
refashioning of Shakespeare and its social and cultural status at times of
intense change and (theatrical) reform.

§

Arranged in reversed chronological order, the four chapters in this book
identify and discuss periods of intense negotiations over and about the
norms that have regulated the acoustic production and reproduction of
Shakespeare on the English stage over the last four hundred years. The
intervening periods, briefly summed up in each chapter, were characterized
by acoustic uniformity. Acoustic uniformity is of course an abstract
oversimplification. There were indeed times, including, for example, from

---

[16] I borrow this phrase from Le Page and Tabouret-Keller 1985.

the mid-nineteenth to the mid-twentieth century, when the delivery of Shakespeare's lines in performance seemed to shift from a more rhetorical, melodramatic diction to a more relaxed and naturalistic style of speech. These shifts are best exemplified by contemporary responses to the voice and style of delivery of actors, like John Gielgud, whose career spanned the late nineteenth and the first half of the twentieth century. By the mid-twentieth century, John Gielgud had come to be heard as a distant echo of his nineteenth-century predecessors, some of whom were famously blood relations – Ellen Terry, for example, who reached celebrity status while acting next to Henry Irving at the Lyceum Theatre in the 1880s and 1890s, was his great aunt. However, when Gielgud had first started performing at the turn of the twentieth century, he had been associated with the new and more naturalistic style of acting promoted by William Poel (1852–1934) and Ben Greet (1857–1936).[17] However, these relatively minor acoustic shifts remained well within the range of variations that contemporary speakers would recognize as StP. Voices that carried the slightest regional or foreign inflection were at this time regarded as aberrant and the tendency was for such acoustic anomalies to be smoothed out and corrected. These periods of *relative* acoustic standardization are contrasted to periods of *comparably* intense acoustic change in each of the four chapters in this book.

Chapter 1 argues that the rise in the number of foreign-language productions of Shakespeare since the late twentieth century has stimulated debate over the desirability of acoustic diversity on the Shakespearean stage more generally. Foreign-language productions have developed a new acoustic sensibility in English-speaking audiences, who have been challenged to make sense of 'Shakespeare without its language'. The traditional perception that Shakespeare becomes lost in translation has slowly been replaced by an appreciation of how differently Shakespeare signifies on stage, when Shakespeare is liberated from the straightjacket of acoustic normativity. Chapter 1 goes on to discuss a selection of late twentieth and early twenty-first century productions which similarly highlight a link between the steep rise in foreign Shakespeare programming,

---

[17] I discuss Poel's interest in voice and his commitment to vocal reform at greater length in Chapter 2. In his acting editions, *The Ben Greet Shakespeare for Young Readers and Amateur Players*, Greet advised against conventional elocutionary training: 'Do not imitate some of those professors, especially teachers of what is called Elocution and Expression, if by any chance they happen to pronounce it in up-to-date American or cockney British, or tell you it was conceived in any other brogue, accent, or pronunciation than the purest of pure English' (quoted in Dobson 1968: 177).

especially when staged as part of large international theatre events, and an increase in the diversity of accents subsequently deployed on the Shakespearean stage.

Before an increase in foreign Shakespeare programming in the second half of the twentieth century, one other significant source of acoustic variation came from the first experiments with Shakespeare in OP. Chapter 2 connects the earliest OP programmes produced in the 1930s and 1940s for the BBC by Mary Hope Allen, a pioneering radio producer who explored the acoustic potential of traditional art forms when adapted for the new medium, to the emergence of OP as a theatrical practice. OP is generally understood, and often critiqued, as a conservative exercise in acoustic archaeology, aimed at recovering and reconstructing the sound of Shakespeare's language, as originally performed on the early modern stage. As Salmon and Burness put it,

> [n]ow that we have the technical ability to put on a play in roughly the pronunciation of 1600, the desirability of so doing has become less apparent. Since so many of the features of Elizabethan pronunciation have remained in twentieth-century use with utterly different sociological connotations, it is exceedingly difficult to avoid farcical overtones in ways that do not arise with original versions in French, German, or even in Chaucerian English. (1987: 5)

While acknowledging the significant methodological challenges associated with OP, Chapter 2 shows how experiments with Shakespeare performed in OP nevertheless catalyzed efforts to introduce acoustic diversity into Shakespearean performance at times of otherwise absolute and uncontested acoustic uniformity.

As noted above, the alignment between Shakespeare and the speech of elitism predates the rise of RP in the mid- to late-nineteenth century (Mugglestone 2007: 4). This long-established alignment reaches as far back as the mid- to late-seventeenth century, when Shakespeare became firmly associated with court culture and aristocratic patronage, as a result of the introduction of the monopoly on spoken drama that regulated the reopening of the theatres after the Civil Wars in 1660. Chapter 3 focuses on sustained challenges to the monopoly and identifies David Garrick as the most important catalyst for acoustic change in the period. His naturalistic style of acting has often been discussed within the wider context of the Enlightenment and related movements that privileged reason over tradition, and the observation of Nature over prescriptive conventions. Largely overlooked, though, is the impact of his voice, which was notoriously marked by regional inflections, and of his debut as Richard III in one of

London's illegitimate theatres,[18] on two important, related movements, led by the two John Palmers I discuss in Chapter 3. Besides their given and their family names, the two John Palmers also shared a determination to make Shakespeare and spoken drama more widely accessible. The movements led by the two Palmers aimed to widen access to Shakespeare and spoken drama by obtaining licenses for professional actors to perform in provincial theatres across the country and by encouraging non-professional actors and enthusiasts to perform in non-conventional venues, ranging from the stages of illegitimate theatres, also known as minor or private theatres, to smaller performance houses and song and supper clubs.

The last chapter in this book, Chapter 4, reconsiders the sound of Shakespeare's language, and the sound of early modern drama more generally, as originally performed before the closure of the theatres in 1642. As mentioned above, the Restoration marked an institutional alignment of theatrical and court cultures, when the granting of royal patents ushered in tight regulations for the public performance of spoken drama. Accordingly, acting style and delivery reflected the taste and standards of acoustic decorum associated with the ruling elite. Public performance prior to 1642 had instead benefited from a mixed system of patronage, which relied simultaneously on older models of economic support and protection from royal and aristocratic patrons and from the commercial networks generated by the recent rise of theatrical and print industries in early modern London.[19] Playing companies moved fluidly between commercial venues in London to performing at Court or at aristocratic households in the country. While historical phoneticians have tended to disagree about how the players would have sounded, with some arguing for an 'everyman sound, well-suited to writing that was written for everyone' (Crystal 2012), and others for a 'type of speech [that was] used in polite circles' (Kökeritz 1953: 4), Chapter 4 argues that the early moderns were more concerned about the players' ability to fake accents than with the need for the players to conform to any given standard of pronunciation.

After highlighting the transgressive quality attributed by the anti-theatricalists to the voice of the players who first performed Shakespeare on the early modern stage, Chapter 4 goes on to show how national and regional accents were used in a selection of early modern plays, including

---

[18] For more details about the status of illegitimate theatres in the eighteenth and early nineteenth century, see Moody 2000.

[19] Among recent studies about patronage in the age of Shakespeare, see, for example, Whitfield White and Westfall 2002.

Shakespeare. Although sparingly used, and often reflecting stage dialects rather than accurately reproduced acoustic features of variations as spoken by actual speakers at the time, regional and national accents carried connotations that must have been recognizable to contemporary audiences, since they were clearly deployed to achieve specific and nuanced dramatic effects, as two case studies at the end of Chapter 4 set out to demonstrate.

The book concludes by reflecting on how a better understanding of how marked voices have been used on the Shakespearean stage can inform current theatrical practice. The conclusion shows how the principles that inform voice training and the expectations that audiences bring to the theatre are still affected by parameters of acoustic propriety that can be traced back to the alignment of Shakespeare and spoken drama with the speech of elitism in the late seventeenth century. The conclusion proposes not only to reconsider how Shakespeare should be spoken on the contemporary English stage, but also to review the allocation of public funding, which continues to privilege producers of Shakespearean drama who, by and large, reinforce dominant standards of acoustic normativity.

CHAPTER I

'Accents Yet Unknown': The Changing Soundscape of Shakespeare in Contemporary Performance

Non-Standard English (henceforth NSE) accents started to feature more prominently in mainstream Shakespearean productions in the early 2010s. Since then, more directors have curated the voice as a significant aspect of the mise-en-scène and NSE accents have no longer been systematically relegated to comic roles as the default acoustic shorthand to personate the marginal and the uneducated.

The impetus towards achieving greater acoustic diversity on the Shakespearean stage is generally linked to the pioneering work by poets, artists and writers who championed the use of regional accents in mainstream theatre, film and television in the second half of the twentieth century. This chapter argues that this pioneering work with regional accents has been reinforced all along by the steady rise of foreign Shakespeare on the English stage. A closer look at the steep increase in the number of foreign productions of Shakespeare that have either toured to, or that have been produced for, the English stage has highlighted a connection between the alienating, but also liberating, experience of hearing Shakespeare performed in a foreign language and the growing acoustic diversity deployed in English productions of Shakespeare aimed at English-speaking audiences.

This chapter therefore identifies and discusses the correlation between the rise of regional and foreign accents on the English stage, starting with the acerbic response prompted by the first regionally inflected voices to be heard on the Shakespearean stage in the 1960s. This chapter then focuses on key theatrical events, including festivals and anniversary seasons within which foreign Shakespeare featured prominently, showing how these events in turn provoked debate about the need for more acoustic diversity and the deployment of regional voices on the Shakespearean stage. Specific productions are granted more sustained attention than others, which are discussed only in passing, because they exemplify more clearly the benefits and the challenges connected to current attempts to move towards greater acoustic diversity.

§

Even in the 1960s, when new voices were starting to emerge in the writing of post-war playwrights, most actors were still well-versed in what Carol Rutter calls 'verbal camouflage': Albert Finney, Tom Courtenay, Peter O'Toole, Anthony Hopkins and Alan Bates were effectively 'bi-lingual', because they were trained not to use their regionally inflected accent on stage (2003: 247). When exceptionally used on the Shakespearean stage, regional accents caused outrage. Most memorably, Nicol Williamson, who was born in Scotland and raised in the Midlands, used his natural accent to play Hamlet in Tony Richardson's production at the Roundhouse in 1968. In this production, he presented the disaffected prince as a radicalized intellectual, thereby echoing the social movements and student protests that were sweeping across Europe and the United States at the time.

Reviewer John Simon found Williamson's accent objectionable and utterly inappropriate for the role. In his review, 'My Throat is in the Midlands', Simon first remarks on the acoustic quality of Williamson's voice: 'Williamson has a tendency to sound like an electric guitar ... [and his] lips seem to part only for visual effect'. Simon then turns to Williamson's accent:

> It has been called Midlands, North Country and Cockney with a loose overlay of culture. Only Henry Higgins could correctly place it South of the Beatles and North of the Stones and identify the veneer as grammar- or council-school. But even Colonel Pickering could tell that it isn't Hamlet. (1969: 56)

A little concession to 'modernization' still leads Simon to surmise that 'surely Jimmy Porter or Bill Maitland or some other Osbornian professional griper is no conscionable correspondence for the exacting idealist turned cosmic malcontent' (1969: 56). After commenting on Williamson's accent, Simon ends by complaining about his 'equine head', his 'gangling, skulking body', and his legs, which, he claims, if not 'exactly spindly' seemed to him 'obstreperously lower-class' (1969: 56).

Simon's review seems particularly acerbic and backward looking now, conjuring uncomfortable memories of late-Victorian biological determinism and their tragic racial and ethnic applications in the twentieth century. However, Simon's appraisal of the acoustic qualities of Williamson's voice was in fact perfectly in keeping with the then prevailing views on the relative 'prestige value' of regional accents. In his influential 1970 study on 'Evaluative Reactions to Accent', social psychologist Howard Giles did not only confirm that 'regional accents [had] less prestige value than RP', but he also suggested that regional accents themselves, rather than attitudes towards them, were the problem that ought to be fixed:

> [R]egional accent is a social stigma, and therefore two courses of action may be put forward to remedy this situation: (i) an attempt to change people's attitudes away from one of social prejudice for non-standard accented-speech, or (ii) an attempt to teach children competence in the standard accent to such a degree that at least they are able to produce this form in socially-appropriate situations. This latter objective would seem the more efficient method of dispelling the particular social prejudice involved for any significant length of time, and in this way therapy is related to the cause of the problem rather than its symptoms. (1970: 225)

The social psychologist, while seemingly intent on measuring attitudes to regional accents dispassionately and systematically, as befits a scientific enquiry, is in fact echoing the reviewer, who had found that the source of the problem with Williamson's interpretation of Hamlet was not his attitude towards Williamson's accent, but Williamson's accent itself.

Williamson's Hamlet is now regarded as a milestone in the recent history of the reception of the play on the English stage. Samuel Crowl has for example recently argued that '[t]he use of Williamson's native accent was one of the film's most exciting features': 'the very sound of his voice' made Williamson's prince come across as 'decidedly anti-establishment', brimming with 'the cheeky cocky wit of the early John Lennon', suggesting that 'Liverpool was closer to his domain than Whitehall' (2014: 113). But, as Simon's diametrically opposed response shows, Williamson's voice initially came across as indecorous and ultimately unacceptable as a vehicle to represent Shakespeare on the English stage.

An important precedent to Williamson's Hamlet was his role as Vladimir in a 1964 revival of *Waiting for Godot*. As John Calder reports, 'Beckett turned up at rehearsals and was unhappy about the way the production was progressing, the actor retaining his London barrister's accent for the author's reflective tramp. "Where do you come from? Is that your natural voice?" asked Beckett, and when told that Nicol was Scottish, asked if he could not use his natural non-London intonation. That evening Beckett looked pleased, more so as the days passed, and he commented, "There's a touch of genius there!"' (2012).

More important work with regional accents followed, though at first in the context of radical adaptations of other classical authors or works. A prime example is the prominence accorded to Northern English in Tony Harrison's *Mystery Plays Cycle* (NT, 1977) and his *Oresteia* (NT, 1981). Barrie Rutter, who worked closely with Harrison in the 1980s, went on to set up Northern Broadsides in 1992. The company, whose repertory includes Shakespeare, English and European classical plays and new writing, has since then become best known for 'their distinctive northern voice' and for the 'strong musicality and clear narrative journey' of their productions.[1]

The 'verbal attack' (Rutter 2003: 236) that Harrison first and then Rutter waged against the continuing dominance of StP on the English stage has undoubtedly played a key role in refocusing attention on the acoustic dimension of performance and the connotations currently attached to NSE accents. However, as this chapter goes on to argue, the initial impetus towards acoustic diversity introduced by artists who promoted the use of regional voices on the Shakespearean and on the classical stage was amplified by the simultaneous rise of foreign voices and, more recently, of English voices inflected by foreign accents.

In addressing the impact of foreign Shakespeare on English-speaking audiences, this chapter also addresses a gap in current scholarship about non-English Shakespeare, otherwise known as 'Global Shakespeare'. When scholars consider what makes non-English Shakespeare in performance distinctively appealing to English-speaking audiences, they tend to focus on visual and textual features, or on the physical theatricality of music and song, if they focus on sound at all. While discussing Robert Lepage's directorial approach to Shakespeare, Robert Ormsby has, for example, identified features that give Lepage's Shakespearean productions 'a markedly global identity' (2011: 318). Among them, Ormsby highlights the use of unlocalized scenography, of modern translations that simplify and de-localize the original language, and of a heavily cut text as pre-requisites for a wider, international appeal within the so-called Angloworld. Writing about 'Global Shakespeare in a Post-Colonial Market', Kate McLuskie has similarly shown how the 'dynamic physical theatricality' of non-Western Shakespeare appeals to Western audiences, who reductively consume it as the product of 'a purposefully homogenized indigenous culture' (1999: 158). While drawing attention to important creative practices and problematic commercial and ideological processes that affect the reception of

---

[1] For more details, see www.northern-broadsides.co.uk/about-us/. Last accessed: 30 November 2016.

'Global Shakespeare' by English-speaking audiences, 'Global Shakespeare' scholars tend to ignore the potential appeal and radical quality of its complex acoustic otherness. The loss of *semantic* meaning is compensated not only by visually recognizable settings or by physical theatricality, but also by unfamiliar *vocal* sounds, which change the acoustic make-up of the theatrical event. In turn, the acoustic diversity associated with non-English Shakespeare has a profound impact on the (re)constitution of audiences as acoustic communities.

§

'Even Now with Strange and Several Noises / ... We Were Awaked': The Rise of Foreign and Regional Shakespeare on the English Stage

The desire to 'demonstrate Europe's cultural accomplishments' and the need to 'facilitate European regeneration and international communication', which led to the launch of major international theatre festivals on the Continent after the end of the Second World War (Allain and Harvie 2006: 156), was matched in England by an attempt to internationalize theatre programming. Theatre impresario Peter Daubeny, who had been the driving force behind visits from leading foreign companies in the 1950s,[2] was appointed to lead the RSC World Theatre Seasons at the Aldwych Theatre in London in 1964. The Seasons were discontinued in 1973, shortly before Daubeny's death in 1975. Despite launching under the auspices of the quartercentenary celebrations of Shakespeare's birth, the Seasons included precious little international Shakespeare, and probably deliberately so, because, as Robert Shaughnessy has argued, '[their] rationale ... [was] the showcasing of indigenous theatrical traditions ([or,] as Daubeny put it, "the original in the original language")' (2009: 3).

The first foreign Shakespeare production to be included in the World Theatre Seasons was Welcome Msomi's *Umabatha*', a Zulu version of *Macbeth*. This production met with great popular acclaim during its three-week run in 1972, but its reception was nevertheless symptomatic of a fundamental resistance to the sound of Shakespeare 'without its language'. The emphasis in contemporary reviews was on music, dance and costumes

---

[2] Visiting theatre companies invited by Daubeny in the 1950s included the Comédie Française and the Compagnie Edwige Feuillère, the Berliner Ensemble and the Moscow Art Theatre. For further details, see Shellard 1999: 151–2.

as signifiers of authentic African otherness,[3] probably as a direct result of a concerted attempt to insulate London audiences from the sound of Msomi's Zulu translation. As Mervyn McMurtry reports, 'a simultaneous interpretation ... was delivered by Huntley Stuart, a Zulu linguist, via earphone' (1999: 315), drowning out the sound of Msomi's Zulu translation. Had audiences been exposed to Msomi's Zulu translation they may have appreciated how, as McMurtry notes, 'certain [Zulu] idiomatic expressions and conventions' had been 'effectively integrated' with the Shakespearean text (1999: 315). Instead, a fundamental distrust of the very possibility of a meaningful encounter between Shakespeare's language and the foreign sounds of Msomi's Zulu translation kept the two safely apart.

The demise of the Theatre World Seasons in 1975 was followed by a period of staunch conservatism, both in political and theatrical terms. Lucy Neal and Rose Fenton give a bleak account of the 'state of play' of public life and of the theatre industry, which they sought to enrich and diversify when they first launched LIFT, the London International Festival of Theatre, in 1981:

> Margaret Thatcher had won the election and begun her eighteen-year hold on British politics and the public realm. Declaring that 'There is no such thing as society' whilst putting the 'Great' back into Britain, her leadership heralded a culture of free-market private enterprise and union-bashing, with a war in the south Atlantic and Poll Tax riots at home. Britain was in a recession and the arts had to justify their existence in the market place, competing with hospitals and schools. International arts were off the agenda altogether and it is hard to conceive the insularity of British theatre at the time – Peter Brook had abandoned the country in despair at its narrow-mindedness and cultural myopia to work in the more cosmopolitan Paris. (Fenton and Neal 2005: 16)

LIFT brought welcome relief to what *The Times* had described as the 'foreign theatre famine' that followed the end of Daubeny's Seasons in 1973 (Fenton and Neal 2005: 22). LIFT attracted to London world-leading theatre directors, such as Anatoly Vasiliev, and major national companies, like the Abbey Theatre. However, unlike Daubeny's Seasons, LIFT also invited emerging companies whose work was theatrically innovative and politically charged and, even more crucially, it provided a platform for local artists to collaborate with international directors and to

---

[3] Felix Barker, for example, mentioned 'jungle drums' alongside the 'magnificent ebony bodies' of the performers, thus reifying the latter, even while praising their beauty (1972).

produce site-specific theatre not only for, but with, local London communities. As Naseem Khan explains, LIFT was specifically conceived to encourage meaningful encounters with, rather than mere exposure to, different cultures and theatre traditions:

> It is true that London had seen its fair share of international work previously, here and there, off and on. But it had been sporadic and for the most part unpredictable. ... like finding an exotic plant in your mundane backyard. LIFT – to carry on the metaphor – naturalized the plant. The shows they brought over [were] determinedly set in London soil. (Kahn 2005: 62)

As a result, LIFT events prompted critical and passionate engagement rather than curiosity or mere aesthetic appreciation of international productions as exotic artefacts. According to Khan, LIFT brought about 'a change in the way that "foreign" work and "foreign" people too were looked at' and 'started to unpick the old ideas of "authentic" culture, expos [ing] it for the fallacy it really was' (Khan 2005: 64).

LIFT certainly paved the way for site-specific performance that turned many unconventional venues in the capital into performance spaces. LIFT also developed a taste for international theatre in London audiences, which in turn led to the launch of other major international festivals, including the Barbican International Theatre Events (BITE) in the late 1990s. However, Shakespeare productions programmed by LIFT in the first ten years after its inception prompted deeply conservative responses to foreign Shakespeare, even in the context of the radically innovative work sponsored and supported by LIFT. Among them, especially noteworthy were the Compagnia del Collettivo di Parma Trilogy, comprising *Hamlet*, *Macbeth* and *1 Henry IV*, in 1983, *La Tempestat* by La Cubana in 1987, and two productions of *A Midsummer Night's Dreams* by Footsbarn Travelling Theatre and by Comedy Theatre Bucharest in 1991.

Reviewers of the Collettivo Trilogy, for example, were generally impressed by an approach to Shakespeare that combined *commedia dell'arte* with a Beckettian, post-modern theatre aesthetic,[4] but they either ignored the translation and radical adaptation undergone by the text or deplored it as an abomination. Michael Coveney, for example, stressed the eminently 'readable' quality of the theatrical language (1983), while Sheridan Morley simply denigrated the Collettivo's approach: 'I left wishing

---

[4] Michael Coveney (1983) compared the Trilogy to the radical approach of homegrown dramatists, like Edward Bond or Charles Marowitz, who had adapted Shakespeare to the conventions of the British avant-garde theatre in the 1970s.

the company had either liked *Hamlet* enough to do it as written or loathed it enough to leave it well alone' (1983). Neither Coveney nor Morley however paid any attention to the sound of Shakespeare in translation. Other reviewers went as far as arguing that English and foreign Shakespeares are ultimately incommensurable entities. Among them, Robert Cushman wrote:

> We don't have to feel inferior. Shakespeare in English and Shakespeare in foreign [sic] are different animals. Nobody cares if a translation is mucked about with. A British production seeking this degree of license would either have to play against the text to a degree fatiguing to both actors and audience, or paraphrase, which is an abomination There are those rhythms, prose or verse, and we are stuck with them. (1983)

Cushman's notion that Shakespeare can be 'mucked about' in translation reinforced his conviction that English productions do not, and should not take any liberties with Shakespeare's language, since Shakespeare would not be Shakespeare without its language.

Responses to the Collettivo Trilogy showed that their work was either dismissed as 'not Shakespeare' or appreciated in the context of an emerging international aesthetic, which, according to Andy Wood, made it possible for 'a piece of theatre ... [to] mean as much in Caracas as in London' (1991). The increasingly familiar theatrical language used by Il Collettivo stopped even those reviewers who enjoyed their work from wondering how the foreign translation affected their experience of listening to Shakespeare without its language. The foreign translation was either ignored or dismissed as an aberration from the acoustic norms – what Cushan called 'those rhythms' – that were firmly associated with Shakespeare in performance at the time.

Even Fenton, who was publicly outspoken about the need for LIFT audiences to hear and appreciate foreign language theatre, was cautious when it came to programming foreign Shakespeare. In an interview published in *The Independent* in 1991, she urged her readers to be open-minded about foreign language theatre: 'we must be much less protectionist about our language and traditions of theatre and let *all* our antennae work: visual as well as auditory' (Donald 1991). However, the 'End of Festival Report' that year, when LIFT presented two productions of *A Midsummer Night's Dream*, one in English by Footsbarn Travelling Theatre and one in Romanian by Comedy Theatre Bucharest, reveals that Fenton had serious reservations: '[d]on't underestimate the extent to which "a foreign language" puts people off'. In a 'note-to-self', Fenton then added: 'Don't programme two *Midsummer Night's Dreams* in the same Festival, thereby handicapping the foreign language production' (Fenton 1991).

Other enterprising theatre producers wetted London audiences' appetite for foreign language theatre towards the end of the 1980s. Outstanding among them was Thelma Holt, whose award-winning international season in 1987 marked a watershed in foreign language theatre programming at the NT. Holt introduced the use of surtitles by means of 'super-proscenial projection', which, while 'enfold[ing] performance within the spectatorial regimes of world theatre' (Shaughnessy 2009: 6), also made foreign language theatre less forbidding and removed the acoustic barrier of simultaneous translation that had insulated English audiences from foreign language theatre in the past. Reviewers of Holt's Shakespearean offerings, however, continued to focus on their visual rather than their acoustic qualities, thus replicating the types of responses elicited by the Collettivo Trilogy four years earlier. Christopher Edwards, for example, praised Yukio Ninagawa's *Macbeth* for its 'visual flair', its 'sure grip on the dramatic heart of the play', and its 'intense stylization' (1987). Edwards, echoing Coveney's remarks about the theatrical language used by the Collettivo, felt that he could get to the heart of the production by focusing on its visual elements alone.

Direct exposure to the sound of foreign Shakespeare in performance would eventually sensitize English-speaking audiences to the material qualities of the sound of Shakespeare in translation. But the 1980s drew to a close without registering any major change in the interpretative sensitivities of those exposed to foreign Shakespeare. While the first ten years of LIFT and producers like Holt did much to develop foreign theatre programming, responses to foreign Shakespeare in the period show that the translation was at best heard as white noise. It was only during the 1990s that reviewers of foreign Shakespeare productions started to comment on the material qualities of foreign voices. Crucially, it was also during the 1990s that homegrown theatre-makers started to exploit the potential of foreign or regionally inflected voices to diversify the soundscape generally associated with English Shakespeare in performance.

§

The 1990s witnessed a steady increase in the number of foreign productions of Shakespeare on the London stage and beyond. According to Shaughnessy, fewer than a dozen foreign productions had been staged in

London in the twenty-year period following the launch of the World Theatre Seasons in 1964; in the next twenty-year period, the number would rise to about fifty (Shaughnessy 2009: 4). Foreign Shakespeare also began to feature at theatre venues beyond London. The Bath International Shakespeare Festival, for example, started to showcase major international productions, including Eimuntas Nekrosius's *Hamlet* in 1999. Reviewers finally seemed more alert to the fresh challenges and opportunities associated with foreign Shakespeare. Silviu Purcârete's *Titus Andronicus*, which was staged at the Lyric Hammersmith in 1997, is a good example of a production that divided critical opinion in relation to the effectiveness and impact of the Romanian translation. According to *The Express*, 'the Romanian language . . . sound[ed] great. The scorching delivery of words, all seeming to end in 'pu' and 'cu', [was] supplemented by actors giving coyote-like howls of anguish as the action pick[ed] up steam' (Anon. 1997). Alternatively, the alien sounds of the foreign language spoken on stage was lamented as an insurmountable barrier that prevented any level of meaningful communication between the actors and the audience: 'the Latinate sonority of the Romanian language becomes an end in itself; the actors never address each other, or God, or us, as if their stage lives were remotely like real life' (Anon. 1997a). Far from being overlooked as irrelevant or secondary to the visual and physical aspects of its theatrical language, the foreign language translation was now regarded either as integral or ultimately deleterious to the impact of the production as a whole.

One other foreign Shakespeare production, right at the end of the 1990s, was deemed ground-breaking for the way in which it foregrounded the materiality of the actors' bodies, of the props and, crucially, of the voices that featured in it. When Romeo Castellucci's *Giulio Cesare* was staged by Socìetas Raffaello Sanzio at the Queen Elizabeth Hall as part of LIFT 1999, English-speaking audiences were confronted by a production that focused relentlessly on the sheer corporeality of the voice. Quite fittingly for a play that explores the power of rhetoric to shape personal and public identities, Castellucci placed the mechanics of voice production centre-stage: an endoscope inserted through the nose and throat of the actor playing Brutus projected real-time images of his vocal cords, which were shown enlarged and vibrating like an alien-looking organism, primordial and remote, on a screen behind him. Similarly, Mark Antony was played by an actor, Dalmazio Masani, who had had a laryngectomy and who delivered Antony's speech in the forum with the help of a prosthetic valve implanted in his throat. The focus that Castellucci placed on the voice forced his audiences to come to terms with the materiality of the voice and the alien sounds produced by the mechanical enhancement of the human voice.

In keeping with the ethos of his company, which 'rose to international prominence for its radical attack against [text-centred] theatrical traditions' (Guidi and Massai 2017: 277), Castellucci used Shakespeare's play very loosely to 're-sensitise the spectator to Shakespeare's over-produced texts, by presenting us with the raw material that goes to make up drama – text, body, mis-en-scène, the work of performance' (Escolme 2005: 138). To Escolme's list, I would add the actor's voice, because the de-familiarization of the actor's voice is central to 'Castellucci's attack on "simple" and corrupt theatre' (Shepherd 2006: 136), namely on theatre that hides the means through which meaning is produced on stage. Castellucci's attack against the epistemological 'lie' of theatrical literariness, which he associates with the tradition of naturalism in Western theatre, translated into an unprecedented attention to the voice, which, along with sound and music, was curated by his then partner and collaborator, Chiara Guidi.

Guidi's experimental approach to sound and voice did not go unnoticed when *Giulio Cesare* was staged before English audiences in 1999. Review-ers described the 'earth-tilting impact' that this production had on their auditory and spectatorial sensibilities: while one reviewer noted that '[t]he production ambush[ed] the audience, constantly challenging concepts of the body's boundaries in a two-and-a-half-hour surreal sensory overload that [left] you reeling' (Halliburton 1999), another admitted that '[i]n a way that's almost impossible to describe to the Shakespeare purist, the production's sinister beauty shook one awake to the brutality and cruelty in the original, while remaining frustratingly oblique' (Cavendish 2001). What reviewers celebrated and deprecated in equal measure was the sheer power of a production that did not only wrench Shakespeare away from the sounds and familiar accents of the English language but also staged the voice as a grossly material, plastic medium produced by bodily organs and artificially enhanced by sound machinery. Crucial to this production and to its reception was the realization that the sound of a foreign translation could lend fresh insight into the source text and that StP is just one set of sounds out of all the natural and mechanically produced variations that the human voice can produce to make a canonical play like *Julius Caesar* signify anew, in a startling and thought-provoking way.

The increasing numbers of foreign Shakespeare productions in the 1990s went hand in hand with a steady rise of NSE accents in homegrown productions. Besides the founding of Northern Broadsides in 1991, other productions marked a revival of interest in nationally or regionally inflected voices. Irina Brook's 1997 Oxford Shakespeare Company production of *All's Well That Ends Well*, for example, relocated the play to a North African marketplace town, re-imagining it as performed by local storytellers before an improvised audience made up of local shoppers and tourists. Brook accordingly relied on a mixed cast of white, black and Asian British actors in order to diversify the acoustic landscape of her production. Taylor praised 'the wildly varying styles', which ranged from 'the refreshing, earthy directness of the African Widow and Diana (Anni Domingo, Clara Onyemere) to Michael Greco's strutting, would-be Latin lover of a Parolles, who gabbles his treacheries at hilarious top speed' (1997). Other reviewers however found the delivery aesthetically unpleasant and dramaturgically problematic. Michael Billington, for example, granted that, while 'multi-cultural casting [is] admirable in principle, it creat[ed] extreme variation in style'. As a result, 'Rachel Pickup's highly traditional, formally elocuting Helena exist[ed] in a different world from ... Michael Greco's Latinate, mustard-jacketed Parolles or Clare Onymere's bold, physical, improbably virginal Diana planting a smacking kiss on the French King's lips' (1997). In Billington's reading of this production, the 'formally elocuting' Helena stood for a standard of elocutionary *and* sexual propriety, which Billington juxtaposed to the compromised sexual mores of the Latinate Parolles and the 'improbably virginal' Diana (1997). Billington was evidently finding it difficult to imagine a (Shakespearean) world where Helena and Diana could convincingly be played by Rachel Pickup and Clare Onymere. Their dissonant voices, in other words, disturbed his sense of what delivery styles and accents most naturally suit the fictive world of a Shakespearean play, even when the setting is updated.

Other reviewers aimed their criticism at the perceived unevenness in the verse delivery: Jeremy Kingston, for example, described [Helena's] speech as 'intelligently varied', but he found that too many of the lines spoken by other characters were delivered 'without discernible knowledge of their meaning' (1997). Worth mentioning is that the production seems in fact to have caused no confusion or incomprehension even among younger members of the audience, as attested by Taylor's comments about his '10-year-old guest' becoming quickly 'engrossed and enchanted' by the production (1997). Billington, unlike Kingston, did not find the delivery of Shakespeare's language unclear or deficient *per se*. He rather found the range of voices used in this production unsettling because, as he went on to explain, 'Shakespeare's story seems more European than African'. What eluded Billington altogether, and what started to emerge from Taylor's review, was the realization that this production offered an exciting remapping of the vocal acoustics of Shakespeare's play, whereby Helena, who is socially eccentric to the world of the court of the King of France, was the only character who spoke in StP. The use of different accents to question and complicate their connotations as markers of class and national identity clearly irritated those who expect English Shakespeare to function as the golden standard of elocutionary propriety, but was interestingly praised by Taylor for 'establishing its own kind of imaginative integrity' (1997).

Responses to Brook's *All's Well That Ends Wells* echoed reviews of an earlier production of *King Lear*, directed by Max Stafford-Clark towards the end of his artistic directorship at the Royal Court in 1993. In this production, Adrian Dunbar played Edmund as a disaffected 'khaki-uniformed Ulsterman with more of a political than a familial chip on his shoulder' (Hassell 1993). Dunbar played Edmund using his native Northern Irish accent, a rare and notable exception over a long and successful career that has involved performing several Shakespearean roles in StP. Most recently, when he played York in the BBC second series of *The Hollow Crown* (2016), he was praised in *The Telegraph* for 'speak[ing] the verse with lyricism, lucidity and complete plausibility' (Davies 2016). Worth stressing here is that, while Dunbar's acquired RP is heard and decoded by reviewers as entirely plausible, his native Northern Irish accent was paradoxically criticized for sounding 'artificial' back in 1993. Ian Shuttleworth, for example, complained that '[his] transparently artificial Ulster Edmund must [have left] most of the audience groping for a handle upon his characterization' (1993), while Morley observed that 'none of [characters] seem to be inhabiting the same universe, let alone the same play' (1993). Anticipating Billington's response to Brook's *All's Well That Ends Well*, Morley found that the range of accents deployed in Stafford-Cark's *King Lear* undermined any coherent 'sense of place and time' (1993). Like Billington, Morley registered acoustic diversity as an implausible and lamentable breach of aesthetic decorum, instead of wondering why Stafford-Clark chose to represent the fictive world of *King Lear* as a place where people speak differently. Morley simply faulted the acoustic diversity in this production as jarring and dissonant, and did not even consider the possibility that Dunbar's accent might productively activate parallels between the catastrophic 'division of the kingdom' in ancient and modern times.[5]

---

[5] A similar accusation was levelled at a 'Moving Theatre' production of *Antony and Cleopatra*, which was directed by Vanessa Redgrave at the Riverside Studios in 1995 and which otherwise got fairly

The 1990s also marked a time when British Black, Asian and Minority Ethnic (henceforth BAME) actors started to attract critical attention for their forays into the dramatic canon. In 1991, Yvonne Brewster, founding artistic director of Talawa, one of the major and most successful black theatre companies in the UK, argued eloquently for the right of black actors to perform Shakespeare 'straight', in response to critical reviews of her production of *Antony and Cleopatra*:

> Because it's an all-black company, critics expected . . . a kind of zingy sappy snappy approach, an Afro rap musical, a Tony and Cleo. They said, as if it was an accusation, 'But you relied completely on the text.' Of course I did. Shakespeare is not a bad writer, I said. It's dangerous to feel you can't do the plays as Shakespeare wrote them. But oddly enough, it's the English who feel you've got to do something with Shakespeare. As black actors, you can do versions – like *Trinidad Sisters* (instead of *Three Sisters*) and *Playboy of the West Indies*. That's cool. But if you do it straight, you're treading in areas you don't have a right to be. (Goddard 2010: 249)

Proving to the theatre industry that BAME actors could perform Shakespeare 'straight' and that they could (and should) be cast in mainstream productions of Shakespeare meant proving, first and foremost, that BAME actors could perform Shakespeare in StP. Any departure from StP was going to be regarded as a lack of skill or training rather than as a legitimate desire for acoustic diversity, as some of the actors raised and trained by Brewster went on to discover. David Harewood, for example, who had been offered his first Shakespearean role by Brewster in her production of *King Lear* for Talawa in 1994, became the first black actor to play Othello at the NT in 1997. The director, Sam Mendes, chose to evoke an early twentieth-century British colonial context as a setting for this production. Responses to Harewood's delivery of Othello's lines suggested that racial prejudice sadly belonged to Britain's colonial past as much as to the theatrical present of this production. Some reviewers enthused about Harewood's Othello finally looking the part, thus reinforcing the racial stereotype of the 'blacktor' as muscular, physical and hyper masculine,

---

favourable reviews. Rhoda Koenig at *The Independent* was the most outspoken reviewer to take a stance against the multicultural cast and the diversity of accents in this production: 'The casting call might have been held at the United Nations, what with black and white Romans and Egyptians speaking in French, Scottish and gypsy-restaurant accents. Some speak the verse for sense, some for music and some for neither' (1995). Once again, NSE accents were heard and decoded as poor delivery or attributed to a lack of understanding on the part of the actors.

looking 'strapping' and 'handsome', oozing gleaming charisma (Brantley 1998).[6] However, other reviewers regretted that Harewood did not sound right. Alistair Macaulay, in the *Financial Times*, noted that Harewood had a 'mannered way of pausing before or after keywords'. 'He is one of those actors', he added, without specifying what type of actors he had in mind, 'who seem to be speaking in an alien tongue' (1997). It is quite staggering that Harewood should be criticized for sounding different from earlier Othellos, even in a production that was meant to foreground racial otherness within an intolerant, colonial context.

Jatinder Verma, founder of Tara Arts, the first company in the UK to champion a multicultural, specifically British-Asian approach to theatre making, has also often stressed the need to prove that British Asian actors can perform Shakespeare 'straight' and that they should resist the temptation to '"Bollywood-ise" it, complete with cod-Indian accents' (Verma 2008). Tara Arts productions of Shakespeare in the 1990s were accordingly devoid of phonetic variation. Even in the 1993 Tara Arts/Contact Theatre Manchester co-production of *Troilus and Cressida*, where Verma envisaged 'Troy as the besieged East (Bosnia, British Asians), and the Greeks as the triumphalist West at its most self-confident and xenophobic', Andrew Mallet was praised for performing Troilus 'in the classic English style of strong enunciation and upright presence (and very well too)' (Wainwright, 1993). Paradoxically, the widespread expectation that companies specifically set up to promote BAME actors on the English stage should conform to the convention of delivering Shakespeare and the classics in StP meant that, at least in the 1990s, experiments with non-conventional world-English accents were the exclusive prerogative of companies who, like the Oxford Shakespeare Company directed by Irina Brook in 1997, did not have to prove their theatrical pedigree.

The first productions to feature regional and lower-status accents in the 1990s were similarly criticized for their lack of plausibility or for failing to meet the prevailing aesthetic and artistic standards associated with Shakespearean performance. Guy Retallack's 1998 production of *Richard III* at the Pleasance was, for example, performed in an accent described in *The Evening Standard* as 'pure Bethnal Green' (Anon. 1998). The East London accent used in this production jarred even with reviewers, who, like Taylor, had found the range of World English accents in Brook's production of *All's Well That Ends Well* 'wildly varying' and 'refreshing' only a

---

[6] Tonderai Munyevu uses the term 'blacktor' in his 2018 play, *The Moors*, which I discuss in detail in the Conclusion.

year earlier (1997). According to Taylor, the vocal register in Retallack's production 'diminish[ed] the grand endangering dimension of the original by presenting it as the world of the Krays'. 'Too much is flattened out', he continued:

> The famous line dropped here, 'A horse, a horse! My kingdom for a horse!' would have to be changed to 'Horse and Jockey, the Horse and Jockey! This pub for the Horse and Jockey!' to indicate the extent which a great tragedy finds itself scaled down. (1998)

Echoing Billington's and Morley's critical reviews of Brook's and Stafford-Clark's productions, Taylor objected to Retallack's notion that Shakespearean tragedy and the world of the Krays can possibly belong together. Nor would he credit those who enjoy this type of spatial and acoustic relocation of Shakespeare with sound aesthetic judgment: '[t]his production', he concluded, 'will appeal to *The Bill*-watching, *This Life* generation' (1998), namely to those members of the audience who would generally enjoy popular TV drama rather than 'straight' Shakespeare or classical theatre.

The only exception to the general rejection of regional variations in the 1990s was the critical and popular acclaim enjoyed by Barrie Rutter's Northern Broadsides. Since its inception in 1992, Rutter's company has promoted the use of regional voices. As Carol Rutter has argued, 'voices like [Barrie] Rutter's [had] never been cast as Shakespeare's royals, at least not at the Royal Shakespeare and National Theatres'; Rutter's company therefore set an important precedent by 'claim[ing] Shakespeare's "elite" text for "popular" speech' (2003: 236). Similarly, reviewer Irving Wardle hailed the company's commitment to the Northern voice as 'a thrilling departure in classical performance' (Rutter 2003: 236), and, on the twentieth anniversary of the company's inception, Andrew Dickson commended Rutter for 'taking theatre out of gilded proscenium cages and to new – especially rural – audiences' (Dickson 2012). However, Rutter's investment in the Northern voice has aimed to reverse rather than to deconstruct the traditional alignment of English Shakespeare with the speech of elitism. The systematic replacement of received pronunciation with Northern voices has effectively relocated Shakespeare into the rural North, 'making Verona', as Carol Rutter puts it, 'as naturally a suburb of Barnsley as Barnes, and the Nile a river that runs through Leeds before emptying in the Thames' (Rutter 2003: 238). The Northern voice has also been promoted as lending an earthy, rough materiality to Shakespeare's lines: in Barrie Rutter's words, 'the Northern voice shifts the centre of gravity of the spoken text from the head, the intellectual, to the visceral' (Rutter 2003: 250). Despite the innovative and politically charged quality of its work, Northern Broadsides has therefore reinforced the notion that the Northern voice suits popular modes of artistic expression. Northern Broadside nevertheless set an important precedent at a time when the delivery of Shakespeare on the English stage was still pretty uniformly aligned with the speech of elitism.

Responses to early experiments with NSE accents on the Shakespearean stage in the 1990s are particularly striking in light of the fact that attitudes to phonetic variation were starting to change. Phoneticians were by now reporting a decline in the prestige value accorded to StP. As J. C. Wells noted, RP was 'increasingly perceived as exclusive and formal' especially among 'younger people ... [who] no longer defer[red] to it in the way their elders ... did' (1999: 38). Paul Foulkes and Gerard Docherty even admitted that they could 'no longer assume that speakers of non-standard varieties automatically orient[ed] themselves towards the standard' and that, '[g]iven the changing status of RP, [phoneticians] might perhaps reassess the continuing role of RP as an educational norm' (1999: 12). The 1990s also marked the rise in popularity of a new modified regional variation, which David Rosewarne had influentially, if controversially, dubbed Estuary English in 1984. Estuary English, an intermediate variety of RP and Cockney, the working-class regional variation spoken by the working classes in East London, was hailed as a source of momentous phonological change in the pronunciation of the English language. Still according to Foulkes and Docherty, most of the phonetic changes first recorded in the late 1990s 'stem[med] from non-standard varieties as ... spoken in the south-east of England'. The 'London's working-class accent', they continue, 'is today the most influential source of phonological innovation in England and perhaps the whole of the English-speaking world' (1999: 11).

Very little, if any, of the excitement reported by the media at the time, however, translated into a sustained change in attitudes towards regional accents when used on the Shakespearean stage. Isolated examples of carefully curated, inflected voices in Shakespearean productions in the 1990s came up against a great deal of critical resistance. As Alan Cruttenden reported in 1994, 'the British [were still] particularly sensitive to variation in the pronunciation of their language. ... Such extreme sensitivity', Cruttenden added, 'is apparently not paralleled in any other country or even in other parts of the English-speaking world'. The level of sensitivity to pronunciation reported by Cruttenden in the mid-1990s was going to persist well into the early twenty-first century, when a sudden influx of foreign Shakespeare refocused artistic efforts and critical attention on the need to diversify the sound of Shakespeare in contemporary performance.

§

'Half to Half the World Opposed': Remapping Foreign and English Shakespeare in the Early Twenty-First Century

Renewed impetus towards the internationalization of English Shake-speare in performance came from the global ambition that shaped two mega-events organized by major theatrical institutions in the early twenty-first century: the Complete Works Season (henceforth CWS), led by the RSC between April 2006 and March 2007, and the World Shakespeare Festival (henceforth WSF), which was also led by the RSC, but involved other large theatre companies, during the Cultural Olympiad in 2012. These two mega-events, in turn, prompted fresh discussions about the importance of uncoupling Shakespeare from StP and the need to move towards greater acoustic diversity on the Shakespearean stage.

The CWS was launched to mark the end of an important chapter in the history of the company and its main house, the Royal Shakespeare Theatre, which would be demolished in mid-2007 to reopen on the company's 50th birthday in March 2011. The CWS had two main components: the commissioning of a new edition of Shakespeare's *Complete Works*, which was edited by Jonathan Bate and Eric Rasmussen and published by Palgrave Macmillan in 2007, and the staging of the entire Shakespearean canon in a single season. Both components of the CWS were visionary and unparalleled in scope.

Bate and Rasmussen's edition of the *Complete Works* offered freshly edited versions of the play texts as first printed in the First Folio of 1623. The *Complete Works* was advertised as the first modern edition, which, 'being commissioned by a Shakespearean acting company', relied on the Folio as the first early edition to be 'authorized by Shakespeare's own acting company' (Bate and Rasmussen 2007: 55). The First Folio actually included plays that were re-set from earlier quarto editions, thus compli-cating the notion of what theatrical authorization or theatrical provenance might actually mean in the context of the transmission of Shakespeare's plays into print.[7] However, Bate and Rasmussen did break new editorial ground by arranging the plays in the order in which they were printed in the Folio and by prioritizing the Folio version of plays that survive in more than one early edition, thus marrying traditional textual scholarship with innovation. Similarly, the CWS combined theatrical tradition and innovation, by undertaking the most extensive international collaboration ever attempted by the RSC since its foundation in 1961.

International companies invited to perform in languages other than English during the CWS included major national institutions with an established international profile: among them, the Berliner Ensemble performed *Richard II* in German; the Münchner Kammerspiele performed *Othello*, also in German; and the Ninagawa company performed *Titus Andronicus* in Japanese. Other productions were the result of international collaborations: Tim Supple presented his British Council sponsored production of *A Midsummer Night's Dream*, performed in English and several Indian languages by an Indian and Sri Lankan cast; Cheek by Jowl presented their production of *Twelfth Night* in Russian, in collaboration with their long-term partner, the Chekhov International Theatre Festival from Moscow; and Yellow Earth with the Shanghai Dramatic Arts Centre performed *King Lear* in English and Chinese, with dual language surtitles. A small number of grass-root and experimental companies also took part in the CWS: the Brazilian company Nós do Morro, patronized and trained by the RSC's own legendary voice coach, Cecily Berry, performed *The Two Gentlemen of Verona*, in Brazilian Portuguese, while Song of the Goat presented a compressed, 75-minute version of *Macbeth*, where lines from the English texts were interspersed with snatches of ancient polyphonic Corsican songs. Overall, eleven out of the thirty-seven main productions staged as part of the CWS were performed, at least partly, in languages other than English.

What prompted the RSC to enlist the collaboration of so many and so different international companies and directors? Michael Boyd had successfully pitched the CWS to the RSC Board shortly after becoming artist director in 2003. When asked what led him to propose such an ambitious project to the Board, he explained that his 'decision was partly inspired by [his] late school days when [he] moved to Edinburgh'. He then added that

> The Edinburgh Festival, with its extraordinary hothouse experience of shifting from a Swiss mime clown to the Comédie Française to a Russian

---

[7] For an overview of 'The Making of the First Folio', see Massai 2007: 136–79, esp. 136–40.

theatre company in the space of two days [had] shaped [his] appetite [for international theatre]. (Smith 2007: 13)

After Edinburgh, Boyd became British Council Fellow at the Malaya Bronnaya Theatre in Moscow in the late 1970s, when the theatre was under the artistic directorship of multi-award winning Russian director, Anatoly Vasilievich Efros. The time he spent in Moscow informed Boyd's own sense of the deeply political role of theatre in society and the benefits of ensemble work (Crompton 2012). It must have also persuaded Boyd about the need for a national company like the RSC to have an international profile, not only through international touring but also through sustained collaboration with other leading companies worldwide. Unlike his predecessor, Adrian Noble, who had attempted to transform the RSC into an international corporation selling Shakespeare as a product of British culture for a globalized, mass-entertainment market (Kidnie 2009), Boyd invited visiting companies from overseas, as well as from across the UK, in order to diversity and internationalize the traditionally text-based, naturalist approach to Shakespeare championed by the RSC.

At least in one important respect, though, Boyd's investment in innovation through international programming was a direct response to the radical changes introduced by Noble. Noble's planned overhaul of the RSC, also known as 'Project Fleet', would have involved a complete transformation of the physical, logistical and artistic make-up of the company. His attempt to turn a national, heavily subsidized company into a more dynamic corporation, in keeping with the globalization and commercialization of the theatre industry, was threatening to undermine the company's core identity, which is informed by its commitment to ensemble work, to outreach and to the fulfilment of a social agenda that sees Shakespeare more as shared cultural capital than as a globally marketable commodity. Noble had also initiated a gradual withdrawal from the company's official London home at the Barbican Arts Centre, in favour of temporary arrangements with more central London West End venues and more touring overseas.[8]

The Barbican's main response to the gradual withdrawal of the RSC from its programmes was the launch of the first Barbican International Theatre Events season (henceforth Bite). Bite was going to prove a major, critically acclaimed undertaking, and had a profound impact on the

---

[8] On Adrian Noble's directorship, see Kidnie 2009: 45–64; on the company's earlier ethos and structure, see Sinfield 1994: 182–205.

programming, staging and reception of Shakespeare on the English stage. Set up as a six-month festival in 1998, when the RSC started to cut the number of productions transferring to the Barbican, Bite became an all-year-round venture in 2002, when the RSC stopped performing at the Barbican altogether. Starting from 2002, Bite brought some of the best international directors of Shakespeare and their companies to London. Among them, a Catalan *Macbeth* directed by Calixto Bieito in 2003, a Russian *King Lear* directed by Lev Dodin in 2006, and a Dutch version of Shakespeare's Roman plays, called *Roman Tragedies*, directed by Ivo van Hove in 2009. According to Maria Shevtsova, Bite turned out to be 'of immense service to theatre-makers and theatregoers ... in Britain':

> [By] invit[ing] some of the most interesting theatre in the world, whether it is established or breaking through to prominence or still on the edge, waiting to be caught up in the international circuit, ... Bite has helped to inspire makers of theatre working in Britain to explore their art in greater depth and breadth. (2010: 293)

As early as 2003, Dominic Cavendish reported that '[b]oth Graham Sheffield, artistic director of Bite, and Louise Jeffreys, then Head of Theatre, burn[ed] with a conviction that London need[ed] a dedicated space for international work'. Cavendish realized that Bite had not only sprung out of the new programming opportunities made possible by the withdrawal of the RSC but that Bite was also changing attitudes towards 'foreign Shakespeare' at the RSC:

> We're back to Shakespeare. Bite's programmers can't avoid straying into RSC territory; directors from round the world want to tackle the Bard, and audiences, from wherever they hail, want to see his work. ... Small wonder that Michael Boyd, the new RSC supremo, has been holding constructive talks with Graham Sheffield about bringing the company back for regular seasons. He would seem to understand, rather better than his predecessor, that the world's most famous dramatist fits incredibly easily under an internationalist umbrella. (2003)

Cavendish, in other words, did not only appreciate the fact that foreign Shakespeare was an exciting alternative to the quintessentially English brand of Shakespeare in performance associated with the RSC, but he also predicted that the excitement generated by Bite would affect programming at the RSC. The CWS was a calculated response to the experimental and international approach to Shakespeare showcased by Bite.

The CWS became a genuine theatrical watershed in its own right. Prior to it, the pioneering curatorial approach to the voice undertaken by some directors in the 1990s seemed all but forgotten. In 2002–3, for example, the under-classes in Nicholas Hytner's NT production of *Henry V*, starring Adrian Lester in the title role, spoke in regional or inner-city accents: Bardolph (David Kennedy), Pistol (Jude Akuwudike) and the Hostess (Cecilia Noble) sounded like modern-day East-Enders, while Nym was played by Robert Horwell in his natural North-Yorkshire accent. Just as predictably, the French sported stage French accents, while Robert Blythe and Tony Devlin played Fluellen and Macmorris in their native Welsh and Northern Irish accents. National stereotyping was downplayed by local editing of the text and by the excision of Jamy, which drastically reduced both the comic and the subversive potential often associated with these characters (Penlington 2010: 245); in all other respects, though, this production simply juxtaposed the higher ranking English characters, whose speech was normatively marked by prestige phonetic variations, to lower class and foreign characters, who were just as conventionally marked by lower status and put-on stage accents.

When Hytner went on to direct *1* and *2 Henry IV* at the NT in 2005, he once again resorted to conventionally marked voices to conjure a familiar sense of national identity, qualified primarily by class and only secondarily by geographical differences. Black British actors Jeffery Kissoon and David Harewood played Northumberland and Harry Percy but spoke in StP, thus sounding exactly like every other character in the King's all-white party. Though factional and splintered, the ruling class was, at least acoustically speaking, perfectly uniform. The carriers in *1 Henry IV* 2.1 (Harry Peacock and Elliot Levey), along with Gadshill (Thomas Arnold) and Chamberlain (Ian Mitchell) just as predictably spoke in a lower-class accent, tinged with a light Essex inflection. Hal (Matthew MacFadyen) in 2.4 mimicked the cockney accents of the waiting staff, including Francis (Darren Hart) and the Vintner (Robert Blythe), while the motley crew of country soldiers recruited by Falstaff and Bardolph in *2 Henry IV* 3.2 – Davy (Ian Gelder), Mouldy (Alistair Petrie), Shadow (Michelle Dockery), Wart (Darren Hart), Francis Feeble (Elliot Levey) and Peter Bullcalf (Harry Peacock) – had very strong, camped-up Gloucestershire accents.

Similarly, even while Boyd was planning the CWS, RSC in-house productions staged under his artistic directorship were still acoustically conventional. Jonathan Slinger, for example, did not get to use his North-ern accent when he played Puck in Greg Doran's 2005 production of *A Midsummer Night's Dream*, even though the mechanicals predictably spoke in a strong regional Brummie accent. Just as unsurprisingly, Slinger spoke in his natural Northern voice when he played the comic servant

Dromio of Syracuse in Meckler's 2005 production of *The Comedy of Errors*. Boyd's own 2005 production of *Twelfth Night* was the only production that offered a refreshing, if minor, departure from the dominant acoustic norm in the early 2000s. By casting two Scots, Forbes Masson and Meg Fraser, to play Feste and Maria in their native accents he added a love interest and psychological complexity to their relationship: the phonetic variation in their voices suggested a potentially shared background, and their status as outsiders in Illyria, where all the other characters spoke in StP, made Feste's disappointment at being rejected in favour of the boorish Sir Toby all the more harrowing.

Foreign accents in Shakespearean productions in the early 2000s were used just as conventionally as regional or lower-status variations. In a 2004 production of *The Winter's Tale* by the Creation Theatre Company from Oxford, Leontes (Andrew Harrison) and Hermione (Sasha Waddell) put on Russian accents to double as Old Shepherd and Son in Bohemia. Their Russian accents were all but gone when they returned as Leontes and Hermione in act 5. As noted by reviewers at the time, the Russian accents reinforced the traditionally comic interpretation of the characters who populate Bohemia:

> Waddell ... and ... Harrison have a chance to demonstrate their comic range ... as the Old Shepherd and his son in an Eastern European version of pastoral life. Their performances are sufficiently distinctive to avoid confusion when they return as the royal couple in the final scene, with all traces of Russian accents expunged. (Loveridge 2004)

Foreignness, signified as a departure from StP, inevitably came across as comic and stereotypical and, as the reviewer pointed out, the tragic roles played by Waddell and Harrison at the Sicilian court were neatly juxtaposed to their comic roles.

In the wider context of these acoustically conventional productions, the CWS offered a unique opportunity for international companies to be heard performing alongside the RSC. Some felt that the contributions by international companies were unfairly sidelined: Katherine Duncan-Jones, for example, pointed out that 'these companies often appeared for barely a week, and sometimes for only a couple of days' and that '[t]he brevity of such appearances severely moderated the apparent generosity of their inclusion in the larger Stratford season' (2007: 359). However, the sound of a wide range of voices, either foreign or marked by regional or foreign accents, had a profound impact on audiences and critics alike. As Peter Kirwan reported, 'language', or 'the process of speaking and hearing

Shakespeare' in languages and registers other than English or StP, was a major aspect of Shakespearean performance that the Complete Works season 'opened up to debate' (2007: 99).

The sound of Shakespeare in the non-English productions showcased by the CWS was indeed the primary focus of critical responses to the overall event. Reviewers of Ninagawa's *Titus Andronicus*, for example, commented on how the sound of the Japanese translation suited Ninagawa's stylized, semi-operatic approach. As Alastair Macaulay put it, '[i]f . . . spoken in English, the extent of its theatrical artifice would seem ludicrous' (2006). In the same spirit, Charles Spencer noted that '[t]he explosive guttural sounds of Japanese . . . seem exceptionally well suited to the play's churning violence' (2006). Echoing Spencer, Terry Grimley observed that '[t]hough it might take a moment to adjust to it', the soundscape of Ninagawa's production 'suit[ed] the material to exhilarating effect' (2006).

Spencer was similarly impressed by the Washington-based Shakespeare Theatre Company's production of *Love's Labour's Lost*: 'The language is treated with respect and is for the most part extremely well spoken (Shakespeare sounds great with an American accent)' (2006a). Conversely, Barbara Gaines's production of *1 & 2 Henry IV* from the Chicago Shakespeare Theatre did not get uniformly positive reviews, at least partly because some of the actors attempted to put on affected, Anglicized accents. Taylor wrote extensively about the plight of American actors who feel, or are made to feel, the need to anglicize their accent to perform Shakespeare on the English stage:

> [Gaines's productions] feel constrained by an unnecessary deference to Englishness. It's not just that they look embarrassingly old-fashioned, with terrible long wigs and black-leather ye-olde-cum-modern uniforms that were all the rage at the RSC in the 1970s. More hampering are the weird, semi-anglicised accents affected by several of the leading actors. As Sir John Falstaff, Greg Vinkler. . . [gives] a genuinely engaging performance, marred for me, however, by the fact that Vinkler has overlaid his native tones with an inappropriate veneer of English gentility. . . . Likewise, given that Jeffrey Carlson plays the unreformed Prince Hal with the body language and nervous sniggers of a contemporary slacker, why has he been told to mangle the vowel sounds that come naturally to him? (2006)

Having regretted the 'verbal camouflage' attempted in this production, Taylor went on to note: 'the irony, of course, is that the American accent is much closer to how Shakespeare would have sounded than English RP' (2006). The overall result, in Taylor's view, was that Gaines's productions 'came across more as a skilled imitation than something that has found its own voice' (2006).[9]

Entirely novel in reviews of the CWS was the realization that Shakespeare's language is not merely a vessel that neutrally conveys the meaning of his works and that becomes redundant or meaningless in translation. Reviewers like Taylor and Spencer began to consider the possibility that Shakespeare's language is in fact a complex system of signs whose material texture and rhetorical complexity take on additional connotations when marked by foreign accents or translated into a foreign language. Rather than harping on what is *lost* in translation, thus clinging to a mode of *linguistic* understanding that privileges the recognition of the familiar, both from a semantic and a phonetic point of view, reviewers started to celebrate what is *found* in translation, namely a mode of *non-linguistic* understanding that relies on the sound of the foreign language translation as much as on other non-linguistic aspects of the *mise-en-scène*, such as gestures, blocking, visual imagery and stage design.

The production that most forcibly encouraged this new mode of non-linguistic understanding of Shakespeare's language in performance during the CWS was Tim Supple's Indian and Sri Lankan *A Midsummer Night's Dream*. Although sponsored by the British Council and conceived by a British director, Supple's *Dream* was designed, rehearsed and first performed in India in the first half of 2005, before it toured internationally in 2006. Performers spoke in their native languages; similarly the theatrical language of this production was informed by theatrical practices and conventions drawn from across the Indian subcontinent. The result was an astonishing feast of languages and theatrical traditions, which, far from coming across as artificial, reflected the multilingual and multicultural contexts from which this production originated. In the words of the director,

> [a]crobats from Delhi worked with dance masters from Kerala; realistic actors from Mumbai worked with folk actors from Tamil Nadu; musicians from Manipur, Kolkata and Tamil Nadu played together. And Shakespeare's words flourished in dialogues between English and Malayalam;

---

[9] Other reviewers echoed Taylor's astute reading of the verbal soundscape of Gaines's productions. Spencer, like Taylor, found the attempt to Anglicize the actors' natural North American accents counter-productive: 'Several of the leading actors ... attempt English accents. This is entirely unnecessary for, as Peter Hall has observed, Shakespeare sounds terrific with an American voice, and the attempt at anglicisation results in some extremely weird, pseudo-genteel vowel sounds. Prince Harry frequently becomes "Prince Hairy", and Falstaff announces that he'll be "henged" rather than hanged before going to sleep behind the "erras" (arras)' (2006b).

> Tamil and Hindi; Gujarati and Sinhala; Marathi and Kannada. India is a multilingual nation: our production would be multilingual too. (Supple 2006)

The rich variety of languages and sounds offered audiences a unique acoustic experience, which, in Peter Foster's words, 'outstrip[ped] the need to understand every word' (Supple 2006).

Being placed in a position of 'linguistic non-understanding' enabled English-speaking audiences to experience aspects of Shakespeare that signify semiotically rather than semantically in performance. Or, as Supple put it, 'seeing and hearing the *Dream* come alive in seven languages and the multitude of approaches of an Indian cast ... scoured clean my perception of the play', generating a level of reception and interpretation that went 'beyond the clichés so ingrained in the way we speak and hear Shakespeare' (2006). Reviewers picked up on Supple's attempt to 'scour clean' our sense of what Shakespeare should sound like in performance. Ian Shuttleworth, for example, felt that the language mix 'prove[d] no barrier whatever to understanding; moreover', he added, 'we [could] appreciate the poetical sonorities of whatever language [was] being spoken at the time.' Gordon Parsons even compared the experience of listening to Supple's production to the surprise and pleasure that Shakespeare's original audiences must have experienced as they were first exposed to the aural thickness of his language:

> its colourful vivacity, its strangeness to the British eye and ear and the total commitment of a cast to a play largely untrammelled by the weight of tradition ... must be the kind of theatre experience that the Bard's first audiences must have relished. (2006)

What is striking in this comment is the novel realization that a different 'Shakespeare' from the one the 'British ear' has been attuned to since the rise of StP in the eighteenth century can emerge from the sonorities and rhythms of Shakespeare performed in other languages.

Of course some reviewers felt misled into unfamiliar territory, 'cheated' into watching productions that they did not recognize as 'Shakespeare'.[10] On the whole, though, the revival of Supple's *Dream* in the context of the CWS, at a time when Stratford audiences and reviewers were exposed to a significant range of foreign voices or voices inflected by foreign accents,

---

[10] See, for example, Hallmark: 'Language barrier broke midsummer spell. . . . On so many levels it was awesome ... But why, oh why, was such a large chunk of the play performed in seven different Indian languages – without any translation? Surely the Bard's power flows through his mastery of language, and when I couldn't understand it, I ended up feeling cheated' (2006).

triggered a novel appreciation of Shakespeare's language delivered in 'accents yet unknown'. Supple's *Dream* was probably the production that came closest to fulfilling Boyd's own understanding of the benefits of performing foreign Shakespeare on the English stage: 'there's been a sort of war in British theatre – partly a xenophobic war', waged on the premise that 'all foreign Shakespeare is bad Shakespeare because there is not enough respect for the author's words. ... I consistently refuse to see them as mutually exclusive'. (Smith 2007: 14) Boyd understood that foreign Shakespeare does not involve a loss but a transformation of Shakespeare's language into 'something rich and strange', which in turn re-moulds its original texture into equally suggestive sonorities.

More generally, the CWS promoted a different appreciation of Shakespeare's language in performance. As Elinor Parsons put it, 'language is too often taken to be simply a matter of vocabulary and syntax'. What the CWS demonstrated, in Parsons' words, was that '[e]ngagement with Shakespeare's text should be extended beyond "words, words, words" with more emphasis placed upon the sound and rhythm of what characters say' (2007: 7–8). The 'sound and rhythm' of the foreign Shakespeare productions presented in Stratford in 2006–2007 stimulated a different hearing mode in English-speaking audiences, and especially in Stratford audiences, who had never been exposed to such a wide range of voices, accents and performance styles before.

This different mode of appreciation of Shakespeare's language in performance had a palpable impact on the use of regional accents on the Shakespearean stage. The use of regional voices in productions presented as part of the CWS was still quite limited and mostly confined to productions that explicitly updated Shakespeare,[11] but the need to start using regional voices emerged in discussions about the CWS more generally. In an interview with Jim Burke, Irish actor Finbar Lynch reiterated the urgent need for a radical acoustic reform of the Shakespearean stage: 'I think ... that Shakespeare ... done in an actor's own accent is closer to the original, because Elizabethan English wasn't ironed out in the way that RP is. But even now', he added, 'there are people who think that we should lose our

---

[11] The Cardboard Citizens' *Timon of Athens* represented a welcome departure from the conventional use of StP in the English productions presented as part of the CWS. This production reimagined the play as a motivational workshop and the actors, who shared a background of homelessness and marginalization, got to use their own accents. Their accents effectively punctured the patronizing rhetoric peddled by the facilitators and the fact that several actors played Timon, using accents ranging from StP to English and foreign variations, amplified Timon's personal plight to encompass other types of dispossession.

accents when playing lords or aristocrats' (Burke 2006). Sadly, Lynch did not get to use his native Irish accent when he played Cassius in the production of *Julius Caesar* that Sean Holmes presented as part of the CWS. In this production, a generic Irish accent was conventionally used for the 'Second Commoner' (the Cobbler) in the opening scene.

However, the legacy of the CWS had a lasting impact on subsequent productions staged on national and regional stages across the country. Peter Kirwan, for example, detected a connection between the vocally experimental quality of Conall Morrison's 2007 RSC production of *Macbeth* and lessons learned during the CWS. '[T]he legacy of the Festival continues', he observed, while writing about this production, and the fact that it featured 'a cast drawn from around the world' and that it 'play[ed] with accent and multiculturalism within Shakespeare' (2007: 102).

Equally significant is the fact that in 2008 David Tennant got to use his natural Scottish accent to play Berowne in Greg Doran's *Love's Labour's Lost*. Tennant's Scottish accent, familiar to cinema and television audiences in the UK and beyond, was deemed not only appropriate but highly desirable for a character like Berowne, in a play like *Love's Labour's Lost*, whose extensive wordplay, puns and the self-consciously literary quality of its language can alienate modern audiences. According to Billington, Tennant successfully used his natural accent to 'express ... pragmatic skepticism' (2008), a fitting response to the King of Navarre's plan to shun the company of women in order to devote three years fully to scholarly endeavours. Spencer in *The Telegraph* also found that, by '[s]-peaking in his natural Scottish accent ...', his Berowne shoots from the quip ... and somehow manages to transmute even the most unpromising lines into genuine laughter' (2008). Also in 2008, Tennant played the title role in Doran's production of *Hamlet*, but he did not use his Scottish accent for the foremost tragic role in the Shakespearean canon. Interestingly, Taylor complained about a decision that would have seemed entirely uncontroversial before the CWS refocused attention on the drawbacks of acoustic normativity on the Shakespearean stage: 'It's a pity ... that Tennant is using an RP accent rather that his natural incisive Scots lilt that might promote greater intimacy of rapport' (2008).[12]

In this respect, Hytner's 2011 production of *Hamlet* at the NT proved more daring, and it did so in ways that harked back to Williamson's

---

[12] Tennant went on to use his Scottish accent when he played Benedick alongside Catherine Tate's Beatrice in Josie Rourke's production of *Much Ado about Nothing*, which opened to critical and popular acclaim at the Wyndham Theatre in London in May 2011.

landmark interpretation of Hamlet's role in the 1960s. Rory Kinnear's Hamlet, anticipating his approach to Iago in the 2013 NT production discussed later in this chapter, spoke in a light Estuary accent. His accent set him apart from the other characters at Claudius's court. As a result, he sounded openly anti-establishment. Kinnear, who was educated at St Paul's School and then read English at Oxford, normally speaks in StP, both on and off stage. His Hamlet therefore sounded like someone who, appalled by the moral standard of the world he was born into, had turned his back upon it by toning down his accent. Kinnear's put-on accent was a calculated decision, in keeping with Hytner's updating of the play, which transformed Shakespeare's early modern rendition of an old Nordic story about prince Amlodi or Amleth, into 'something we recognise as the world we know' (Hytner 2011).

Another NT production, also staged in 2011, registered important changes in the soundscape of 'English' Shakespeare in performance. Dominic Cooke's *The Comedy of Errors* turned the cavernous depths of the Olivier Theatre into a sounding box that reverberated with regionally marked and foreign accents, punctuated by the singing, in an foreign language, of popular songs, including 'Madness', 'People Are Strange' and 'Paranoid' (Purves 2011). Lenny Henry, as Antipholus of Syracuse, and Lucian Msamati, as Dromio of Syracuse, spoke in a thick Nigerian/West African accent, while their Ephesian twins spoke in distinctive English accents, the master in a middle-class/Surf London (South London) accent and the servant in a heavy Cockney accent. Reinforcing the updating of Epheseus as a modern-day version of multicultural and multi-ethnic London, Claudie Blakley and Michelle Terry as Adriana and Luciana came across as stereotypical 'Essex WAGs teetering on impossible heels' (Purves 2011), while their maid (Clare Cathcart) spoke in an exaggerated stage Spanish accent. Some reviewers recoiled from the sight and sound of what struck them as an 'extended urban nightmare' (Billington 2011):

> There's a strong sense of a multicultural society throughout, with a bewildering mix of acute accents, which is some ways succeeds rather too well in evoking modern Britain: many-hued, richly diverse, and, er, nobody can actually understand anybody. (Hart 2011)

This review shows how the fear of being placed in a position of 'linguistic non-understanding' by a major Shakespearean production on the main stage at the NT channelled more general anxieties about the state of multiculturalism in contemporary Britain. The blend of familiarity and strangeness detected and lamented by some reviewers was directly linked to the kind of dislocation experienced by the main characters in Shakespeare's comedy of mistaken identities: those who look familiar, or even familial, turn out to be strangers, causing Shakespeare's characters – as much as some reviewers – to doubt their ability to understand the world around them.

The wide range of marked voices in Cooke's production captured the accents spoken in present-day London. Quoting a survey carried out by Sue Fox, Mara Logaldo found that

> the urban slang spoken in London is actually less and less identifiable with Cockney or with other variants of vernacular London English (LE), differing in vocabulary and accent, and is increasingly influenced not only by Standard American English, as would seem more predictable (given the pervasive influence of this variety worldwide), but by the dialects imported by immigrants, especially English-lexicon ones like Jamaican Creole, with inflections of Bangladeshi, Gujarati, and even Arabic. The process is mainly the outcome of the huge immigration of Afro-Caribbeans and Asians from the 1950s onwards, which has resulted in language or dialect contact between white and second- or third-generation black children, adolescents, and teenagers. (2010: 120)

Cooke's production effectively evoked the soundscape of contemporary London, as described by phoneticians like Fox and Logaldo. By doing so, this production activated aspects in the fictive world of Shakespeare's play that speak directly to the challenges faced by multiculturalism in the UK (and beyond) in the wake of a global resurgence of fundamentalism, conservative nationalism and sectarianism.

The comic resolution of the play in the context of Cooke's updating showed how a convergence of diverse voices can generate what Paul Gilroy calls 'a shared culture' that 'mediates the relationship between ... different ethnic groups that together comprise ... Britain' (1987: 294–5).[13] The acoustic diversity built into Cooke's production constituted a close theatrical counterpart to Gilroy's notion of a new 'ethics of antiphony' (1993: 200). The reciprocal interchange, or antiphony, generated by the use of different foreign accents and regionally inflected voices on the main stage of the NT resembled the sort of 'language or dialect contact' described by Fox and Logaldo, which, in turn, triggers important changes in the

---

[13] As Gilroy explains, '[t]he effects of the ... penetration of black forms into the dominant culture mean that it is impossible to theorize black culture in Britain without developing a new perspective on British culture *as a whole*. ... An intricate web of cultural and political connections binds blacks here [in the UK] to blacks elsewhere. At the same time, they are linked into the social relations of this country' (1987: 205).

cultural connotations associated with phonetic variations as markers of class and national identities.

The legacy of the CWS played an important role not only in the curatorial work that went into the acoustic make-up of individual productions staged in its wake, but also in the organization of the next mega-event to include a record number of foreign-language productions. Deborah Shaw, who had headed the Bath International Shakespeare Festival in the early 2000s, before being appointed Festival Director during the CWS in 2006–2007, was now put in charge of the WSF that took place in 2012 as part of the Cultural Olympiad. Shaw's long-term commitment to bringing world theatre to Britain informed the Festival's large-scale investment in foreign Shakespeare.

Statistically, the WSF nearly doubled the number of foreign Shakespeare productions staged in England up to that point in time. Between March and August 2012, audiences in London and at venues across the country had a chance to listen to Shakespeare performed in eleven African languages, thirteen Asian languages and sixteen European languages other than English (including Welsh), as well as in Māori, Mexican and Argentine Spanish and Brazilian Portuguese.[14] The RSC and Shakespeare's Globe alone, as just two of the several partners that took part in the Festival, showcased a staggering number of international companies. As part of the Globe to Globe 2012 Festival (henceforth G2G), Shakespeare's Globe invited thirty-seven companies to perform all the plays most commonly attributed to Shakespeare in languages other than English over a period of six weeks, from late April to early June. The RSC opted instead for in-house mini-seasons and large international collaborations. Three shipwreck plays – *The Comedy of Errors*, *Twelfth Night* and *The Tempest* – were, for example, staged as part of the 'What Country, Friends, is This?' Trilogy. *A Soldier in Every Son: An Aztec Trilogy* was instead co-produced with the National Theatre of Mexico, but performed in English, alongside *Richard III* and *King John*, as part of the *Nations at War: The Struggle for Absolute Power*. *Troilus and Cressida* and *Two Roses for Richard* were also co-productions, performed respectively in English with the Wooster Group, from New York, and in Brazilian Portuguese with the Companhia Bufomecânica, from Rio de Janeiro.

Both approaches to festival programming – hosting visiting companies versus international collaborations – proved at their most interesting when

---

[14] For a full list of WSF productions by language, see 'Appendix 1: Productions by Country and Language', in Edmondson, Prescott and Sullivan 2013: 271–4.

English jostled for attention with other languages, whether as interpolations within foreign language productions staged during the G2G or as inflected by the different companies who participated in the WSF. Snippets of English were smuggled into some of the foreign productions staged at G2G, despite a strict ban on English imposed by the organizers, who were obliged to follow the guidelines issued by the funding body (the London Olympic Games Organizing Committee) for this event. As a result of this controversial ban, companies who would normally use English when performing Shakespeare in their own countries had to perform entirely in other languages. Some of the companies who occasionally ignored the ban made their use of English all the more significant and suggestive.

Among the companies who occasionally ignored the ban, London-based Two Gents Productions (henceforth TwoGents) proved by far the most interesting and thought-provoking. TwoGents were invited to revive their production of *Vakomana Vaviri Ve Zimbabwe* (*The Two Gentlemen of Verona*), which had premiered at Ovalhouse, South London, in 2008. The invite was however conditional on the company's willingness to perform it not in English and Shona, as they had done in 2008 and on tour since then, but exclusively in Shona, the language most commonly spoken in Zimbabwe, the country of origin of the company's two founding actors, Denton Chikura and Tonderai Munyevu. Directed by German-born Arne Pohlmeier, TwoGents had always performed Shakespeare in two-men English versions, interspersed with Shona, for mixed audiences in London, across Europe and the UK, and in Zimbabwe. Having dutifully had their script translated into Shona by poet translator Noel Marerwa, TwoGents nevertheless retained enough English to ensure that their mixed audiences heard key moments in their productions in both languages. By doing so, they managed to retain their distinctive approach to Shakespeare's language, which combines the company's eccentricity of acting style and diction with their commitment to performing Shakespeare in English.

Their sophisticated understanding of the politics that inform the delivery of Shakespeare's language on the English stage had already emerged quite clearly in the opening sequence of the 2008 version of their *Vakomana Vaviri Ve Zimbabwe*. In this earlier version, Chikura and Munyevu had burst onto the stage shouting at their audience in Shona. It soon became clear that they were personating cab drivers trying to secure the custom of unwitting members of the audience by offering them competitive fares. Chikura and Munyevu quickly switched to English to decide whether it was sensible for them to speak Shona, given that the customer/member of the audience they were addressing was 'a white'. However, addressing this customer/member of the audience in English proved just as fraught. Chikura's claims – 'I speak proper English', 'I speak Shakespearean English' – and Munyevu's cutting reply – 'No you don't' – seemed specifically meant to catalyze any potential resistance on the part of those members of the audience who were used to hearing Shakespeare delivered in StP. Chikura's further claim that 'Shakespeare [was his] grandfather' provoked Munyevu to retort that 'No, [Shakespeare] was not [his] grandfather'. Chikura's reply, 'I'll show you', framed the entire production as an attempt to show Munyevu (and the audience) that he could and would perform Shakespeare in English, though inflected by the accents, sounds, songs and traditions of a different language and (theatrical) culture.

Other key moments in this earlier version of *Vakomana Vaviri Ve Zimbabwe* had drawn the audience's attention to the inflected quality of the English spoken by Chikura and Munyevu. One such moment occurred in 4.1, when Chikura and Munyevu recruited three members of the audience to play the Outlaws. The three unsuspecting spectators were carefully selected because of their gender and their race. The first of the Outlaw scenes thus became the perfect pretext for Munyevu to ventriloquize a high-pitched white female, a booming baritonal black male and a white male who spoke in StP. The accent, tone and register used to deliver Shakespeare in mainstream English productions was thus evoked to signal the distance between a normative 'English' Shakespeare and this company's unique brand of Shakespeare in performance, which is neither normatively English nor straightforwardly foreign, but rather a brand new type of non-mainstream, intercultural English Shakespeare.

Although duty-bound to perform in Shona during the G2G, TwoGents managed to deliver Shakespeare's text in translation while inflecting both Shona and English with accents that would sound non-standard to their Festival audience. For their revival of *Vakomana Vaviri ve Zimbabwe*, Marerwa was asked to produce an archaic and literary translation that would make Shakespeare's language sound remote to modern Shona speakers. Chikura and Munyevy often strayed from the Shona translation to interpolate English not only to supplement the sparse surtitles used at the Globe during the Festival but also to allow both Shona speakers and non-Shona speakers to share the experience of hearing Shakespeare in a linguistic register that was simultaneously familiar and strange.

TwoGents also modified and expanded the original opening sequence in order to emphasize not only the intercultural quality of their approach to

Shakespeare, as they had one in 2008, but also the fundamental hybridity of their subject-positions as Zimbabwean actors, who would normally perform Shakespeare in English in fringe venues, and were now invited to perform Shakespeare on the Globe stage, but in Shona. Chikura and Munyevu took their time to stage their entrance at the Globe Theatre. While the audience chattered expectantly, Chikura lifted one side of the trapdoor on the main stage and peered out, seemingly shocked by his surroundings, thus stressing the significance of their temporary relocation from a venue like Ovalhouse to the Globe Theatre. Chikura then disappeared from view, closing the trapdoor behind him. Most members of the audience may not have noticed him at all at this stage. A few seconds later, though, Chikura flung the same side of the trapdoor open and instantly secured the attention of all members of the audience as the door landed on the stage with a loud bang. The whole theatre fell perfectly silent and all eyes focused on Chikura, who, still looking overwhelmed, climbed onto the main stage followed by Munyevu. Sporting Elizabethan costumes – Munyevu wore deep-brown velvet doublet and hose with a dark-brown cape flung over one shoulder, while Chikura wore an open white shirt over knee-length hose – they stood still for a few long moments, looking nervous and ill at ease.

By protracting their entrance, Chikura and Munyevu drew attention to their complex status as insiders and outsiders, and not as mere visitors on the Globe stage. Their surprise on entering the stage, the huge trunk they hoisted onto the stage, and their entrance from the cellarage, which was used in Shakespeare's own time to admit demons, ghosts and other liminal creatures on to the main stage, suggested Chikura and Munyevu's status as travellers and outsiders. However, their choice to wear not only period costumes, but costumes that they had borrowed from the Globe's own collection of meticulously manufactured artefacts for original practice productions, simultaneously marked Chikura and Munyevu as 'authentically' Elizabethan and as in-house company actors. Other companies chose to stage their entrance at the Globe either by paying homage to Shakespeare's original home (some actors kissed the stage) or by waving national flags or singing national anthems, thus breaking another ban on any reference to belligerent nationalism, which – the organizers felt – would run against the spirit of internationalism and communality in which Festival had been conceived. TwoGents were the only company who did not cast themselves in the role of either deferential or defiant guests, opting instead to position themselves as playful, intercultural go-betweeners.

After a long pause, Chikura and Munyevu finally took a bow, acknowledging their role as performers, to the great relief of the audience, who applauded and cheered on finally being acknowledged as spectators. The opening sequence was however far from over. TwoGents continued to tease the audience by drawing attention to the distinctive features of their approach to Shakespeare. They first proceeded to take out their props from the trunk and to hang them, slowly and ceremoniously, on a rope tied to the two columns that flank the entrance to the tiring house (or discovery space) at the back of the Globe stage. After carefully placing a thumb piano on the base of one of the two columns, Chikura smiled confidently at the audience and readied himself to speak. Much to everyone's amusement, the language that came out of Chikura's mouth was not Shona, but the first line of the English prologue that TwoGents had used to open their inaugural production in 2008: 'Two friends, both alike in dignity / In fair Zimbabwe where we lay our scene...'. Peals of laughter rose from the yard, while Munyevu, staring sternly at Chikura, proceeded to translate the same line in Shona. Taking turns, and blatantly contravening the ban on English, they delivered the entire version of the original prologue line by line, first in English and then in Shona.

When the action of the play finally got underway, Chikura and Munyevu switched to Shona. Most visiting companies avoided using English, and their audiences depended entirely on the sparse surtitles shown on two digital boards placed on either side of the main stage. As a result, speakers of the foreign language being used on stage stood out quite clearly from those who may have been familiar with the play but did not understand the language. The ban on English, in other words, split the audience into two palpably different groups: one who identified more immediately with the performers, laughed at their jokes and responded more directly and emotionally to the action being performed on stage, and another who watched both the performers on stage and the foreign language speakers in the audience, as if the latter were part and parcel of the spectacle of 'foreignness' that was unfolding before them in the Globe. Conversely, TwoGents kept switching to English, albeit briefly, speaking in an informal, acoustically inflected register, thus giving their audience an opportunity to hear a textured, accented Shakespeare that departed both from modern spoken Shona and from StP, as routinely used on the English stage.[15]

Other WSF productions used a range of NSE accents, but they did not prove as popular with the critics or their audiences as *Vakomana Vaviri ve Zimbabwe* had done on the Globe stage. An RSC production of *Troilus and Cressida*, co-presented with The Wooster Group, New York, is a good

---

[15] For a more detailed discussion of this production, see Massai 2017.

case in point. The Wooster Group, like TwoGents, regard the performer's voice not as a mere vehicle through which meaning is conveyed to the audience, but as a source of meaning in its own right. The company's approach to canonical playwrights, including Racine, O'Neill and Chekhov, as well as Shakespeare, has routinely privileged the voice over textual interpretation. As company performer Kate Valk put it, when asked to describe their trademark approach to the classics, 'we don't sit around the table a lot and break down the text. It happens on our feet because Liz [director Elizabeth LeCompte] needs to hear it in the room' (LeCompte *et al.* 2013: 128). Hence Gerald Siegmund's apt and helpful description of their work as 'a theatre of voices' (2005: 178).

The Wooster Group's approach to *Troilus and Cressida* was, in other words, perfectly in keeping with this company's sustained interest in the voice, and can best be understood in the context of their work with Shakespeare, and of their 2005 production of *Hamlet*, more specifically. Their production of *Hamlet* placed just as much emphasis on how modulations of the voice can carry connotations that exceed and transform the meaning of the source text. This production had been conceived not as a new interpretation of Shakespeare's tragedy, but as a live reconstruction of John Gielgud's 1964 *Hamlet*, starring Richard Burton as Hamlet and Gielgud himself as Old Hamlet. The Gielgud Burton *Hamlet* was filmed and shown in cinemas across the United States on 23 and 24 September 1964. The Wooster Group in turn repurposed a recording of this production, working especially on the sound of Shakespeare's lines as delivered by the original performers, 'editing out long pauses' or 'adding pauses where pauses had been left out' (LeCompte *et al.* 2013: 128). The edited video and sound recording was then projected onto the back of the stage and used as a palimpsest by the Wooster Group performers, who spoke over, and often suppressed, or parodied, or simply accompanied, the voices of the original performers. The Wooster Group, who had been attracted to this production by the calibre of 'some of the greatest English performers ... involved in it' (LeCompte *et al.* 2013: 122), explained that they were less interested in establishing 'whether Gertrude knows that Claudius killed her husband' (LeCompte *et al.* 2013: 128) than in measuring their own voices up against those of their famous British predecessors. Their approach to *Hamlet* thus focused less on what Shakespeare's lines might mean than on how they have been or can be spoken.

Gielgud's 1964 *Hamlet* offered the Wooster Group a prime opportunity to show how powerfully voice resonates on the Shakespearean stage.

As scholars have repeatedly observed, Gielgud's and Burton's modes of delivery in this production were distinctively 'Janus-like', respectively 'looking squarely back to Edwardian traditions' and 'coming from film' (Cartelli 2008: 156). Gielgud's voice embodied a 'traditionally classical, melodic approach' to the delivery of Shakespeare's language on stage (Folkerth 2002: 3), which harked back to the acting styles associated with earlier generations of Shakespearean actors. Richard Burton came from a very different background: born Richard Walter Jenkins Jr into a coal-mining, Welsh-speaking household in Pontrhydyfen, near Port Talbot in South Wales, he was trained by his English teacher, Philip H. Burton, whose patronym Richard adopted as a tribute to Philip's fostering and influence over his formative years as a young student with a driving passion for language and for Shakespeare. Philip realized the potential of Richard's vocal ability and memory skills, and decided to transform his rough, but powerful, voice to conform to mid-twentieth-century standards of phonetic propriety. Melvyn Bragg writes eloquently about the time that Philip and Richard spent together:

> They practised in the living room on psalms and Shakespeare . . . Philip also took Richard out on to the hills and up to the top of the Welsh mountains like master and disciple in some biblical parable. The boy would speak . . . the Chorus from *Henry V* and [he] would go further and further away from him, forcing him not to shout but to make certain [he] could hear him. . . . The voice changed: darkened, soared over the valley. . . . He was accent perfect. (1989: 37–8, 40)

Burton may have brought the freshness associated with his delivery on film to his performance as Hamlet in 1964, but his voice was as trained and constructed as Gielgud's, though in accordance with mid-twentieth rather than late-nineteenth and early twentieth-century variations of RP.

The Wooster Group responded to the textured quality of Gielgud's and Burton's voices, as well as to their acting styles, and worked carefully to modulate their voices to those of the original performers in order to create a layered soundscape of different accents and registers. According to Elizabeth LeCompte's own recollection of the rehearsal process, accents were one of the company's primary concerns:

> At first, I thought, 'We can't do English accents!' . . . [The actors] were imitating the English accents, and it sounded copied – badly copied; an affectation rather than something deeply felt. But then, slowly, as they stripped away the English accents and stayed with the exact shape of the language and the metre of their particular performance, they began to invest it so deeply that, when they would go into an English accent, it was fine.

But that took ... a year, and I never knew it was going to happen. (LeCompte *et al.* 2013: 125–6)

Gielgud's and Burton's accents, which conveyed multiple temporalities in conforming to different British models of phonetic propriety, became a point of departure, with occasional moments of identification, in ways that beautifully evoked a long tradition of negotiations over Anglo-American cultural identities as mediated through the appropriation and reception of Shakespeare on both sides of the Atlantic.

The Wooster Group's investment in voices, sound and accents as sources of theatrical interpretation and cultural meanings re-emerged as a defining feature of their collaborative production of *Troilus and Cressida*. RSC actors, directed by Mark Ravenhill, played the besieging Greeks and the Wooster Group played the besieged Trojans. The two companies only met for a five-week period of shared rehearsal, having worked on the production independently beforehand. In the production itself, the two companies performed as warring enemies, using clashing acting styles: the RSC actors wore modern military desert camouflage and delivered their lines naturalistically in StP, while the Wooster Group wore fake wigs, body suits and feathered headgear, and spoke through head-mikes in the accents of Native American Indians from the upper Midwest, who could be seen in filmed recordings shown on small videos at the back of the stage. Everything about the appearance, diction and acting style used by the Wooster Group suggested a presentational, or citational, approach not only to Shakespeare's play but also to the composite subject position they performed as mostly white actors, playing Shakespeare's Trojans as Native American Indians.

Some reviewers found the clash of styles and registers aesthetically and theatrically unbearable: Billington described the production as 'less [of] a collaboration than an awkward stylistic collision' (2012), and even those who appreciated the self-consciously constructed quality of the Wooster Group's approach deemed their work, and the production as a whole, to be 'half-baked, pointlessly baffling, ill-conceived and sophomoric' (Prescott 2013: 217). The same reviewers also objected to the fact that a production should 'at least give us an idea of what the work is about' (Billington 2012) and that it should add up to a satisfying theatre-going 'experience' (Prescott 2013: 217). However, other reviewers found that the clash of registers suited the notoriously problematic quality of Shakespeare's bitterly satirical play, where both Greeks and Trojans fall short of the martial or romantic ideals associated with them in earlier classical or vernacular incarnations of the myth of the fall of Troy.[16] Jane Shilling, for example, felt that the production 'buil[t] a powerful sense of beleaguered humanity' and, though 'not an ideal production … – whatever that might be … [it was] intelligent, engaged, and an honourable realization of a play full of intractable questions' (2012). One other significant contribution this production made to the WSF as a whole was the forcible demonstration of the visual, acoustic and ideological distance that divides different approaches to Shakespeare in contemporary performance. What is at stake in the sound of the spoken word on the Shakespearean stage? The Wooster Group and their collaboration with the RSC, as much as the participation of TwoGents in the G2G, showed that accents, inflections and the modulations of the performer's voice can be used to reinforce acoustic normativity and the crippling social and national stereotypes that acoustic normativity supports, or that they can be used to de-familiarize English-speaking audiences from the sound of Shakespeare in performance, as a first step towards their gradual dismantling.

Conversely, two other WSF productions, this time produced in-house by the RSC, showed how detrimental and untenable a conventional, a-critical approach to accents to signal stereotypical national identities had become, especially in the wake of productions where voices had been carefully curated. These two productions – Greg Doran's *Julius Caesar* and Iqbal Khan's *Much Ado about Nothing* – were lambasted for their politically incorrect use of put-on African and Indian accents by their British black and Asian cast. Doran was criticized for 'set[ting] the play in an unspecified, nameless African country:' '[a]re we to assume', as Monika Smialkowska put it, 'that Africans in general are like the figures represented here' or that they speak in the 'generic "African English" … accents in which the characters spoke' (93) in this production? Similarly, Khan was taken to task for using generic stage accents:

> With this production of *Much Ado*, we have a parody or pastiche of 'internationalism', with apparently second-generation British actors pretending to return to their cultural roots in a decidedly colonial way. Not ever intended as offensive or racially subversive, this *Much Ado* is

---

[16] See, for example, Ann Thompson on Geoffrey Chaucer's *Troilus and Criseyde*: 'Chaucer is careful to give the maximum value and attractiveness to his presentation of romantic love, while simultaneously reminding us through his constant irony that it is not the highest good. … Chaucer … is sure of his ultimate standards, but [unlike Shakespeare], he does not ridicule or condemns his characters for not measuring up to them' (1987: 160).

> nevertheless unable to offer anything other than the veneer of Indian
> culture, served on a bed of Bradford or Birmingham Anglicized rice.
> Overlong and overindulgent, it does little other than cement the comedy
> caricature of India in the British psyche. (Quarmby 2016)

The difference this review draws between representation and caricature is important in the context of recent debates about the opportunities and challenges associated with intercultural performance.[17] As Kate Rumbold has cogently put it, 'the RSC often sets plays in foreign locales, without the expectation that every member of the production team and cast be from that country. However, as she went on to add, it is also possible that, 'in the hyper-global context of the WSF – and particularly, of the Globe to Globe Festival – … the internationalism of the play came under new scrutiny' (2013: 151–2).

As with the CWS, the most important legacy of the WSF seems to have been a new alertness to the importance of venue and context to the reception of signifiers like regional and foreign accents, as used in the charged cultural space of contemporary English Shakespeare in performance. No matter how much (or how little) curatorial attention theatre artists bestow on unconventional colour, gender and accent casting, its reception and effectiveness will be gauged in relation to the context within which the target audience decode these crucial identity markers.

Instructive in this respect were local responses to the Festival programming in Newcastle and Gateshead. The Festival programming in the region included 'official, franchised, branded events', which, as Adam Hansen and Monika Smialkowska have noted, failed to 'engag[e] … with

---

[17] 'Intercultural' became a byword for cultural imperialism in the 1990s, when postcolonial critics such as Rustom Bharucha criticized Western directors who plundered non-Western traditions in order to inject new life and new energy into Western drama. For more details, see Bharucha 1993. Refocusing the debate on the increasingly globalized quality of culture and of world theatre cultures more specifically, William B. Worthen extended Bharucha's critique of intercultural performance to what he referred to as 'globalized Shakespeare'. Worthen argued that 'globalized commerce' is the main framework within which 'globalized Shakespeare' is produced and consumed and that the framework of 'globalized commerce' can therefore turn Shakespearean performance into intercultural productions which in fact erase cultural difference in the name of a universal, transcultural Shakespeare. However, Worthen also conceded that 'performance forms and practices can, on some occasions, retain their history' (2003: 123) and that 'theatre practices [can] be deployed with different kinds of force in different locations, [and can] do different kinds of work in different local and global registers' (2003: 129). Even Bharucha has more recently admitted that, while 'some appropriations are misappropriations of other people's cultural texts, contexts, and histories, … not every appropriation is necessarily imperial, colonial, or neocolonial in its methodology, rhetoric, or impact' (2004: 6).

the North East on the level of setting, costuming or dialect' (2014: 108–9). The Shakespeare on offer in Newcastle and Gateshead in 2012 ranged from *In a Pickle*, a pre-school version of *The Winter's Tale* to Doran's 'African' *Julius Caesar*, along with a Tunisian *Macbeth*, *The Rest Is Silent* by dreamthinkspeak, and a handful of amateur productions sponsored by the RSC's Open Stages project. As Hansen and Smialkowska observed, 'there was no clear rationale as to why these particular shows of all the Festival's repertoire were chosen to be presented in the Newcastle and Gateshead area'. They went on to conclude that 'one could be forgiven for feeling that Shakespeare was on tour rather than at home in the region, with companies from elsewhere bringing random offerings to the locals' (2014: 109).

The Tunisian *Macbeth* was the offering that most starkly highlighted the disconnection between what was presented on stage and the range of expectations that audiences from the North East brought to the Festival. As Hansen and Smialkoska pointed out, 'it was a privilege, stimulating and enlightening, to see how Tunisians were using Shakespeare to rethink their lives', but it was not clear to them 'what opportunities the World Shakespeare Festival present[ed] for someone from Jarrow, Fenham, South Shields or anywhere in the greater Newcastle–Gateshead conurbation, to rethink *their* lives using Shakespeare' (2014: 111–12). The lack of productions originating from the North East of England was felt to be deeply regrettable, especially at a time when significant amounts of funding were devoted to showcasing homegrown as well as 'Global Shakespeare' across the country. What interests me most about this critical response to the staging of this Tunisian *Macbeth* in Newcastle is the consequent realization that the region was, in other words, conspicuously missing from local stages at a time when regional Shakespeare could have been more easily brought to national and international attention. And it was primarily the Tunisian *Macbeth*, in all its visual and acoustic otherness, that raised awareness about the marginalization of regional Shakespeare and regionally inflected voices in Shakespeare in contemporary performance.

Productions since the WSF seem to have responded to this enhanced sensitivity to accents and to the need for the contemporary Shakespearean stage to reflect regional diversity and the nation's changing demographics, even more so than in the immediate aftermath of the CWS, as shown by the two productions discussed in the final two sections of this chapter.

§

'A Smack of All Neighbouring Languages': Accenting Parolles in *All's Well That Ends Well*

Nancy Meckler's 2013 RSC production of *All's Well That Ends Well* lent Parolles unprecedented contemporary resonance. Jonathan Slinger played this character, the 'manifold linguist' (4.3.172) who knows a smattering of German, Dane, Low Dutch, Italian and French (4.1.51–2), as 'a closeted gay man hiding behind a fake Sandhurst accent' (Billington 2013a). Slinger reverted to his native accent when alone on stage and during the kidnapping trick in 4.3, when, as Taylor put it, 'he disintegrate[d] . . . from gloating swaggerer to frantic, camp Northern blabbermouth' (2013). While some reviewers like Taylor highlighted the comic potential of Slinger's manifold voices, his Parolles tapped on this character's complexity, which is often overlooked in performance, and highlighted parallels with Helena's character, which are routinely ignored in productions delivered entirely in StP.

   In most modern productions, Parolles is represented either as a comic type, the Plautine *miles gloriosus* or swaggering soldier, or as a self-deluded character, who experiences a moment of genuine self-discovery during the kidnapping trick.[18] These productions tend to read Parolles as a comic foil for Bertram, who is also exposed as a liar and a coward by the bedtrick set up by Helena to force him to accept her as his wife. However, as Meckler's production showed, Parolles can also function as a counterpart for Helena, who, like Parolles, lacks status and social standing, or, as Lafew puts it, 'the commission of . . . birth' (2.3.261) that has 'put such difference betwixt [Bertram's and her] estates' (1.3.109–10). Slinger's use of StP and his native Northern accent (Slinger was born in Accrington, Lancashire) laid bare the class dynamics that inform both Helena's and Parolles's relations to higher-rank characters in the play, highlighting key concerns to do with power, authority and identity, which StP productions quite simply fail to register.

---

[18] See, for example, James Garnon's performance as Parolles in the 2011 Shakespeare Globe production directed by John Dove, who played this character as a comic type, as noted by Billington: 'the comedy is in good hands with James Garnon's popinjay of a Parolles' (2011). At the other end of the spectrum, Greg Doran's Parolles, played by Guy Henry, proved particularly moving in a generally sombre production characterized by a nostalgic harking back to the values of the older generation, which the younger characters learn to appreciate. See, for example, Kidnie: 'Guy Henry's comic inventiveness . . . [was] deepened through his self-knowing dignity after his humiliation at the hands of the Dumaine brothers' (2009: 48).

In Meckler's production, Slinger used StP consistently up to 2.3. While in the play Parolles attempts to disguise his social and personal shortcomings by dressing up (his 'scarfs' are repeatedly mentioned as tokens of his vanity and pretentiousness), Slinger had up to this point managed to hide his insecurities by speaking in StP. Slinger first used his Northern accent when he found himself momentarily alone on stage at the end of 2.3. At this point in the play, Lafew starts to see through Parolles's social pretensions; Lafew 'finds him out' when Parolles overreacts to the former's suggestion that he is Bertram's servant:

LAFEW   Your lord and master did well to make his recantation.
PAROLLES   Recantation! My lord! My master!
LAFEW   Ay. Is it not a language I speak?
PAROLLES   A most harsh one, and not to be understood without
           bloody succeeding. My master!
LAFEW   Are you companion to the Count Rossillion?
PAROLLES   To any Count; to all Counts; to what is man.
LAFEW   To what is Count's man; Count's master is of
           another style.

                                                          (2.3.187–96)

This fraught exchange hinges on the double meanings of the words 'man' (as in 'servant' and 'mankind') and 'count' (as in the title and the verb). Parolles's sensitivity at being regarded as the 'Count's man' confirms Lafew in his conviction that Parolles lacks the 'style' of a 'master' and that he and Count Rossillion are not equal.

Their exchange in this scene also reveals that Lafew had initially believed Parolles 'to be a pretty wise fellow', because Parolles had made 'tolerable vent of [his] travel'. Parolles had, in other words, *sounded* well-spoken and well-travelled enough to gain Lafew's respect, albeit momentarily ('for two ordinaries' [2.3.202], that is, after dining with him just twice [*OED n.*12b]). Parolles' appearance – his gaudy 'scarfs' and 'bannerets' – had then made Lafew question the legitimacy of Parolles' seemingly elevated status (2.3.206). After their brief exchange in 2.3, Lafew concludes that Parolles is 'good for nothing but taking up', that is 'to borrow money from' (*OED*, *v.* 6a). He then adds, punning on the verb 'to take up', that Parolles is actually 'scarce worth' the bending over to be picked up (*OED v.* 1b), thus reducing Parolles to the status of a worthless piece of garbage.

When Slinger's Parolles was left alone on stage to vent his frustration at being so harshly dismissed by Lafew, he did so using his Northern English accent. The sudden switch of accent gave Parolles's outburst additional resonance. When he complained that he 'must be patient' because 'there is no fettering of authority' (2.3.213), he sounded like a social pariah *not only* because of his cowardice on the battlefield but also because of his attempt to fit in at court. Slinger's marked regional accent jarred within the acoustic context of a production that had, up to that point, been performed entirely in StP. The jarring sound of Slinger's regional accent took on a very powerful connotation of social exclusion and made Parolles's character more easily and more immediately intelligible to Meckler's audiences. The sudden change in the acoustic register of Slinger's delivery of his short soliloquy in 2.3 effectively translated an early modern concern with the relative importance of personal worth versus social status into a very contemporary preoccupation with social exclusion, unequal access to education and lack of diversity within the ruling elite and key institutions and organizations. Among them, this production singled out the army, within which Slinger's Parolles tried to get himself established, but also the RSC, where Slinger is generally expected to set aside his regional accent and to use StP in order to comply with the acoustic parameters that are still dominant on the mainstream Shakespearean stage.

The humiliation Parolles suffers in Act 4 acquired a similarly social dimension in Meckler's production. The smattering of languages Parolles speaks at other moments in the play is no use to him in 4.1, where some lords in Bertram's party surprise, bind and hoodwink him, pretending to be a foreign legion among the Duke of Florence's enemies. Their aim is to show Bertram that Parolles is 'a most notable coward, an infinite and endless liar, [and] an hourly promise-breaker' (3.6.9–10). Slinger reverted to his Northern accent in this scene and in his questioning before Bertram in 4.3. This time, Slinger's native accent suggested the breaking down of Parolles's constructed social persona, which he had been using to hide not only his cowardice but also his sense of dislocation, a common plight among those who struggle to get by in a world to which they feel they do not naturally belong.

Generally staged in a comic key, 4.1 and 4.3 came across in this production as cruel bullying. Parolles's capitulation, in turn, did not amount merely to a reversion to type, as Parolles self-identified as a braggart – 'Who knows himself a braggart, / Let him fear this: for it will come to pass / That every braggart shall be found an ass' (4.3.328–30). In this production, Parolles's unmasking made the enforced acknowledgement of his lowly origins – 'Simply the thing I am / Shall make me live' (4.3.327–8) – especially touching and resonant, because it conveyed his sense of exclusion in terms that contemporary audiences could grasp, tapping on social connotations that are still commonly attached to StP and NSE accents, on and off the Shakespearean stage.

§

'Do You Know My Voice?': Accenting Iago in *Othello*

Two recent productions of *Othello* – directed by Nicholas Hytner at the NT in 2013 and by Iqbal Khan for the RSC in 2015 – have also used accents, alongside unconventional casting, in order to revisit the complex interracial dynamics explored in the play. Hytner's production, starring Adrian Lester and Rory Kinnear in the lead roles, used aural rather than visual identity markers to signal otherness, prejudice and exclusion. Kinnear's use of Estuary English was one of the main strategies through which class replaced race to code Iago, rather than Othello, as an outsider. In Khan's production, race was still firmly at the heart of the tragedy, but the casting of Lucian Msamati as Iago, alongside Hugh Quarshie's Othello, transformed Iago's originally racially inflected prejudice against the Moor into a sobering exploration of intra-racial tensions. Msamati's younger and less assimilated Iago spoke in his native Tanzanian accent, while Quarshie's Othello, who performed the lead role in impeccable StP, cut a striking figure as a successful general and a more integrated member of the Venetian elite. Their relationship, fraught from the beginning, gained depth and contemporary resonance in the context of Khan's consistently unconventional approach to the casting of other key roles. Among them, Emilia was played by British-Indian actress Ayesha Dharker in her original accent and Montano was played by black British actor David Ajao, who gave this character greater depth in the improvised 'rap off' sequence added to the nuptial revels in Cyprus in 2.3.

Both productions broke new interpretative ground by combining unconventional casting strategies with a careful curatorial approach to voices and accents. Other Iagos had already spoken in regionally marked accents. Bob Hoskins, for example, played Iago in Jonathan Miller's 1981 BBC production as 'a working-class sergeant' dogged by 'social frustration' (Petcher 1999: 60). Commenting on Hoskins's Iago, Edward Petcher refers to 'a strong tradition of modern Iagos', who have similarly highlighted class as the root of Iago's resentment against Othello:

> In this respect, Miller ... goes back to Frank Finlay's 'solid, honest-to-God N.C.O.' opposite Olivier ... and further to Olivier's own Iago in 1938 opposite Ralph Richardson. This line carries on to Ian McKellen,

> opposite Willard White in Trevor Nunn's 1989 RSC production:
> McKellen's northern accent sets him apart from the rest of the cast,
> particularly Othello and Cassio, who spoke in traditional BBC tones.
> (1999: 60)

In these earlier productions, Iago did not seem as starkly juxtaposed to
Othello, because Othello was still the primary target of exclusion and
prejudice. However, the casting of Lester as Othello in Hytner's production significantly mitigated Othello's racial otherness. By the time he
played Othello in 2014, Lester had built his reputation as one of the most
prominent classical actors in contemporary British theatre by playing key
leading roles in major gender-blind and colour-blind productions, including Rosalind in Cheek-by-Jowl's milestone production of *As You Like It* in
1991 and the title role in Hytner's *Henry V* at the NT in 2003. As
Billington has rather crudely, but effectively, put it, 'Lester is a fine classical
actor, who just happens to be black' (2013b), or, as Christina Patterson has
more sensitively argued, 'few black actors have moved beyond racial
stereotypes as deftly as ... Lester' (2009).

The casting of a black Iago was also not entirely unprecedented. The
Shakespeare Theatre Company in Washington DC had cast black actors
Avery Brooks and Andre Braugher as Othello and Iago, alongside Fran-
chelle Stewart Dorn as Emilia, in 1990–91. However, this earlier production had not offered a radically new reading of the play, as Khan's did in
2015. This production extended, or at best inverted, the sense of exclusion
experienced by these three characters, as Miranda Johnson-Haddad
explains:

> Frequently one of the most obvious visual features of a traditionally cast
> *Othello* is that Othello himself stands out as a solitary figure among the
> white Venetians; his difference is palpable, and in many productions this
> difference is further emphasized by Othello's native African or specifically
> Moorish garb. In this production, however, it was Othello and Iago who
> stood out together. In scenes involving Othello, Iago, Emilia, and Desde-
> mona, it was Desdemona who stood out. (1991: 477)

Subtle variation in the delivery of their lines did highlight slight differences
in the status of these three characters. Brooks, for example, 'delivered many
of his speeches [in a] lilting, mellifluous cadence' (Johnson-Haddad, 1991,
478), which set him apart not only from the Venetians but also from Iago,
who, as a result, seemed more assimilated than Othello. This production
therefore lent fresh insights into Iago's resentment against Othello, as
Angela C. Pao has observed: '[Othello's and Iago's] shared status as
partially assimilated outsiders ... magnify[ied] Iago's sense of betrayal

and rejection when Othello promot[ed] Cassio', which was in turn 'compounded as he watch[ed] Othello solidify his position in Venetian society by marrying a highborn Venetian lady' (2006: 32). A later production, directed by Penny Metropulos for the Acting Company in New York in 1995, had also cast two black American actors, Ezra Knight and Allen Gilmore, as Othello and Iago. However, the lack of a wider rethinking of the implications that this type of unconventional casting can have on the dramatic economy of the play as a whole led some reviewers to assume that they were watching a colour-blind production, while others found the casting distracting (Pao 2006: 40).

What set the two productions under discussion here apart from earlier ones is their combined approach to casting *and* acoustic diversity, on the one hand, and some careful tweaking of the dialogue, on the other. In Hytner's production, for example, the dialogue was substantially cut. The cuts in Act 1 – 135 lines in total – were especially significant. Some cuts were required by the updating of the play: the first act took place in a contemporary, urban setting that resembled present-day London, with punters drinking outside pubs, while military and political leaders had emergency meetings in formal council rooms; once the action moved to Cyprus, the setting changed to a modern-day military outpost and the soldiers wore desert camouflage uniforms and modern weaponry. Most other cuts were however specifically aimed at removing references to Othello's status as an outsider. These cuts included Roderigo's description of Othello as an 'extravagant and wheeling stranger' (1.1.134) and Othello's allusion to his having 'fetch[ed his] life and being / From men of royal siege' (1.2.21–2). In keeping with these cuts, Brabantio's insinuations that Othello had used witchcraft to steal his daughter away from him were drastically toned down. Other cuts lessened Brabantio's power and status. In fact, Brabantio was reduced to a pretty pathetic and isolated figure and other scripted, non-verbal cues in 1.3 indicated that the other characters did not share Brabantio's racist views. When, for example, Brabantio wondered, before the Senate, how Desdemona, 'in spite of nature, / Of year, of country, credit, everything' (1.3.95–6) could have fallen for Othello, all the other Senators were visibly shocked and their body-language suggested that they were distancing themselves from him.

The updating of the setting contributed to deflecting attention even further away from Othello's racial otherness. When Hytner introduced the *Othello* NTLive cinecast on 26 September 2013, he explained that Othello's descent into abject and murderous jealousy only makes sense in his production when understood in the context of the military base of the Venetian army in

Cyprus. He then went on to compare the military base to a bell jar, in order to emphasize the impact of enforced confinement on troops stationed in enemy territory, especially when soldiers have nothing to do but wait. Hytner hired a general, Jonathan Shaw, who had been in charge of the British troops in Basra in 2007, as a military adviser in order to bolster the accuracy and verisimilitude of his directorial vision for this production, where Othello's gullibility had nothing, or very little, to do with the colour of his skin. In the programme notes, Shaw accordingly explained that:

> Duping . . . mak[es] sense once it is understood that [Othello] is a 'military orphan' whose moral code is derived entirely from his military upbringing within a culture which is based on trust; for trust is the basis of all soldering. Othello and Iago have clearly been in many fights together, life-and-death situations, in which each has probably entrusted their life to the other and at some points saved each other's life. Iago has proved his 'honesty' on battlefields around the region; Othello has every reason to trust him implicitly. Betrayal is the most heinous of military sins so it is the last to be suspected. . . . His colour marks him out but, from a military perspective, this is the least interesting point of discord. (2014)

In this important respect, Hytner took *Othello* into a brand new stage in the history of its reception in mainstream British theatre.

   Hytner's approach seems all the more remarkable when considered in relation to earlier NT productions of *Othello*. When white actors used to black up to play Othello, Othello's racial otherness came across either as racist parody or as purely cosmetic. Laurence Olivier's Othello, in John Dexter's 1964 National Theatre production, falls into the first category, as intimated by Lester's comments on his predecessor: '[Olivier's] stage performance . . . [was] doing a very generalized parody. It's colour as character, not just colour as colour. And there is this insulting idea . . . that because the dots of why Othello believes the things that he does can't be joined, people go, "Well it's about colour"' (Rees 2013). Paul Scofield's Othello, in Peter Hall's 1980 National Theatre production, fell into the second category, in that Othello's racial diversity seemed to have no discernible impact on Scofield's interpretation of the role. In fact, Billington implicitly reinforced the bias outlined by Lester above by admitting that he 'could never quite believe that this eloquent, dignified sophisticate would be such a willing dupe' (1980).[19] Lester's Othello, on the other hand, came across as an insider in a contemporary, cosmopolitan

---

[19]   The only other NT production of *Othello*, starring David Harewood in the title role and directed by Sam Mendes in 1997, was discussed earlier in this chapter.

urban setting, where racist views were relegated to old and seemingly out-of-touch characters, like Brabantio. It is in this context that Lester's StP and Kinnear's Estuary English accent acquired more resonance than in earlier productions, where both Iago's regionally marked accent and Othello's racial difference were directly linked to social discrimination.

Similarly, Khan's production offered an original reading of the play because the unconventional casting was supported by the use of multiple accents and other local departures from Shakespeare's text and its perform-ance tradition. Non-verbal communication, for example, played a key role in the opening scene, where Msamati's Iago flinched in response to Roderigo's racist remarks about Othello. As Taylor reported, '[w]hen Roderigo . . . refer[red] to the absent hero as "thick-lips", we [saw] Iago freeze and then decide to make light of it, burbling parodic raspberries through his own lips and cuffing Roderigo with a feigned jokiness' (2015). In Khan's multiracial society, racism was still simmering just below the surface. Even more troubling were the intra-racial tensions that emerged when Iago was once again alone on stage at the end of 1.3. As Dominic Cavendish noted, Msamati's Iago had a clear motive for hating the Moor:

> At a stroke we move beyond black-and-white ideas of racism as a motivator for Iago, and racial difference as the reason for Othello's ruinous suggest-ibility. In this version, they're both outsiders and that makes for a fascinat-ing psychological dynamic. When Msamati tells James Corrigan's doltish Roderigo, spit flecking from his mouth, that he hates the Moor, what might sound like a nonsense (doesn't he qualify as a 'Moor' himself?) acquires an added level of complexity. His Iago repeatedly uses that phrase "the Moor" with a hint of sarcasm. The envy is subtle but unmistakable: why should his boss "own" that identity, while he – short, stocky, a figure of forced affability – must dance humble attendance upon him? Without adding a word to the text, the other's elevated position implicitly rankles more. (2015)

Other significant departures from Shakespeare's text included the nuptial revels in 2.3, when, after Othello and Desdemona retire for the night, Othello's soldiers party on. It was at this point in Khan's production that the action of the play slowed down and improvised signing and new dialogue offered a fresh perspective on Iago, Montano and Cassio. This sequence also made it clear that thinly veiled racial tensions, as opposed to Cassio's lack of 'brains for drinking' (2.3.27), triggered the rioting among the soldiers. Similarly significant was the addition of a traditional African song which, sung by Msamati's Iago, evoked a 'world elsewhere' and the extent to which Msamati's Iago was not at home among the Venetians.

Cassio's crass remarks about Iago's song revealed the same type of casual racism voiced by Roderigo in the opening scene. This time, however, Cassio's racism was not shrugged off and, instead of getting Cassio drunk, Iago and Montano challenged him to take part in an improvised rap competition.

The rapping competition left Cassio feeling angry and humiliated. As Fiona Mountford recalled, '[t]here [was] a magnetic moment during the raucous knees-up in Cyprus when the assembled men start[ed] beat-boxing and sharp race-based undercurrents suddenly bubbl[ed] up out of nowhere' (2015). Far from bubbling 'out of nowhere', the inter- and intra-racial tensions detected by Mountford were carefully woven into this production from its very opening scene, as already noted above. As a result, Iago's resentment was now clearly fuelled by the fact that he felt betrayed by one of his own people. As Taylor perceptively put it, '[t]he fact that Othello has promoted this spuriously liberal white man over him adds a new strand of bitterness to the villain's vengeful hatred'. And, as Taylor continues, '[Iago] evidently feels disdain for Othello's assimilationist approach' (2015).

The inter- and intra-racial tensions that Khan worked into this production affected not only Iago's relationship with Othello and with the Venetians but also with his wife, Emilia. Played by Dharker in a recognizable British-Indian accent, Emilia was not only an outsider among the Venetians but also a stranger within Othello and Iago's community of black officers and soldiers in the Venetian army. Iago's fraught exchanges with Emilia in the play were compounded in this production by the lack of a shared cultural background, which made it easier to understand why Emilia failed to question Iago's motives when she unwittingly helped him to plot Othello's demise. Emilia's accent also set her apart from the other characters and her isolation made her unwillingness to confide in others more understandable. By the time Desdemona asked Emilia's advice in 4.3, Desdemona was herself uprooted and isolated and could no longer make sense of what was happening to her and to Othello, as the latter became increasingly remote and inaccessible.

All in all, Hytner's and Khan's productions represented a daring and radical updating of Shakespeare's play. Their departures from the source play and its performance tradition were not cosmetic changes carried out for novelty's sake; they instead amounted to a coherent, relevant and timely exploration of the failings of multiculturalism in contemporary societies, where integration is tragically undermined by lingering racisms and fresh social and economic divisions. Along with Meckler's

2013 production of *All's Well*, Hytner's and Khan's productions of *Othello* have marked an important point of departure from performance traditions that continue to associate Shakespeare in performance with the sounds and registers of the speech of elitism.

§

To sum up, this chapter has charted the long and largely unexplored rise of accented Shakespeare on the English stage in the late twentieth and early twenty-first centuries, focusing on the impact of foreign productions on how Shakespeare's plays are acoustically re-interpreted and re-presented to modern audiences. Accent is now an increasingly curated aspect of the complex process of non-verbal communication activated by live performance. This new level of acoustic diversity connects the delivery of Shakespeare's language in performance with the English spoken off-stage by contemporary audiences. This chapter has more generally shown how the acoustically diverse productions discussed in more detail in its final two sections represent the culmination of a long and gradual process of acoustic reform that is starting to give back to the English spoken on the Shakespearean stage all its 'native breath' (*Richard II* 1.3.167), in all its current acoustic diversity.

CHAPTER 2

'Lend Me Your Ears':
Experiments with Original Pronunciation

Chapter 1 has argued that the steady increase in acoustic diversity in late twentieth- and early twenty-first-century Shakespearean performance was prompted by groundbreaking work with regional accent but also by an unprecedented level of exposure of British audiences to foreign Shakespeare productions, which in turn led to the wider deployment of carefully curated foreign and regional accents in home-grown productions. This chapter shows that one other important trigger for change came from a series of experiments with OP led by Mary Hope Allen, a pioneering radio producer, who worked for the BBC from 1927 to 1958 (Fig. 1). Her legacy eventually fed into a significant performance tradition that culminated with David Crystal's recent OP productions at Shakespeare's Globe in 2004 and 2005 and at smaller venues in the UK, Europe and the US in the early 2010s. Even more importantly, Allen's OP radio programmes disrupt a simplistic association of OP with conservative attempts to recover the authentic sound of Shakespeare as originally performed on the early modern stage, showing how experiments with OP can in fact disrupt a traditional alignment of Shakespeare with high culture and the speech of elitism.

From their inception, OP studies focused mostly, if not exclusively, on Shakespeare. From the middle of the nineteenth century, scholars based in Northern Ireland and North America started to identify the main differences between modern variations of English and the English spoken in Shakespeare's time. In his *The English of Shakespeare, Illustrated in a Philological Commentary on his 'Julius Caesar'* (1857), George L. Craik explained to his readers how what Shakespeare wrote was 'to be read and construed', because, as Craik put it, '[m]uch of [his] vocabulary has ceased to fall from either our lips or our pens' and 'much of the meaning which he attached to so much of it as still survives has dropt out of our minds' (ix–x). Similarly, in his 'Memorandum on English Pronunciation', appended to his multi-volume edition of the *Complete Works* (1865),

Fig. 1.   Mary Hope Allen.
Held at the University Library in Cambridge (GB 12 MS. Add. 9225). Reproduced by permission of
the BBC Archives and Photo Library Services

Richard Grant White emphasized the profound acoustic alterity that separated nineteenth century and early modern speakers of English: 'our orthoepy would have sounded as strange and laughable to our forefathers, as theirs does to us' (quoted in Crystal 2016a: xxxii).

At this early stage in the development of historical phonology, OP was deemed unsuitable for performance. When English philologist Alexander Ellis embarked on his monumental study *On Early English Pronunciation* (1869–89), he echoed his predecessors by warning his readers that early modern spoken English would have sounded uncouth and off-putting on stage. He concluded that

> [a]s essentially our household poet, Shakspere [sic] will, and must, in each age of the English language, be read and spoken in the current pronunciation of the time, [because] any marked departure from it ... would jar upon cherished memories, and would be therefore generally unacceptable'. (3: 984)

The first philologist to experiment with OP in performance was Daniel Jones. In 1909, he presented a selection of 'Scenes from Shakespeare' at University College London, where he worked as Professor of Phonetics from 1921 to 1949. His solo performance as Prospero and Sir Andrew Aguecheek was enthusiastically received. The reviewer in *Le Maître phoné-tique* hailed Jones's experiment as 'mark[ing] an epoch in the history of Elizabethan representations of Shakespeare'. 'On that day', the reviewer continued, 'Shakespeare was first heard in the pronunciation which may safely be accepted as that used by the poet himself and his fellow actors' (Noël-Armfield 1910: 117). Jones went on to advise on radio programmes about early modern spoken English. In February 1949, he introduced 'Our Changing Speech', and, later on that year, another radio programme called 'The Elizabethan Tongue'.[1] Jones also trained Alfred Charles Gimson, who was to succeed him as Professor of Phonetics at University College London. Gimson advised on a prominent OP production of *Macbeth*, which was directed by Bernard Miles at The Mermaid Theatre in 1952 (and which I discuss in detail later in this chapter).

Jones's contributions to the emergence of OP in radio and theatre may however have been overstated or, at the very least, mistakenly taken to be paradigmatic of what OP can bring to Shakespeare in performance. Jones's approach to OP was in fact quite niche, specialist and informed by a palpable institutional agenda. Especially noteworthy in this respect is the fact that his performance of extracts from Shakespeare in OP at University College London in 1909 was attended by E. R. Edwards, who was then Vice-President of the International Pronunciation Association (IPA), and by University College London Provost, Gregory Foster. As Beverly Collins and Inger M. Mees explain, 'the success of the evening inspired Jones . . . to suggest a Shakespearean evening to Foster as one way of popularizing the idea of a Phonetics Institute for the University of London' (1998: 59–60). Foster, on his part, seems to have 'remembered the success of the evening whenever matters concerned with phonetics came up for later discussion in College Committees' (1998: 60). From the very beginning of his experiments with OP, Jones exploited the legitimizing function of an accent that could be presented as authentically Shakespearean. As Collins and Mees put it, Jones's realization led to a significant shift of emphasis in

[1] For further details, see *The Radio Times*, now accessible digitally via the BBC Genome website at http://genome.ch.bbc.co.uk/search/0/20?adv=0&q=our+changing+speech&media=all&yf=1923&yt=2009&mf=1&mt=12&tf=00%3A00&tt=00%3A00#search and http://genome.ch.bbc.co.uk/search/0/20?adv=0&q=elizabethan+tongue&media=all&yf=1923&yt=2009&mf=1&mt=12&tf=00%3A00&tt=00%3A00#search.

the way in which historical linguistics had operated up to that point in time: instead of the 'usual pattern of philological analysis', which involves 'tracing back individual speech sounds through previous stages of a language', Jones undertook 'the reconstruction of the pronunciation of a given period in a holistic manner, dealing with the complete sound system and attempting to bring this to life' (1998: 58).

Conversely, as this chapter shows, Allen's experiments with OP were in keeping with her lifelong commitment to using sound to explore the boundaries between different art forms and between music and the spoken word. Having established a productive working relation with Cambridge-based linguist Francis George Blandford, Allen integrated OP within her wider experiments with music and the spoken word, as she set off to adapt established art forms to the new medium of radio broadcasting. She deployed OP in creative ways, which aimed to amuse and entertain, and gave rise to an entirely different tradition, which, though largely overlooked,[2] has inspired practitioners to use the radical alterity of the accent associated with OP to reach and develop new audiences for Shakespeare.

§

London Calling – 1600 was Allen's first programme to focus entirely on OP. Originally aired on the National Programme on 15 April 1936, *London Calling – 1600* was conceived as a news bulletin and was described, tongue-in-cheek, in *The Radio Times* as 'an impression – a conjecture – a shot in the dark at what listeners might have heard, had broadcasting been invented in the reign of Queen Elizabeth' (1936: 654, 42). The illustration used to advertise this programme lays out its title and description to look like the title page of an early modern playbook (Fig. 2), with the imprint reading 'Written by Herbert Farieon [sic], and produced by M. H. Allen, and is to be broadcast to-night, April 15, at 10.0, MCMXXXVI'. The layout of the illustration was clearly meant to amuse those readers who were familiar with the bibliographical make-up of an early modern playbook. The title of the programme is centred and set in larger type at the top of the page, while the last line of the programme description foregrounds Queen Elizabeth's name as a marketing ploy, replicating how title pages of early modern playbooks accorded typographical prominence to the royal and aristocratic patrons connected with specific playing

---

[2] Jensen 2008 provides a full and detailed overview of Allen's Shakespearean productions for the BBC, but does not focus on Allen's engagement with OP or on the impact that her work has had on later experiments with OP on the radio and on the stage.

Fig. 2.   Advertisement for 'London Calling – 1600' by Eric Fraser.
Originally Published in *The Radio Times*, April 1936, issue 654. Reproduced by permission of
Immediate Media Co

companies. The wording of the date and time of the broadcast – 'and is to be broadcast . . .' – similarly evokes the wording that early modern London stationers used in the imprints included on title pages – 'and is to be sold at. . .' – to advertise the publisher's address.

The ironic claim to authenticity humorously conjured by the illustration is in keeping not only with the self-deprecating register of the short programme description but also with Gordon Stowell's feature-length essay included in the same issue of *The Radio Times*. In his essay, Stowell teases his readers by promising that "'London Calling – 1600' will be as near genuine Elizabethan as sham Elizabethan ever can be' (1936: 654, 17). Rather than encouraging a documentary, historical or scholarly mindset in its listeners, the essay invites amused critical distance and humour as perfectly adequate responses to the programme:

> [o]n Wednesday evening, put yourself in the place of that Elizabethan listener . . . – who would return at night to his manor house, or his gabled cottage, take off his starched ruff, undo a few buttons of his doublet, and spread himself before a log fire – . . . and see what Herbert Farjeon has provided in the way of contemporary entertainment for him. (1936: 654, 17)

Had the wireless being invented, as Stowell continues, an Elizabethan listener's evening entertainment on the radio would have included:

> [n]ews above all . . . [s]ports commentaries from the bear-baiting pit . . . [r]elays of Master Will Shakespeare's plays from the Globe Theatre . . . [and] jokes – most of them probably of a kind that the BBC would never allow today. (1936: 654, 17)

The essay is illustrated by a drawing by Eric Fraser (Fig. 3). The drawing shows 'Ye House of ye Broadcast' top-centre. Outside its front door, a distraught young man is pleading on his knees: 'I would I were an announcer'. A reproachful Shakespeare leans out of one of the windows and looks unimpressed. 'Ye House of ye Broadcast' is flanked by a market stall selling *The Radio Times*, and, close to a 'Plotte for Sale suitable for a Church', a constable asks a passerby if he has paid for his radio license. The extent to which *London Calling – 1600* was meant to entertain and amuse a wide and varied audience is also suggested by the fact that, when the programme was repeated on 23 July 1936, it was adapted for younger listeners and broadcast as part of the children's hour on the Regional Programme.

Although clearly meant to appeal to a large and varied audience, *London Calling – 1600* was thoroughly researched and backed by the most recent scholarship on OP. Allen's second OP programme was called *Take Your Choice*, and the programme description published in *The Radio Times* refers back to *London Calling – 1600* as follows:

> When *London Calling A.D. 1600*, broadcast in April 1936, was discussed between the producer, M. H. Allen, and the author, Herbert Farjeon, the latter happened to mention that he had seen F. G. Blandford's production

Fig. 3.   Drawing for 'London Calling – 1600' by Eric Fraser.
Originally Published in *The Radio Times*, April 1936, issue 654. Reproduced by permission of
Immediate Media Co

of *Twelfth Night*, Act 1, Scene 5, in Elizabethan English at the Festival
Theatre, Cambridge. It was decided to ask Mr. Blandford to do a scene for
this broadcast, and he came up from Cambridge and took the rehearsals.
(1937, 740: 31)

The programme description, still referring to *London Calling – 1600*,
stresses how, despite being purely conjectural, the accent in which actors
had performed the *Twelfth Night* excerpt had been 'one of the most
effective' features of the programme. From a letter that Blandford sent to
Allen from Cambridge on 21 April 1936, we learn that, besides coaching
the actors in rehearsal, Blandford had also provided Allen with the
'"Shakespearean Pronunciation" booklet that had been printed to be sold
in the theatre as a kind of souvenir programme at the first performance of
Terence Gray's *Twelfth Night* at the Marlowe Society in Cambridge in
1933 (GB 12 MS. Add. 9225).

The same letter informs us that *London Calling – 1600* had proven
popular with listeners. Blandford thanks Allen for forwarding letters from

enthusiastic listeners and then mentions that he has had 'one or two personal letters in much the same vein of appreciation' and 'one or two from habitual listeners who regretted that they had not noticed the announcement of this 'feature' in the programme until they saw the notices of it the next day'. That Blandford should receive feedback on the programme is all the more remarkable, since the listing in *The Radio Times* only mentions his name among 'Those taking part'. Allen annotated this letter and, in a 'note-to-self' added to the top margin, she writes: 'we did a lovely programme' (Fig. 4). The positive reception of the programme is also documented by a review published in *The Listener*, which describes it as 'most enchanting, . . . witty and . . . original entertainment' (Murphy 2016: 134).

Another letter sent by Blandford to Allen on 6 June 1936 shows that he was invited back as OP adviser to Allen. In this letter, Blandford reassures Allen that '[t]he answer to your question is "Provisionally, yes!"' He goes on to explain that he is tied down by teaching in Cambridge in July and that he might therefore not be able to be involved in rehearsals. He however suggests that he is prepared to rearrange his teaching, especially 'to avoid the time of the broadcast so as to allow me to be present at it if I am wanted' (GB 12 MS. Add. 9225). Although Blandford does not specify the title of the programme or the date and time of the broadcast, the date of this letter indicates that he was about to be re-engaged as a consultant on the adapted version of *London Calling – 1600* that was aired in September 1636.

Blandford advised Allen again in the run up to *Take Your Choice*, which was broadcast on 6 December 1937. This programme invited listeners to compare 1.5 in *Twelfth Night* as performed in StP and OP. *The Radio Times* listing attributes the transcription of this scene to Blandford, and mentions that the scene had already been presented on stage in Cambridge (1937: 740, 31). The illustration in *The Radio Times* shows modern-day actors wearing Elizabethan costumes, on the left-hand side, and Elizabethan actors in an early modern amphitheatre, on the right-hand side (Fig. 5). The programme description in *The Radio Times* invites readers to decide whether modern actors could or should aspire to sound more like their predecessors, by stating that 'spoken this way, Shakespeare has a music and a rhythm which Edith Evans, almost alone among actresses, gives it today' (1937: 740, 31). Despite suggesting a parallel between OP and Evans's style of delivery, the programme description primes readers to listen out for and to appreciate the fundamental acoustic alterity of OP.

A feature-length essay included in the same issue of *The Radio Times* informs readers that OP studies are an established field of enquiry and that

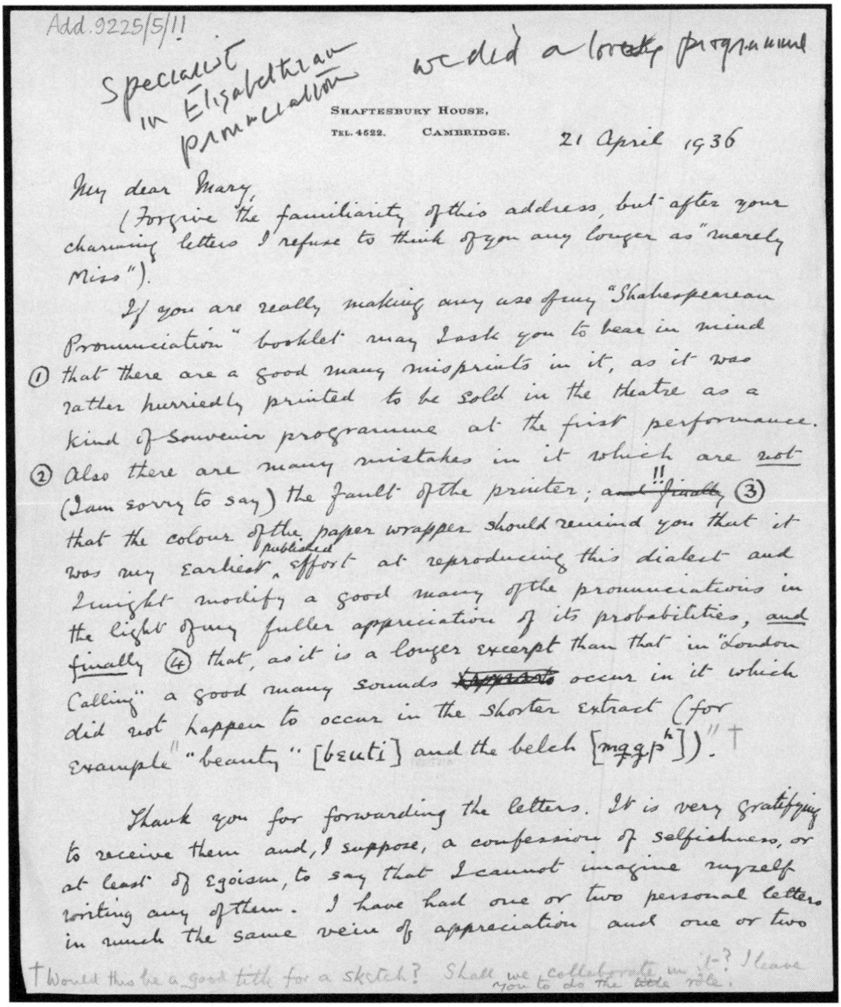

Fig. 4. Letter by F. G. Blandford to Mary Hope Allen, dated 21 April 1936.
Held at the University Library in Cambridge (GB 12 MS. Add. 9225). Reproduced by permission of
Julia Allen-Manheim

Blandford's phonetic reconstruction is based on meticulous research dating back to the mid-nineteenth century. However, listeners are once again warned against the assumption that what they hear is an entirely accurate reconstruction of spoken Shakespearean English:

Fig. 5.   Advertisement for 'Take Your Choice'.
Originally published in *The Radio Times*, 3 December 1937, issue 740. Reproduced by permission of *Immediate Media Co*

The speech we shall hear in the second part of the broadcast is . . . an honest reproduction of all that is known about Elizabethan speech, but nobody (least of all Mr. Blandford) would claim that it is altogether exact. Apart from possible mistakes on the night, there are certain words (though not many) on the pronunciation of which there is no evidence. And the Elizabethan *intonation*, as distinct from accent, is a matter on which there is no authoritative guidance. The rise and fall of the voice must be left to the actor, and it must almost certainly be wrong. (1937: 740, 16)

Far from making any claims to the authenticity of the reconstructed OP, the essay stresses its approximation and admits that Shakespeare himself would most likely not recognize it as his own:

The question really is, would Shakespeare himself understand the second half of Monday's broadcast any better than he would understand the first? The answer undoubtedly is that he would. In the first part he would hardly recognize a line of his work; the second part would probably appeal to him in very much the same way as modern English does to us when spoken fluently, correctly, and with good pronunciation by a foreigner. Remarkably good, but 'just not English'. (1937: 640, 16)

Instead of encouraging listeners to believe that the temporal gap that separated them from how early modern English was originally spoken could be bridged, the essay prepares listeners to hear and appreciate acoustic difference by comparing reconstructed OP to what Shakespeare would have heard, when early modern English was spoken by a foreigner. Exceptionally, the essay goes on to mention Allen's own views (and her co-producer's, Barbara Burnham) on OP:

One appeal from the producers to the listeners. Don't start *comparing* what you hear with other dialects; listen to what it is, not what it is like. Don't try to *spell* the words you hear; there will be vowels intermediate between two modern vowels, and sounds that the ordinary alphabet cannot express. (1937: 740, 16)

This appeal is particularly significant in light of the fact that scholars and commentators interested in OP had, up to that point, tended to invite precisely the sort of comparison with modern regional dialects, which Allen and Burnham regarded as unhelpful and misleading.[3] Avoiding such comparisons allowed Allen and Burnham's listeners to hear OP without associating it with NSE accents and their lack of prestige, especially in the context of the prevailing acoustic norms that dominated Shakespearean performance at the time.

---

[3] Commenting on Jones's experiment with OP in 1909, a reviewer in *The Observer* had, for example, observed how 'the effect of the old pronunciation on the ear was very pleasing. It strongly resembles the broad, rich dialect of the West of England, with a strong admixture of the Lancashire speech' (quoted in Crystal 2016a: xxxv).

To sum up, while *London Calling – 1600* had aimed to amuse the well-informed and entertain a wider and varied audience, *Take Your Choice*, which was broadcast as the second episode of the new, groundbreaking series 'The Experimental Hour', invited its listeners to appreciate OP for its intrinsic otherness. Far from revealing 'an obsession with bringing to life, or re-enacting, the speech and the sound of Shakespeare's age' (Greenhalgh 2011: 549), Allen's programmes paved the way for an experimental use of an accent that departed not only from how Shakespeare was spoken on the mid-twentieth-century stage but also from any variation of modern English pronunciation more generally.

Allen's pre-war original pronunciation programmes seem all the more significant in light of the conservative turn that took place in radio programming and in Shakespearean performance during the Second World War. Allen herself began to produce a much more mainstream series called 'Shakespeare's Characters', thirty-minute programmes that could be run with a small cast. As Michael Jensen explains, when 'Britain became deeply involved in the war, the BBC, [which] had produced two or three full-length plays a week' switched mostly to 'shorter versions, . . . usually in abridgement of one hour or less, . . . to make time for war news' (2008: 171–2). Radio Shakespeare in wartime was not only shorter, but it was consistently performed in StP. One important way in which radio Shakespeare aligned itself with the imperatives of a country at war was by reinforcing the well-established association between Shakespeare and Englishness. Accent was the main means by which this association was evoked on a medium, like radio, that relies solely on aural channels of communication to reach its target audience.

Particularly prominent was the use of StP in Shakespeare programmes broadcast by the World Service (or the Overseas Service, as it was known back then), probably because these programmes reached out to English-speaking audiences across the world and could create a sense of community and allegiance among them. A good example is 'Shakespeare's Birthday', a programme broadcast on 23 April 1942. This programme included extracts from *As You Like It, 1 Henry IV* and *Henry V*, and was introduced and performed by Peggy Ashcroft, Robert Donat, Edith Evans and Ralph Richardson.[4] By April 1942, England had witnessed multiple Nazi invasions on the Continent and had repelled large-scale seaborne and airborne attacks. Despite a British victory in the Battle of Britain, the Blitz continued and Germany had yet to suffer its first major defeat. It is hardly

---

[4] For more details, see the Overseas Services magazine, *London Calling* 1942: 132.

surprising, therefore, that the first extract should focus on the 'green world' of the Forest of Arden, indulging in the memories of those 'golden days' when the young were carefree and could afford to spend their time growing up and falling in love with each other. Similarly, the second extract reminded listeners of the 'warm and rumbustious' world of the Boar's Head tavern in Eastcheap, where Prince Hal and Falstaff, royalty and commoners come together to eat, drink and waste their time in idleness. The third extract is instead a call to arms. The extract, 'Once more unto the breach, dear friends, once more', is introduced by harrowing references to the war and to the need to fight it not only by air or at sea, but by playing Shakespeare in London and in hundreds of other towns across England, in factories, hospitals, military camps and mining villages, in order to ensure that Shakespeare's vision for England, darkened by the war, would shine brilliant and unclouded again.[5]

The delivery is especially striking in this third extract, where the clipped, precise, formal and high-sounding diction of the actors parallels the prowess of Henry's and Churchill's soldiers. Vocal decorum and military competence are linked by being associated with true breeding: if the limbs of Henry's soldiers are 'made in England', the actors go as far as to identify themselves as members of Shakespeare's original company. They claim to be the very actors who were at Will Shakespeare's elbow and who delivered his lines in the sunshine at the Globe on Bankside. They also claim to be the actors who played Shakespeare in the flickering light of the candles and oil lamps in Drury Lane in the eighteenth century, or against the soft hissing of the gaslights at the Lyceum Theatre in the nineteenth century. Their voices, carried by radio waves across the world by a medium that transforms performance into a 'theatre of the mind', span not only space but also time in order to revive that true ideal of Englishness that, in 1942, was associated with 'Shakespeare's vision for England'. But radio produces sounds rather than visions, and it was the voice that was charged with the daunting task of evoking an ideal for which many had died and many more were going to continue to fight.

It is the paradoxical quality of the actors' claim to acoustic authenticity, which I find particularly fascinating, because it is of course a convenient fiction. As I will go on to show in Chapter 4, Shakespeare's actors did not sound like Peggy Ashcroft or Ralph Richardson. And not only because standards of English pronunciation change over time, but also because of

---

[5] These extracts are held as digital recordings in the BBC Archives, and can be requested via the Listening and Viewing Service at the British Library (www.bl.uk/help/listening-and-viewing-service).

the different status accorded to Shakespeare and to playacting more generally in the early modern period. As I mentioned in my introduction, the association between Shakespeare and StP dates back to the eighteenth century and does not apply to the early modern period, when actors and playacting were deemed low-status, if not positively disreputable. When Shakespeare's actors spoke in an elevated register, they did not only sound different from Ashcroft and Richardson, but, by doing so, they were in breach of acceptable standards of acoustic social decorum. More generally, instead of alerting listeners to the temporal and acoustic gap that separated them from Shakespeare and the English spoken by Shakespeare and his contemporaries, as Allen had done in the 1930s, wartime Shakespeare radio programmes encouraged them to identify with, and draw strength from, Shakespeare as a source of cultural and, by association, of military prowess.

Allen returned to OP towards the end of her career at the BBC.[6] In 1949, she enrolled Daniel Jones to introduce *The Elizabethan Tongue*, a forty-five-minute programme consisting of extracts from Shakespeare's plays.[7] Jones also published a feature essay in *The Radio Times*, where he explained how historical phoneticians went about reconstructing accents from periods predating the rise of recording technologies (1949: 1367, 31). Jones's contribution to this programme bears the mark of Allen's approach in lacking the legitimizing, institutional overtones of his early experiments with OP. That Jones's contribution to *The Elizabethan Tongue* programme should bear the marks of Allen's approach to OP is not surprising, given the key role she played as producer. According to Val Gielgud, who, by 1949, had been Head of Productions at the BBC for twenty years, the role of the radio producer was more wide-ranging in those days than at present: '[t]he period between the assignment of a play to a radio producer and its production varie[d] from six weeks to three months'. It was during this period, as Gielgud explains, that

> [the producer's] labour, for the most part 'unhonoured and unsung' [made] all the difference between ultimate success and failure. Most important of all [was] the detailed study of the script, its interpretation, and in consequence the decisions taken regarding the 'approach' of the various actors and the basic tempo and graph of the production as a whole. (1957: 113)

---

[6] During the war, Allen revisited her earlier work on the acoustic dimension of Shakespeare's London in a programme called *Shakespeare's Country* (first broadcast by the Home Service on 5 September 1940), giving her listeners another chance to enjoy 'the sights, sounds, and people that Shakespeare knew, as described in his own verse and prose' (https://genome.ch.bbc.co.uk/16b977844e194aaeae99b11c8fe90d61).

[7] https://genome.ch.bbc.co.uk/5b8b858bdcb14ad29b66c6ca2e46a75b.

Fig. 6.   Mary Hope Allen (third from left), recording *The Tempest*, 3 March 1945.
Reproduced by permission of the BBC Archives and Photo Library Services

Contemporary photographs do indeed show Allen hard at work in the recording studio, effectively directing her actors (Fig. 6).

It is finally worth stressing that the work that Allen produced throughout her career at the BBC was consistently experimental. Viewed in the larger context of her overall output as a radio producer, her OP work appears similarly driven by her determination to surprise and entertain her listeners. Rather than using OP to legitimize and elevate radio as a new medium that reached large audiences, cutting across geographical, class and economic boundaries, she experimented with Shakespeare and Shakespearean English in ways that invited amused participation and curiosity. First hired by the BBC in 1927 as a cataloguer in the Play Library, Allen, who had previously worked as a freelance journalist, copy writer, book reviewer and drama critic, read all plays in the repertory at the time to decide which ones were more readily adaptable to radio (Jensen 2008: 171; Murphy 2016: 132). She then negotiated a producing role for herself directly with BBC founder and first director general, Lord John Reith (Murphy 2016: 133). Shortly after its foundation in 1928, she was transferred to the Research Section, whose 'undefined roving commission [was] to browse over the whole field of programmes, to initiate ideas, [and] to experiment generally' (Gielgud 1957: 27). Allen's first high profile programme while based in the Research Section was called *Russian Twilight* (first broadcast on 4 October 1929).[8] Besides producing the programme, she had been specifically responsible for 'intertwin[ing] … the music … with words and sounds'. Her contribution to this programme set the tone for her later work, which has aptly been described as 'lyrical and avant-garde' (Murphy 2016: 133, 134).

While working on *Russian Twilight*, Allen had also been involved in another successful, experimental programme called *Yes and Back Again* (first broadcast on 11 December 1931), which *The Radio Times* described as 'a fantasy', written by Allen's fellow Research Section colleague, E. J. King Bull, and loosely based on 'The Story of this Book' from Walter de la Mare's anthology *Come Hither* (1931: 428, 874). Allen's private correspondence shows that she had proposed the idea for the programme to de la Mare, along with King Bull,[9] in 1928 and that Allen was the one producer who continued to work with de la Mare for the next ten years.[10] In 1931, Allen became involved in producing another programme, which showed the remarkable scope of her experimental ambitions. In *La Boîte à Joujoux* (first broadcast on 17 November 1931), dancer and actress Lydia Lopokova had read a monologue written by Allen to accompany Claude Debussy's pianoforte suite. As the blurb in *The Radio Times* explains, this suite, 'seldom performed in concerts, and … never … produced as a ballet', 'form[ed] the theme of a new kind of radio production, … [which,] next to an actual ballet … [gave] Debussy's gay ballet … the most vivid and delightful interpretation' (1931: 424, 535). A postcard sent by Lopokova to King Bull earlier in 1931, and now held along with Allen's papers and private correspondence at the University Library, Cambridge, shows that Lopokova had been impressed by Allen's ideas for this programme and had been persuaded to perform in it as a result: 'I think that M.A.'s ideas are very nice. I have recited [her monologue] through and I am attracted and want to try it with music. Thank M.A. for her genial fancy. I feel she has caught my personality and I like the feeling of it!' (GB 12 MS. Add. 9225).

When the Research Section was closed down in 1933, because 'eventually seen as too high-brow' (Murphy 2016: 133), Allen was transferred to the Drama Department, but, as shown above, she brought the highly

---

[8] For more details, see *The Radio Times* 1929: 314, 38.

[9] See a letter sent to Allen by de la Mare dated 11 December 1928 among Allen's private papers and correspondence at the University Library in Cambridge (GB 12 MS. Add. 9225).

[10] See, especially, two letters sent to Allen by de la Mare in January 1930 and July 1938, as representative of their close working relationship (GB 12 MS. Add. 9225).

experimental quality of her approach to programming with her, as she turned her attention to OP. After the war, besides *The Elizabethan Tongue*, she produced another programme, which shows her uncanny foresight in terms of anticipating future trends that would change the soundscape of Shakespeare in performance. In *Hamlet, the Closet Scene*, first broadcast by the Third Programme on 25 March 1947, Allen cast English and French speaking actors to play the roles of Hamlet, the Queen, Polonius and the Ghost. The French actors used a translation by Andre Gide. Later that year, the programme was repeated in a slightly expanded version to include Spanish actors, who performed a translation of this scene by Salvador de Madariaga.[11] These programmes attest to Allen's sensitivity to the material, acoustic features of Shakespeare's language and to how OP and other languages can be used to develop new audiences for Shakespeare. This last programme, which Allen produced for the BBC, drew on her original intuition that the foreign quality of OP could appeal to, as opposed to turn off, listeners who may not have had access to, or may not have felt drawn to, Shakespeare as it was still traditionally performed on the mid-twentieth-century stage.

§

Allen's approach to OP seems even more radical when considered along-side attempts by late nineteenth- to mid-twentieth-century theatre practitioners to depart from the contemporary standards of pronunciation used on the Shakespearean stage. Well-known, for example, is William Poel's commitment to reviving early modern staging practices at the turn of the twentieth century. Less familiar are Poel's views on how he felt Shakespeare should be spoken on stage. While similar to Allen in wanting to reform the sound of Shakespeare in contemporary performance, Poel was oddly unaware of, or not interested in, the potential for change offered by OP.

Like Allen, Poel was a pioneer, not an antiquarian. Poel did advocate the need to pay closer attention to surviving evidence about the staging of drama in Shakespeare's time. In 1881, he set up The Shakespeare Reading Society, whose aim was to produce annual recitals using the texts preserved in the earliest editions of Shakespeare's works. The Elizabethan Stage Society, which started to operate in 1893, was similarly conceived as a

[11] For further details of both programmes, see digital entries at http://genome.ch.bbc.co.uk/search/0/20?adv=0&q=hamlet+the+closet+scene&media=all&yf=1923&yt=2009&mf=1&mt=12&tf=00%3A00&tt=00%3A00#search

proper 'play-producing society, . . . staging productions of non-commercial drama' inspired by early modern staging conditions and practices (O'Connor 2013: 29). However, as recent scholars have established, Poel, like Allen, was not driven by an impulse towards reconstructing Shakespeare as originally performed on the early modern stage, as his disregard for 'antiquarianism or architectural accuracy' suggests (Falocco 2010: 12). Like Allen, he was interested in original practices for their performative potential and because he believed that they would lend fresh insights into Shakespeare's plays.

Also noteworthy is that, although Poel is primarily remembered for championing the benefits of the thrust stage and continuous perform-ance,[12] he, like Allen, also placed considerable emphasis on how the actors' voice could be used to re-sensitize his audience to the sound of Shake-speare's language. In his own words, Poel believed that, while 'the atmosphere . . . of Elizabethan drama [was] created through the voice, that of modern drama [was created] through the sight' (Sprague 1947: 32). He also thought that 'Shakespeare's verse was spoken on the stage of the Globe easily and rapidly' and that, 'unless English actors [could] recover the art of speaking [his] verse, his plays [would] never again enjoy the favour they once had' (Poel 1913: 57).

As Marion O'Connor has pointed out, 'the aural dimension of perform-ance preoccupied him throughout his long career' (2013: 21). And yet, unlike Allen, he never attempted to perform Shakespeare and his con-temporaries by using the findings made available by recent OP scholars. He instead insisted that his actors should avoid the grandiloquent 'redundancy of emphasis' that dominated the late nineteenth-century stage and 'destroy[ed] all meaning of the words and all resemblance to natural speech' (Poel 1913: 58). According to Poel, a more natural style of delivery suited Shakespeare's language both in terms of pace and clarity. Poel's approach was therefore genuinely innovative and experi-mental, both visually and aurally, at a time when many theatre critics and commentators lamented the way in which contemporary directors reduced Shakespeare to pure spectacle. Writing about Herbert Beerbohm Tree, George Bernard Shaw for example memorably summed up his impatience with a directorial approach that ignored the nuances of Shakespeare's language as follows:

---

[12] For more details, see, for example, Sprague 1947 or Falocco 2010.

Confronted with a Shakespearian play, he stares into a ghastly vacuum, yet stares unterrified, undisturbed by any suspicion that his eyesight is failing, quite prepared to find the thing simply an ancient, dusty, mouldy, empty house which it is his business to furnish, decorate, and housewarm with an amusing entertainment. And it is astonishing how well he does it. Totally insensible to Shakespear's qualities, he puts his own qualities into the work. When he makes one of Shakespear's points – which seldom happens – it is only because at that particular moment Shakespear's wit chances to coincide with his own. (1920: 3–4)

Echoing Shaw's appeal to rediscover the beauty and complexity of Shakespeare's 'dying tongue', Poel added a polite note to Shaw's tirade, explaining how Shakespeare's language should 'be spoken with dramatic intelligence and significance, so as to be a real delight to the listener' (Shaw 1920: 18–9). In this respect, though never resorting to OP, Poel anticipated Allen's impulse to develop new audiences for Shakespeare by disrupting the visual and acoustic norms that informed theatrical performance at the time.

§

The radical and innovative quality of Allen's approach to OP stands out even more clearly when compared and contrasted with mid-twentieth-century productions that were directly affected by the legacy of Jones's approach and used OP for its legitimizing function. Among them, the most revealing is Miles's production of *Macbeth*, which was performed in OP twice nightly for six evenings at the Mermaid Theatre in St John's Wood, North London, in September 1952. As mentioned above, Gimson, who had been one of Jones's students, acted as phonetic adviser for Miles. Along with two other colleagues, J. D. O'Connor and Gordon Arnold, Gimson prepared a phonetic transcription of the text and a recording, which the actors listened to and attempted to reproduce by imitation.[13] Bertram L. Joseph, author of *Elizabethan Acting* (1950), advised the actors on gesture and movement (Crystal 2016a: xxxvii; O'Connor 2002: 93). Voice and gesture were therefore carefully curated to suit the Mermaid Theatre, a venue that Miles had carefully reconstructed to evoke the architectural features of an early modern playhouse.

'Neither a public theatre nor a club, [where] tickets were sold in return for donations' (Anon. 1952a), the Mermaid Theatre was described by those who visited it as offering a unique theatrical experience:

---

[13] This recording is in the holdings of University College London Library.

Fig. 7.   Duff House, as No. 43 Acacia Road, St John's Wood.
Reproduced by permission of Ben Frow

The country-style gate of No. 43 Acacia Road, St John's Wood, protects a straight drive leading up to a squarish house ... [that] was formerly a school ['Duff House', see Fig. 7] ... The Mermaid Theatre ... adjoins it ... in the back garden. (Gosling 1952)

A contemporary photograph (Fig. 8) shows 'a spacious and lofty hall, sixty feet by thirty', that had been used 'some fifty years earlier ... for the Christmas play' (Bryden 1969: 43), as the construction of the theatre got underway. Another photograph (Fig. 9) captures the imposing, if austere appearance of the stage of the Mermaid, which had been designed by Walter Hodges and Michael Stringer at the Nettleford Studios and then

Fig. 8.   The First Mermaid Theatre, at No. 43 Acacia Road, St John's Wood; under
construction, in 1951; Bernard Miles and Josephine Wilson, bottom right.
Reproduced by permission of Ben Frow

erected in St John's Wood for the 1951 and 1952 seasons. The hall itself
'was transformed into an auditorium holding 200 people', with 'the
audience [sitting] on forty pitch-pine forms . . . and arranged in sharply-
raked tiers', facing a 'high, trestled open stage and tiring house' (Bryden
1969: 43). The first season opened on 9 September 1951 and included a
production of Henry Purcell's opera *Dido and Aeneas*, fifteen recitals as
well as a production of *The Tempest* and a special performance of the
opening scene of *Hamlet* performed in OP (Bryden 1969: 43). The
Mermaid theatre was modified just before the opening of the 1952 season,
which included Miles's OP production of *Macbeth*, when 'a "roof
hut" [was] built above the auditorium so that "apparitions" and the like

Fig. 9.   The Stage of the First Mermaid Theatre, at No. 43 Acacia Road, St John's wood;
designed by Walter Hodges and Michael Stringer.
Reproduced by permission of Ben Frow

[could] be lowered on to the stage in the correct Elizabethan fashion'
(Anon. 1952b).

Miles's efforts to recreate a visually and aurally authentic Elizabethan
experience for his audience had been driven by a precise agenda, which had
clear affinities with the 'institutional impulse' that had led Jones to experiment with OP at the beginning of his academic career. From its very
inception, the Mermaid Theatre was conceived as a project meant to boost
Britain's post-war efforts to regain a sense of its national and global
identity, in the face of a slow economic recovery and housing shortages
at home and the dissolution of the British Empire overseas. Miles and his
wife, Josephine Wilson, started to plan the first Mermaid after they

performed with a small company for the Home Fleet on the Orkneys in 1945. In their own words,

> [It was] playing on catapult decks, on top of gun turrets, on bare platforms slung between destroyers, indeed wherever there was space for half a dozen people to stand upright [that] we suddenly began to develop a strong taste for closer contact with our audience. (Miles and Wilson 1951: 2)

The experience of performing outdoors and in close proximity to their audience gave Miles and Wilson a taste for the potential benefits associated with the thrust stage on which Shakespeare's plays had originally been performed. Two years after their performance on the Orkneys, they saw a production of *1 Henry IV* in the Harrow School Speech Room and were struck by the 'highly skilled attempt to reproduce the exact stage conditions of Elizabethan times'. That production proved an important turning point during the planning stages of the Mermaid Theatre, because, as they were to explain later on, it had shown them that until then they 'had seen Shakespeare only in adaptation' (Miles and Wilson 1951: 12). This production, in other words, crystallized their understanding of original practices as a more 'authentic' approach to Shakespearean performance.

The gradual rediscovery of early modern conditions of theatrical production at a time of great military and civilian effort and of renewed hope for the nation strengthened Miles's and Wilson's determination to revive the type of indigenous theatre-making that had prompted the rise of the 'Golden Age' of British drama in the sixteenth and the seventeenth centuries. 'The picture frame . . . [is] not a native growth', they argued:

> It was really born in Italy and was imported into England at a time when we had a wonderful theatre of our own, a theatre as homegrown as the great drama of which it was the technical nursery and as inseparable from that drama as a cricket bat is from a game of cricket. This is the theatre we have never yet seen. (Miles and Wilson 1951: 9)

The son of a market gardener, Miles came to think of the conditions of production in an Elizabethan playhouse as 'a rare native growth, which deserv[ed] to be replanted for its own sake as well as the fruits it [might] bear' (Miles and Wilson 1951: 12). This botanical metaphor, repeatedly used by Miles in his own writing about the first Mermaid Theatre, linked original practices not only to a point of origin located in the nation's own past, but also to its native soil, which should be carefully farmed to ensure a revival of the best that British theatrical traditions could offer in the present.

Two years later, in 1949, while Miles's and Wilson's friend, Norwegian opera singer Kirsten Flagstad, was visiting them at 43 Acacia Road, they drafted a 'light-hearted document' that stipulated that if Miles and Wilson managed to turn the hall into a theatre, Flagstad would sing in Purcell's *Dido and Aeneas* in the opening season. Miles and Wilson started converting the hall shortly thereafter. The building of the Mermaid Theatre proved quite timely, because it coincided with the planning for the Festival of Britain, which was to take place in summer 1951 and which evidently bolstered Miles's and Wilson's investment in the whole venture:

> Ideas now came thick and fast. Why not build the Elizabethan stage we had so long dreamed of and use it as the setting for a short season of music and drama sometime during the Festival of Britain? Why not build a dozen Elizabethan theatres and send them all over the world to speak for Britain through the mouths of great poets and composers? Our imagination suddenly ran wild! (Miles and Wilson 1951: 2)

Janus-like, the Mermaid Theatre looked both back at the past as the point of origin of homegrown, national traditions of theatre-making and to a new future for Britain, when those traditions could be revived and function as popular exports advertising British ways of life to the world. In this respect, the Mermaid Theatre was perfectly attuned to the cultural agenda that shaped the Festival of Britain. As Becky Conekin explains, 'the Festival's imaginings of the future and the past were not "at odds"; rather they were mutually reinforcing' and 'particular representations of the past bolstered particular representations of the future and vice versa' (2003: 80). The Festival's imaginings of the past were also specifically British: while the Great Exhibition of 1851 had been thoroughly international in scope, the Festival aimed to 'create new meanings for the terms "Britain" and "Britishness"' (Conekin 2003: 8) and actively promoted an ideal of Britishness that 'was dependent on beliefs, stories, and discourses constituted' around the idea of '"belonging" to a place':

> Britons were British because they 'belonged' to Britain – there was something about their 'island' home that made them unique and different people; this something was related to both the soil and the sea – the land and the 'islandness' of Great Britain. (Conekin 2003: 31)

The soil featured as a central trope both in Miles's and Wilson's thinking about the revival of original Elizabethan theatrical practices and in the way in which the Festival's organizers constructed ideas of national culture. The very notion that nationality is rooted in blood and land, and should therefore be understood as the birthright to inhabit 'bounded territorial space' (Anderson 2006: 173), was compounded with the idea that culture and tradition can also become inscribed into the land, and be grown and flourish into recognizably British ways of life.

This convergence of cultural and ideological agendas might explain why mixed reviews of Miles's Elizabethan productions did not prevent the project from receiving significant institutional support. Looking forward to the 1952 season, which included Miles's *Macbeth* performed entirely in Elizabethan pronunciation, a review in *The Manchester Guardian* auspiciously observed that 'it [began] to look as if [Miles's] idea of a permanent Elizabethan playhouse in London [might] flourish for a long time, as he had planned' (Anon. 1952a). Revealing the levels of anticipation related to the impeding opening of the second season at the Mermaid, another review in *The Manchester Guardian* informed its readers that the recording prepared by Gimson's team at University College London sounded 'smooth, less exaggerated than has sometimes been heard, and with pleasant Midland, West of England, and Irish undertones' (Anon. 1952b).

The tendency to try to hear OP as approximating modern regional dialects, which Allen had tried to discourage among her listeners back in the late 1930s, emerged in other contemporary reviews, though not as an endorsement of Miles's choice to revive Shakespeare in OP. In 'A Throne for Two', Ivor Brown, writing for *The Observer*, found the accent entirely off-putting. According to Brown, Miles's attempt to perform *Macbeth* 'in the supposed pronunciation of the time' resulted in 'Mummerset': 'It seems, to my ear, an ugly mess, but even those who find it pleasing must admit that it impedes the acting' (1952). Brown appreciated the fast pace of Miles's heavily cut production and admitted that, despite the 'tiresome word-sounds, the experiment was well worth making.' However, he felt that 'the poetry was diminished' and pleaded 'no more of that Mummerset mixture, and far more relish of the mighty line'. Brown conceded that OP 'may give purists pleasure', but he also stressed how it made 'the speaking of verse perhaps even more difficult for the lesser fry' (1952).

Despite the mixed views expressed by contemporary reviewers, the grander season of 1952 attracted the attention of the City of London authorities. The Lord Mayor, Sir Leslie Boyce, spotted an opportunity to channel the energy and curiosity generated by the Mermaid Theatre to boost civic pride, as he was planning the celebration for Elizabeth II's coronation in 1953. Miles was invited to move his replica stage to the Royal Exchange. The 1952 season at the Royal Exchange was arranged by the Gresham Committee and included matinees for city workers, Saturday morning performances for school children and evening performances for all. The profits went to charities and to the Mermaid Theatre, with a view to ensuring continuity to Miles's project (Anon. 1952c). The following summer, Miles moved the replica stage to the piazza facing the Royal

Exchange and offered a thirteen-week season as part of the celebration for the Queen's coronation. The 1953 season included productions of *As You Like It* and *Eastward Ho!*, as well as revivals of Purcell's *Dido and Aeneas* and *Macbeth*, though, crucially, the latter was no longer performed in OP. The season proved exceptionally popular and was attended by over 70,000 people over a thirteen-week period (Bryden 1969: 44).

The support of the City of London and the popularity enjoyed by the 1953 season gave Miles enough momentum to plan the building of a permanent Mermaid Theatre in the City. Miles received strong additional backing from private sponsors (Bryden 1969: 46) and was able to start building his new theatre in Puddle Dock in 1956. The opening of the second, permanent Mermaid Theatre at Puddle Dock in 1959 was marked by grand civic celebrations. As Ronald Hastings reports, 'a four-year-old girl, who played the live mermaid, was rowed up the Thames by the Westminster Sea Cadets and unloaded at Puddle Dock into the welcoming arms of the Lord Mayor, Sir Harold Gillets' (1969: 4) (Fig. 10). Miles's efforts paid off, at least in terms of raising his public profile: he received a CBE for his services to the theatre in 1953, was knighted in 1969, and eventually received life peerage in 1979 (Morley 2004).

In artistic and ideological terms, though, Miles's theatrical experiment proved less groundbreaking and innovative than it set out to be. In some respects, Miles did manage to introduce important reforms inspired by early modern theatrical practice. It is for example important to stress that, although the second Mermaid Theatre soon started to offer a mixed programme of early modern and modern plays, with a leaning towards comedy and light entertainment, it gave London its first commercial thrust stage. As Ronald Bryden remarked, on the tenth anniversary of the second Mermaid,

> [It is] quite extraordinary to remember how, ten years ago, the lack of a proscenium stage seemed a disadvantage, a makeshift to be glossed over. Even in those Elizabethan revivals it staged with such special verve . . . why didn't we recognize it as the playhouse of the future? I hope we have now; and that its special relationship with its audience and the new drama growing up in Britain will continue, floribundantly, into the next decade. (Bryden 1969: 7)

The second Mermaid Theatre strayed considerably from the first one in St John's Wood, but, as this extract shows, it did introduce some important and lasting changes.

The legitimizing function that Miles attributed to original practices, and to OP among them, was however ever present as one of the core principles

Fig. 10.   The Lord Mayor, Sir Harold Gillets, at the opening of the Second Mermaid
Theatre at Puddle Dock, 1959.
Reproduced with permission of Ben Frow

that shaped his theatrical ventures. Even the site where the second
Mermaid was built had been chosen to reinforce and promote Miles's
commitment to offering his audiences a more authentically British theatrical
experience. As Bryden points out, Paddle Dock 'had a very early theatrical
connection: across the street to the north in Printing House Square, once
stood the famous Blackfriars Theatre'. Bryden goes on to mention that 'a
house bought by Shakespeare in 1611 ... is described in conveyance as

"abutting upon a streete leading down to Puddle Wharfe on the East Part'". And, last but not least among the site's credentials, Bryden reminds his readers that 'in 1613, actor Philip Rosseter had planned his Puddle Dock playhouse, but residents petitioned, and he was evicted' (1969: 44). Despite the early modern theatrical credentials of its new site, and the popularity of its thrust stage, the second Mermaid Theatre never resurrected Miles's early experiments with OP, which proved too challenging in the context of Miles's increasingly commercial and populist agenda.

§

The two different approaches to OP explored in this chapter are still affecting how the reconstructed accent associated with it is reproduced on the Shakespearean stage and how contemporary audiences hear and decode it. Occasionally, these two approaches are activated simultaneously, not only by the practitioner's own agenda, but also by the specific sets of cultural and economic forces that operate in the spaces where OP work is performed. The OP productions curated by Crystal and by his son, Ben Crystal, since the early 2000s would, for example, seem to oscillate between reclaiming and resisting the authorizing function associated with early experiments with OP by the likes of Jones and Miles. Crucially, though, when asked why OP productions have a role on the contemporary Shakespearean stage, Crystal mentions access and ownership, using arguments which resonate with the tenets that were already informing Allen's approach in the 1930s and 1940s:

> What I find most fascinating about OP is the way audiences everywhere (I've seen about 15 plays done in OP around the world to date) report that OP gives them a sense of ownership that the tradition of presenting the plays in RP (. . . as heard from Olivier, et al) did not. (2016b)

Crystal attributes the increased accessibility of OP not so much to the profound alterity of the accent associated with it, as Allen had done in the 1930s, but to similarities with modern regional inflections, thus encouraging a mode of listening that Allen had resisted. According to Crystal, his audiences feel closer to Shakespeare, when performed in OP because it 'contains echoes of their own speech':

> Virtually everyone says, after listening to OP, 'we speak like that where I come from'. What they're noticing are the sounds in OP that are closest to their own backgrounds. The closeness makes them more receptive, and thus a second comment is also common (including those who speak English as a second language): the plays become easier to understand. (2016b)

Despite insisting on its 'closeness', rather than on its alterity, Crystal, like Allen, finds in the acoustic diversity of OP a vehicle to re-present Shakespeare as relevant and accessible to a wider, more varied audience.

Like Allen's OP radio programmes, Crystal's OP productions have reached and entertained large audiences. In 2011, Rob Gardner directed an OP production of *Hamlet*, starring Ben Crystal in the title role, for the Nevada Repertory Company at the University of Nevada. David Crystal voice coached the actors, while Eric Rasmussen, Foundation Professor of English at the University of Nevada, advised as dramaturg. This production attracted large local audiences: twenty-one sold-out shows took place over a period of three weeks to great popular and critical acclaim. According to Rasmussen, who had initiated the project by inviting the Crystals to work on this production, members of the audience interviewed by local newspapers and on local TV stations thoroughly enjoyed listening to Shakespeare in OP. No one complained about the accent being difficult or off-putting and most remarked on its novelty as a positive aspect of this production.[14]

The reception of David Crystal's work with OP was more uniformly positive in Nevada than it had been in London, when Crystal was first invited to advise on a short run of OP shows included in a repertory production of *Romeo and Juliet* directed by Tim Carroll in 2004 and on an OP production of *Troilus and Cressida* directed by Giles Block in 2005. According to a reviewer of the OP *Romeo and Juliet*, OP had undermined 'the actors' ability to . . . act their roles':

> While some were more hamstrung than others in this respect, there was a staggering thoughtfulness to the lines that could only have resulted from the difficulty of remembering a whole new part. Most culpable here were Joel Trill's barely comprehensible Escalus and Tom Burke's Romeo, who managed to render his hormonally challenged, pubescent lover entirely passionless. As he met Juliet for the first time, a scene in which the text, at least, fervently articulates the most lyrical surges of ardor, he was concentrating so intently on getting the OP right, that he sounded quite bored. James Garnon's Mercutio appeared to know that the description of Queen Mab was about something but his laborious effort to remember his OP clearly overwhelmed the logic of the speech. (Smith 2004: 146)

What is striking about these comments is not only their emphasis on the lack of clarity but also the fact that they reflect the informed views of someone who is thoroughly familiar with the text and with the history of

---

[14] In conversation with Eric Rasmussen, October 2018.

its critical and theatrical reception. Audiences in Nevada, made up mostly by members of a general public rarely exposed to Shakespearean verse in performance, did not complain about not understanding the accent or Shakespeare, as an effect of listening to the play in OP. The different responses to Crystal's OP productions in London and Nevada are in keeping with how voice theorists attribute the perceived lack of clarity in marked voices to cultural expectations rather than to any material features intrinsical to them.

Similar views were expressed by reviewers of the 2005 production of *Troilus and Cressida*. John Lahr in *New Yorker* reported experiencing 'a certain fascination' with this production:

> As *Troilus and Cressida* unfolds, the rolled "r"s, the elided pronouns, and the longer, tenser vowels give the audience a frisson of extra drama. The earthy regional sounds ruffle the familiar strut of Shakespeare's eloquence and root the language more in the belly than in the larynx. As the antique idiom washes over the mostly roofless auditorium, the audience struggles to suss out the odd bouquet of sound, savoring the hints of Irish, Yorkshire, and Welsh, each with its own verbal spice. (2005)

However, for all its mixture of exotic and local/regional appeal, the accent was again thought to get in the way of clarity of diction, appreciation of the poetical quality of the Shakespearean verse and a basic understanding of the language:

> Still, sound must also serve sense. ... The actors here aren't feeling the words they strain to pronounce. ... The barbarous vanity of the two swaggering Greek warriors Ajax and Achilles is almost lost; the irony between word and deed is unfocussed. ... By my estimate, only about thirty per cent of the production, which is unamplified, is comprehensible; the waves of words produce a mesmerizing static, sort of like listening to poetry underwater. (2005)

Once again, the perception of a lack of clarity and understanding is surprising, especially when this reviewer admits to having a copy of the text with him, which he followed as he watched this production: 'I had to read along to get the full meaning' (2005). Comparing responses to OP as performed on the Globe stage in London and in Reno, Nevada, can help us reflect on what one means by 'getting the full meaning' of Shakespeare's language in performance. Audiences who can be assumed to have brought a more limited familiarity with the text of the play and with the play in performance relished the novelty of the language *and* of the accent, while audiences attuned to listening to Shakespeare in StP found the language hard to understand *because of* the accent in which it was delivered. A final telling comment by Lahr – 'Now that I have heard the play in OP, next time I look forward to seeing it' (2005) – shows that he was reading in order to compare the sound of OP to the written text of the play at the expense of all other aspects of the production. What this review suggests, therefore, is that one of the pitfalls of staging OP productions in major theatrical venues is not its intrinsically difficult, and therefore non-commercial, quality, but the fact that audiences at these venues have a very specific set of expectations as to how Shakespeare should sound in performance in order to be understandable and aesthetically pleasing.

Staging OP productions at the Globe is even more challenging than in other major theatrical venues in London and beyond, because the Globe is of course associated with experimenting with original practices more generally. Especially when it first opened, the Globe had to work very hard to convince its critics that the impetus behind their programmatic commitment to experimenting with original practices was to test what Shakespeare's plays looked and sounded like in a reconstructed early modern playhouse and not to recover the authentic look and sound of Shakespeare as originally performed in the first Globe Theatre. Resistance to using OP on the Globe stage would therefore seem to stem from an understandable unwillingness to be dragged back into old debates about authenticity and its discontents. Sceptical responses to the use of OP on the Globe stage seem similarly fuelled by a growing impatience with practitioners who exploit OP for its legitimizing function, as Jones and Miles did in the early and mid-twentieth century.

Although trained by Gimson at University College London, Crystal seems to bring to OP some of Allen's more creative and experimental approach to it. When Crystal pays homage to earlier scholars and practitioners who inspired him, he does not mention the academic context within which he first encountered historical phonetics; he instead refers to a pioneering theatrical experiment with OP, which, according to Crystal, paved the way for later work with OP in the theatre, including his own. In his preface to *Pronouncing Shakespeare: The Globe Experiment*, Crystal singles out a 1952 production of *Julius Caesar*, directed for the Marlowe Society by John Barton, while the latter was still a student in Cambridge:

> If this book were being dedicated to any one person, it would have to be [to Barton], for his production of a Shakespeare play in Elizabethan pronunciation that took place in 1952, when I was eleven and had yet to see my first Shakespeare play. (Crystal 2005: xi)

It is rather fitting that Crystal, who trained at University College London as a linguist, should instead associate his own work with OP with John Barton and the Marlowe Society Theatre in Cambridge. The Marlowe Society Theatre is the venue where Gray's 1933 OP production of *Twelfth Night* was originally staged. And, as explained above, this was the production which, phonetically curated by Blandford, inspired Allen to bring Shakespeare in OP to the much larger audiences reached by radio in the 1930s and the 1940s. Barton was therefore continuing to work within a tradition of practitioners who had used OP for its potential to entertain.

Barton never returned to OP, once he embarked on his long career at the RSC. The mid-twentieth century was still a time when, as Crystal himself has pointed out, 'RP was the dominant voice of British theatre', and 'putting on … plays in [non-standard] accent was unimaginable' (2013: 15). Nowadays, though, the main obstacle preventing OP from playing a more central role in contemporary Shakespearean performance stems from its association with earlier practitioners who exploited it for its institutional, legitimizing function. This chapter has identified and discussed an alternative tradition, within which OP was instead used creatively and experimentally to develop new audiences for Shakespeare at a time of otherwise absolute acoustic uniformity. All in all, though, while foreign and regional accents are increasingly being used to achieve nuanced dramaturgical effects and to diversify the soundscape of Shakespeare in contemporary performance, as argued in Chapter 1, OP is facing greater challenges that might sadly confine it to isolated experiments, more in line with the institutional imperative that informed Jones's early work with OP than with the ethos underlying Allen's pioneering approach in the 1930s and 1940s.

CHAPTER 3

David Garrick's 'Sonic Revolution': Hegemony and Protest, 1737–1843[*]

Before the first experiments with OP discussed in Chapter 2 began to challenge the acoustic uniformity that dominated the English stage in the twentieth century, Shakespeare in performance was well and truly bound up with the accent of Southern English people educated at preparatory boarding schools and public schools. The earliest extant audio recordings from the period[1] attest that late nineteenth-century actors were by then speaking their Shakespeare in RP, either because they had been privately educated or because they took elocution lessons aimed at refining their regional or lower-status accents. Historical phoneticians have established that 'the accent we now know as Received Pronunciation ... emerg[ed] in England [at] the beginning of the nineteenth century' (Crystal 2005: 27), but that it only 'came to social prominence during the period of the expansion of public (fee-paying) school education from around the 1870s, in the latter part of the Victorian era' (Fabricius 2006: 111). However, the link between Shakespeare and StP goes even further back to the mid-eighteenth century, when the need to move towards a standard, supra-national accent was strenuously advocated, especially for professional roles that required public speaking or to perform spoken drama on the stages of the so-called 'legitimate theatres'. 'Legitimate theatres' had been set up as a direct result of the duopoly granted by Charles II to Thomas Killigrew and William Davenant in 1660, whereby only their two companies, the King's Company and the Duke's Company, were licensed to stage plays in London.[2] The terms of the duopoly were qualified, but also reinforced, by the Licensing Act of 1737, which survived until the Theatre

---

[*] I borrow the phrase 'Sonic Revolution' from Holland 2007: 259.
[1] See, for example, the historical recordings gathered in Various Artists 2000.
[2] For a full text of the patents issued to Killigrew and Davanent 'for the representations of Tragedys, Comedys, Playes, Operas, and all other entertainments of that nature', see Hotson 1928: 199.

Regulation Act of 1843.[3] The very notion of 'legitimate theatres' had strengthened the related idea that spoken drama was the 'preserve of elite groups' (Greenslade 2012: 232), and that elite speakers were the best arbiters on how spoken drama, included Shakespeare, should sound on stage.

This chapter shows that the alignment of Shakespeare with the speech of elitism was however a deeply controversial process and that the rise of StP in the eighteenth century was mired from the very beginning in a fierce dispute as to what variation of spoken English should be taken to constitute that very standard. This chapter also argues that the controversy was to a large extent shaped by contemporary responses to David Garrick's popularity as the foremost Shakespearean actor on the mid-eighteenth-century London stage and to the 'natural' style of delivery with which he became associated, following his debut at Goodman's Fields, White Chapel, in October 1741. Garrick's voice sparked a debate about what acoustic standard suited the eighteenth-century stage, but it also triggered two parallel movements against the ban on spoken drama. These movements, headed by the two John Palmers who are discussed in detail in the second half of this chapter, led to groundbreaking attempts to bring Shakespeare and spoken drama, performed in a range of regionally and socially marked voices, to larger and more varied audiences in venues beyond Central London. Before RP became firmly associated with the delivery of Shakespearean and spoken drama on the London stage in the mid- to late nineteenth century, Garrick's 'sonic revolution' ushered in a period of radical acoustic diversity, while standards of correct pronunciation were still being passionately debated and contested.

A representative intervention in the debate is a pamphlet by Scottish orthoepist James Buchanan, called 'An Essay towards Establishing a Standard for an Elegant and Uniform Pronunciation of the English Language throughout the British Dominions, as practised by the Most Learned and Polite Speakers' (1766). Buchanan's pamphlet, though largely in keeping with the work produced by other contemporary elocutionists, was harshly criticized. Among others, William Kenrick, the author of *A New Dictionary of the English Language*, tellingly sub-titled '*containing ... [the] Pronunciation in Speech, according to the present Practice of polished Speakers in the Metropolis*' (1773), focused his invective on 'the ridiculous absurdity in the pretensions of a native of Aberdeen ... to teach the natives of London to speak and to read (1784: I). Kenrick's attack suggests the extent to which

---

[3] For further details about the Licensing Act of 1737, and other intervening legislation prior to 1834, see Milhous 2004.

deciding what constituted a model of standard pronunciation was regarded as the prerogative of a select group of speakers. 'Standard', as in 'Standard English', already meant 'metropolitan' and 'elitist'.

Like Buchanan, Thomas Sheridan, a born Irishman, who divided his professional life as an actor and theatre manager between London and Dublin, was mocked for trying to dictate to the English how to speak their own language.[4] Sheridan had sided with other leading orthoepists in promoting 'the English spoken in London at court and in stage circles during the reign of Queen Anne' (Mahon 2001: 75), while condemning all regional dialects as 'sure marks, either of a provincial, rustic, pedantic, or mechanical education; and therefore [as] hav[ing] some degree of disgrace annexed to them' (*Course of Lectures*, quoted in Spoel 2001: 63). Despite the conventional quality of his views, Sheridan, like Buchanan, was however deemed unsuited to act as an arbiter of acoustic decorum because of his nationality.

Attacks against Sheridan revealed not only a national, but also a social bias. He was, for example, accused of running 'the worst school of oratory' during his time at the Smock Alley Theatre, in Dublin, when he opposed Spranger Barry's plan to open a second theatre there (Anon. 1758: 20). The arguments used against Sheridan catalyzed simmering class tensions. Sheridan was more specifically blamed for misleading 'gentlemen bred under his care [who] may mistake [his] imperfections for excellencies'. Among Sheridan's imperfections, his 'unnatural and false tones' were singled out as especially pernicious, as they were associated with 'an affected pompous diction and delivery, which we know very well by the name of Theatrical; a manner that is always ridiculous, as it is unnatural, and tends to turn ordinary subjects into burlesque' (Anon. 1758: 20). Barry, on the other hand, who had performed in Dublin in 1754 to the 'general satisfaction' of the more discerning members of the audience, had the support of 'the nobility and gentry, as well as citizens of the greatest eminence', who praised him for his 'voice, person and deportment' (Anon. 1758: 45). The breach of acoustic decorum on stage was therefore linked to social impropriety, to a lack of genteel taste and manners, and, ultimately, to a transgression of social boundaries.

Sheridan defended himself by attacking his enemies but also his former allies, including Garrick, with whom he had often been compared, because

---

[4] Spoel reports sarcastic comments made at Sheridan's expenses for his efforts 'to teach all the delicacies of English intonation . . . in his strong Irish brogue' (2001: 57).

of similarities in their 'natural' style of acting and the clarity of their delivery (Thomson 2004b). In his *Elements of English* (1786), Sheridan denounced 'a very improper pronunciation', which '[had] of late gained ground, owing to a provincial dialect with which Mr. Garrick's speech was infected' (quoted in Holland 2007: 28). Worth stressing, though, is how other contemporary orthoepists had extolled the acoustic quality of Garrick's voice: John Walker, fellow actor and elocutionist, had, for example, considered Garrick's 'manner of . . . delivery to be the modern standard of true pronunciation' (Boaden 1831–32: 651) and had dedicated his *Dictionary of the English Language* to Garrick in 1775.

Walker's and Sheridan's disagreement over the merits and drawbacks of Garrick's diction confirms that any given accent is never inherently clearer, or naturally and phonetically superior, and that the connotations attached to accents vary not only over time but also across social groups or members of the same professional community. The debates among mid- to late eighteenth-century orthoepists reveal that the rise of StP involved complex negotiations about what constituted a 'naturally' superior English accent. Similarly, the delivery of the spoken word on the mid-eighteenth- to the mid-nineteenth- century English stage regularly split public opinion along emergent class divisions. As Julia Swindells has put it, revisiting E. P. Thompson's work on elite and popular cultures in the period, 'class relations were being newly forged within the theatres themselves, in ways which were crucial in deciding the character of the British nation, giving a language and form to political as well as dramatic performance and engagement' (2001: 150). Or, as Angie Sandhu explains in even more general terms, '[m]atters of government, commerce, art, literature, and colonial management all, it seemed, required a degree of morality, refinement, and perspicacity that could only be found in particular people who were busily transforming themselves into those who could and should be recognized as . . . newly forming cultural elites' (2014: 13–14).

Building on the work of these scholars, this chapter highlights the tensions that accompanied the gradual distancing of the English stage from the Court and the higher ranks of English society, with which the theatre had become firmly associated since Charles II had introduced the theatre duopoly in 1660. This chapter also addresses and develops recent work on 'illegitimate' forms of theatrical entertainment by eighteenth-century theatre studies specialists, including Joseph Donohue, Jane Moody and David Worrall. While these scholars have argued that the competition introduced by unlicensed theatrical activity from the 1730s to the Theatre Regulation Act of 1843 bolstered theatrical creativity and innovation, as well as theatrical political agency,[5] I focus more specifically on how regionally and socially marked voices on the mid-eighteenth- to the mid-nineteenth-century stage acted as a major catalyst for theatrical (and social) reform in the period.

§

Enter David Garrick, 'According to Staffordshire Custom'[6]

The grandson of French Huguenot refugee David de la Garrique (later rewritten as Garric and then Garrick) and the son of army officer Peter Garrick of Lichfield in Staffordshire, David Garrick (1717–1779) was apprenticed as a wine trader to his uncle, who was also called David and ran a commercial enterprise in Lisbon. David was back in Lichfield within a year but resumed wine trading, if only briefly, after moving to London, having unsuccessfully started training in the legal profession at Lincoln's Inn in 1737. David showed no inclination to pursue either a business or a law career; he instead started to mingle with some of the most prominent figures from the contemporary London stage, including actor and theatre manager Henry Giffard and actor and playwright Charles Macklin (Thomson 2004a).

Giffard and Macklin had a profound influence on the young Garrick. It was Macklin's groundbreaking performance as Shylock in February 1741 that inspired Garrick to challenge the declamatory style and set rhetorical gestures associated with older and well-established actors, like Colley Cibber (1671–1757) and James Quin (1693–1766).[7] And it was Giffard who, on 19 October 1741, offered Garrick the opportunity to play the title role in a production of *Richard III* at Goodman's Fields, in Great Ayliffe Street, near White Chapel. This production proved an overnight sensation and transformed Garrick's burgeoning passion for amateur dramatics into a life-long career in the theatre.

Despite his rise to stardom and his proficient management of Drury Lane from 1747 until his retirement, shortly before his death in 1779, Garrick was the target of sustained criticism throughout his career. Those who regarded themselves as arbiters of good taste and champions of aesthetic and social decorum condemned his acting style as vulgar, coarse

---

[5] See especially Donohue 2004, Moody 2000, and Worrall 2006 and 2007.   [6] Sheridan 1786: 28.
[7] For further details on the innovative qualities of Garrick's acting style, see, among others, Benedetti 2001: 47–54.

and acoustically inappropriate. Garrick did represent the main point of departure from an acting tradition that reached back from Cibber and Quin to Thomas Betterton. The latter, the most renowned actor in the Restoration, had been praised as 'the epitome of neoclassical dignity and rhetoric, and had adapted the French style of declamation, favoured by the court, to the English stage' (Benedetti 2001: 47). Garrick, on the other hand, introduced a new style of acting that struck his admirers as more 'natural', because more effective in capturing the infinite variety of human nature, as observed in everyday life. As Gefen Bar-On Santor has recently argued,

> [Isaac] Newton's achievement in discovering precise and predicable [sic] regularity in the physical universe inspired broad cultural optimism about the possibility of ascertaining truth in other areas of investigation. In an age that preceded the separation of art and science and in which the behavioural sciences were yet to develop, people saw in Shakespeare's characters much of what they saw in Newton's laws of motion and his law of universal gravitation: precise descriptions of underlying principles, what Samuel Johnson described as 'just representations of general nature'. . . . [And] the actor most widely celebrated . . . for his embodiment of Shakespearean characters was of course Garrick. (2014: 217–8)

Not everybody however agreed on the merits and revolutionary qualities of Garrick's acting style. Even Macklin, a great innovator in his own right and a source of inspiration for Garrick, found it too bald and ultimately unseemly. Macklin turned from keen supporter to harsh critic after falling out with Garrick, as a result of the outcome of the actors' strike in autumn 1743, when Charles Fleetwood, then manager at Drury Lane, welcomed back in time for the new season Garrick and all the other 'rebel' actors, but not Macklin. His criticism of Garrick's acting, though at least partly motivated by a personal grudge, did chime with the disapproval expressed by others. Like other critics, Macklin commented on the coarseness of Garrick's animated and life-like gestures and the uncouth style of his diction. Besides, as Leigh Woods has pointed out, Macklin's attack on Garrick resonated with 'an inherent class bias . . . translated into aesthetic terms' (1984: 18, 19).

The class bias that emerges from Macklin's attack on Garrick had wider implications, related not only to the latter's personal and social background, but also to the circumstances of his debut at Goodman's Fields in 1741. The duopoly introduced by Charles II in 1660 had protected the interests of the patent holders, thus contributing to a steady decline in the quality of the theatrical offerings on the London stage. As Judith Milhous puts it, '[t]he stodgy condition of drama in the 1720s unquestionably reflected the complacency and collusion with which the two companies were run' and led to 'the burgeoning of often unlicensed theatrical activity' (2004: 120). Enterprising theatre managers, including Giffard, had found ways to circumvent the duopoly, by staging spoken drama as part of benefit performances, by subscription, or by charging entrances only for musical entertainments that preceded or followed dramatic performance.

The first theatre in Goodman's Fields had been built by Thomas Odell, who had secured a patent on the understanding that it would support itself by subscription. Giffard took over two years after the theatre opened in 1729, and built a larger theatre in 1732. He marked the opening of his new theatre by staging Shakespeare's *1 Henry IV*, an all-time favourite in the repertory of the patent companies. As Donohue argues, Giffard openly and defiantly 'challenged the West End theatres at their own game' (2004: 16). It was the vitality of fringe theatres like Goodman's Fields that led the patent holders to demand a tightening of the legislation that regulated dramatic performance.

The Licensing Act of 1737 was accordingly passed to reinforce the existing ban on spoken drama and to introduce heavier penalties for those in breach of it. As the Act stated,

> every person who shall, for hire, gain, or reward, act, represent, or perform, or cause to be acted, represented, or performed, any interlude, tragedy, comedy, opera, play, farce, or other entertainment of the stage, or any part or parts therein, in case such person shall not have any legal settlement in the place where the same shall be acted, represented, or performed, without authority by virtue of letters patent from his Majesty, his heirs, successors or predecessors, or without license from the lord chamberlain of his Majesty's household for the time being, shall be deemed to be a rogue and a vagabond within the intent and meaning of the said recited act, and shall be liable and subject to all such penalties and punishments, and by such methods of conviction, as are inflicted on or appointed by the said act for the punishment of rogues and vagabonds (Pickering. 1761: 17, 140)

The specificity of the types of 'entertainment of the stage' listed in the Act was meant to put an end to all dramatic performance 'acted, represented or performed without the authority' granted by a royal patent and the punishment, in keeping with the old Vagrant Act of 1714, included financial penalties and incarceration. Actor and theatre manager James Lacy (1696–1774), who would go on to co-manage Drury Lane with Garrick, but had previously worked at Odell's Goodman's Fields, was one of the first actors to fall foul of the new legislation. In December

1737, he openly defied the Act by offering 'lectures' at the York Buildings in Villiers Street, which were effectively staged readings 'in all but name'. As a result, he was arrested and remained in jail for a considerable length of time (Brayne 2004). As late as the 1830s, shortly before the 1843 Theatres Regulation Act revoked the legislation introduced in 1737, not only actors, but also members of the audience, could be arrested for congregating in public venues that offered any type of dramatic performance, since the Act extended to 'any house or place where wine, ale, beer, or other liquors [were] sold or retailed' (Pickering 1761: 17, 142). Journalist and theatre manager John Hollingshead (1827–1904) reports seeing 'actors from Mrs Harwood's penny gaff being marched through the streets of Shoreditch, in the costumes of *Othello*, with eighty members of the audience to Worship Street Police Station' (Barker 1971: 22–3).

Giffard was understandably deterred by the Licensing Act of 1737 and put Goodman's Fields up for sale (Donohue 2004: 16). However, theatrical activity soon restarted to flourish, using the same loopholes that had been invoked by enterprising theatre managers like Giffard before 1737. It soon became clear that 'the acting of plays', when offered free of charge, 'was not in itself an illegal thing, and the government had no basis in law for suppressing [it]' (Milhous 2004: 121). Accordingly, Giffard put on a production of *Richard III* on 19 August 1741, circumventing the letter of the law by charging only for 'A Concert of Vocal & Instrumental Music' offered on the same night. The young Garrick shared the risk with Giffard. As mentioned above, the risk paid off: '[b]y the end of the month', as Donohue explains,

> Garrick had become the best-known actor in London before almost anyone knew his name, and Giffard's theatre had turned into an easterly magnet for theatre-goers captivated by the prodigious talent and unorthodox style of the suddenly famous young actor (he was 24 years old). (2004: 24)

It is not an overstatement to claim, as many have done since,[8] that this production changed the course of British theatre history, as well as Garrick's personal and professional fortunes.

Most remarkable about Garrick's London professional debut is the near-illegal status of the venue where it took place and its location in the popular East End of the City. Also unprecedented was the wide range of enthusiastic spectators that it attracted from opposite ends of the social and geographical spectrum. According to the anonymous author of 'The Case

---

[8] See, for example, Benedetti 2001: 47–70, esp. 58–61 and Caines 2008: xvii–xxix, esp. xix–xxii.

of the Stage in Ireland', 'every night the house was crowded with wives, daughters, apprentices, journeymen and servants, who, to secure good places, stole thither at four o'clock in the afternoon' (Anon. 1758: 30), while Garrick's biographer Arthur Murphy (1727–1805) noted how '[f]rom the polite ends of Westminster the most elegant company flocked to Goodman's Fields, insomuch that from Temple Bar the whole way was covered with a string of coaches' (1801: 1, 25–6). It was precisely this level of criss-crossing of geographical and social divides that most upset Garrick's harshest critics.

One of them was Horace Walpole, the son of Prime Minister Robert Walpole, who had been the prime mover behind the passing of the 1737 Act, following the rise in satiric attacks against him in fringe theatres across London in the earlier 1730s. In a letter to Horace Mann in 1742, Horace Walpole expressed his outrage at the fact that 'all the run is now after Garrick, a wine-merchant, who is turn'd player at Goodman's Fields'. Walpole's snobbery was compounded by his aesthetic aversion to Garrick's acting style, which he saw as an act of mimicry, as opposed to the high dramatic school he associated with Betterton and his theatrical descendants: '[h]e plays all parts, and is a very good mimic' (Woods 1984: 19). According to Walpole, Garrick's much praised ability to imitate nature was in fact symptomatic of a lack of intellectual and acting skills that allowed actors trained in the grandiloquent tradition associated with Betterton to reflect the highest and most refined qualities of human nature, as represented in the dramatic works by ancient and modern classics. According to Moody, in this context 'dramatic genres became categories of major ideological dispute and Shakespeare a major cultural weapon' (2000: 5).

Walpole's censure of Garrick's acting style anticipated the type of criticism that kept re-emerging at later stages in Garrick's career. As mentioned above, most of the criticism focused on his voice. As the anonymous sender of a letter to Garrick put it, 'the correctness of speaking [is] of such importance, that no force or propriety of gesture, no expression of the countenance, how exquisite soever, can compensate for the want of it' (Boaden 1831–32: 111). Comments on Garrick's voice were indeed a constant feature in critical responses to his increasing popularity. The following year, while Garrick was working at the Smock Alley Theatre in Dublin, another anonymous critic, who identified himself with 'the most judicious and discerning part of your audience', complained about the way in which Garrick pronounced the letter 'a'. The register of the critic's comments is condescending and smacks of social snobbery:

I cannot imagine what your objection can be to the letter *a*, that you should change it into an *e*, both in the English language and the Latin; or what fault you can find with the English word *matron*, that you should be obliged to make it Greek. Does not Horatio sound much better than the little word *Horetio*? It is said that Horatius Cocles, when he could no longer withstand the fury of his enemies, leaped into the Tiber. But what did he do this for? Was it not for a name? Yes, surely; but never for the name of *Horetius*. Should we, in the Latin tongue, generally change the letter *a* into *e*, the language would certainly lose much of its force and grandeur. (Boaden 1831–32: 12)

The critic's reference to the pronunciation of the letter 'a' in English and Latin, along with his extended reference to Roman history, insinuates a lack of classical education on Garrick's part. The critic goes on to argue, half-mockingly, that since Garrick's pronunciation cannot possibly be 'allowed upon the English stage', he 'must certainly have learned it from the sailors in his passage from England' (Boaden 1831–32: 13).

Also in 1742, Garrick was unfavourably compared to Quin in an anonymous tract written in rhyming couplets, called 'A Clear Stage, and no Favour: Or, Tragedy and Comedy at War, Occasion'd by the Emulation of the two Theatric Heroes, David and Goliah. Left to the impartial Decision of the Town'. Although the part of the poem spoken by Garrick credits him for first teaching 'dull *G—dm—*'s *F—ds* to grow polite', it also gives Quin a winning line of defence, when the latter claims that 'no crackt Accents [his] firm Period break', while '*Puffs*' must Garrick's 'way precede, / [so] That England may his foreign Actions read' (Anon. 1742: 9, 10).

A letter sent more than a decade later to Garrick by Theophilus Cibber (1703–1758) harped, once again, on Garrick's lack of social status and foreign descent. The son of actor, writer and theatre manager Colley Cibber (1671–1757), Theophilus was following in his father's footsteps and did not only see Garrick as an upstart, but also as a competitor: 'is it not . . . a little hard', Cibber exclaims, 'that an *Englishman*, the Son of an *Englishman*, . . . who, in his Theatrical Capacity, as Author and Actor, has been judged one of the greatest Ornaments of the *English* Stage . . . should be obstructed . . . by the Son of a *Frenchman*?' (Cibber 1755: 16–7). The emphasis on the Cibber's national and theatrical lineage exposes, by contrast, Garrick's status as an interloping foreigner and threatening outsider. Also worth pointing out is the fact that Colley Cibber was not only a representative of the grand theatrical tradition that Garrick's contemporaries associated with Betterton; he was also closely associated with the Hanoverian court and with 'leading members of the Whig oligarchy', including Robert Walpole, who was Cibber senior's 'regular drinking and gambling companion at White's Gentlemen's Club' (Salmon 2004). Theophilus Cibber's attack against Garrick is therefore also implicitly loaded with the same class bias that had first emerged in the 1740s, when Garrick had first risen to fame.

In short, the 1750s revealed the same blend of veneration and criticism that had characterized Garrick's reception in the 1740s. Representative of the lavish praise bestowed on Garrick in the 1750s is the well-known 'Poetical Epistle from Shakespeare in Elysium, to Mr. Garrick, at Drury-Lane Theatre', where he is commended for his ability to speak a new 'language of the heart'. The 'Epistle' also contrasts formal 'elocution', which 'feebly' fails 'to move the soul', with 'eloquence', which Garrick is urged to 'foster', 'as a tender child', 'from the stage', since it is 'banish'd from the schools' (Rolt 1752: ll. 152, 164, 172–4). In this poem, which is often quoted as marking the highest point of Garrick's popularity on the eighteenth-century stage and his growing association with the cult of Shakespeare as national poet, Garrick is regarded as naturally superior to actors schooled in the formal arts of rhetoric and elocution. The myth of Shakespeare's 'natural' genius for playwriting overlaps here most prominently with Garrick's 'natural' genius for playacting.

However, only a year before the 'Epistle' was published, a dramatic satire called *The Theatrical Manager* had once again anonymously attacked Garrick, insisting on his modest origins and unorthodox acting style. Vaticide, a thinly veiled caricature of Garrick, admits to being a man of fashion: 'As every thing now is governed by fashion, so it is the Fashion for me to govern; the whole Town is in my Disposal – I am the Man in Taste, and that's sufficient' (Anon. 1751: 4). 'Yet', Vaticide adds, 'the Thought of what I was, hangs heavy upon my Spirits' (Anon. 1751: 31). Garrick's lack of social credentials is set against the social background of Buck and Dangle, two gentlemen who have dissipated their patrimony and turned to Vaticide for employment. Buck drives the point home, by complaining that they have to 'solicit . . . the capricious Man', who 'not long ago was in some Degree no more than a Servant' (Anon. 1751: 36). When Dangle voices a feeble objection to Buck's character-assassination, by pointing out that Vaticide is 'much admired for his Conversation', Buck retorts:

> That sprightly Turn is owing to the Multitude of People he converses with, that he borrows from all sorts a Rhapsody of uncommon Expressions, and pours them out as incoherently as a Parrot'. (Anon. 1751: 36)

Garrick's ability to imitate human nature is critiqued for amounting to mere parroting. This stab at Garrick echoes Walpole's claim, ten years earlier, that Garrick was a 'mimic' rather than an actor.

Also replicating the satirical tone of the earlier attack on Garrick's mispronunciation of the letter 'e' is another invective, which, as late as the 1750s took Garrick to task for mispronouncing the letter 'i'. In his 'To David Garrick, Esq; The Petition of I' (1759), John Hill reminds Garrick, on behalf of the petitioner, that the latter was 'treated with Distinction and Respect' in antiquity, and that,

> to her, one called the STAGYRITE, decreed the Palm, where Strength should be combined with Elegance; that PLATO, surnamed THE DIVINE, gave her the same Preeminence for delicate Distress; that she was the peculiar Favourite of VIRGIL and of HORACE; that SUETONIUS, ARNOBIUS, and PLINY, respecting her as a soft, nervous, smooth, and well sounding Letter, displaced her Brothers often in her Favour; and universal ROME established her the Sound for Gentleness and soft Humility. (Hill 1759: 4)

By referencing a long list of classical authors who paid due respect to the letter 'i', Hill deploys the same rhetorical strategy used in the letter sent to Garrick in 1742, where the anonymous author had evoked classical antiquity to expose Garrick's lack of formal training. Hill then links classical antiquity to the theatrical tradition from which Garrick had marked such a spectacular point of departure, by reminding the latter that the petitioner had been

> the Favourite of the Theatre from its Establishment in BRITAIN: that to her BOOTH and BETTERTON, once celebrated in the Paths of Tragedy, owed more than to all her Family beside . . . [and] THAT your Petitioner [had] continued in this Estimation on the Stage at all Times till the present Government. (Hill 1759: 5)

Garrick's 'present Government' on the English stage has led to the petitioner's disgrace, who 'cannot but esteem it cruel and *unnatural*, that [Garrick] should have determined never to pronounce her, in the most forcible of her associations' (Hill 1759: 6; my emphasis). Worth stressing is the contradictory use of the term 'natural' or 'unnatural' in relation to Garrick's acting style, and in relation to Garrick's pronunciation more specifically. While his supporters deemed his style groundbreaking for its ability to capture the nuances of human nature and emotions, his detractors refer to it as either 'natural', that is uncouth, unschooled and parrot-like, or 'unnatural' because 'unorthodox' and in breach of classical and current standards of taste and propriety.

Equally worth noting is Hill's use of quotations from Shakespeare to prove that Garrick's pronunciation was ultimately unacceptable:

> Your Petitioner does, and must conceive, the original and natural Pronunciation of the good Word FIRM, to be at least as elegant, and as expressive of the Sense, as the coarse boggy FURM, which you have introduced into its place, and which your many Excellencies, fixing the Stamp of Judgment upon Folly, have forced into the Throats of others. (Hill 1759: 6)

The word 'firm' is cross-referenced in a footnote to a line from Shakespeare's *The Winter's Tale*, as adapted by Garrick in his *The Winter's Tale: Or Florizel and Perdita, a Dramatic Pastoral* (1756). Hill transcribes this line as Garrick spoke it on stage: 'Walk I on Land, FURM Land?' The onslaught against Garrick continues, as Hill gives more examples of how Garrick mangles Shakespeare's lines. The petitioner, he continues, 'requests, nay she demands, to be no longer banished from the sacred Name of VIRTUE who, since she is doomed to lose her Being in the present Age, should be allowed to keep her Name immaculate' (Hill 1759: 6–7). This time the word 'virtue' is cross-referenced to Hamlet's speech in the closet scene: 'Calls VURTUE Hypocrite'. The petitioner then comes to her sister E's defence, claiming that 'not the Strength of HERCULES can keep her in her place', having explained that she 'feels no less Apprehensions to her Cousin EA, whom not the steadfast EARTH itself can fix in her Possession', giving one last Shakespearean line in a footnote, this time from *Romeo and Juliet*: 'Turn back dull URTH, ROMEO' (Hill 1759: 7–8).

In the final section of the 'Petition', Hill explains that the petitioner would not have approached Garrick, 'if it were on the Theatre alone [that] she and her Family were threatened with annihilation'. However, since 'the Stage takes nothing now from Life, ... and Life takes every Thing from the Stage', the Petitioner concludes that the 'Danger' of Garrick's mispronunciation 'grow[s] universal' (Hill 1759: 11). Becoming more direct and openly offensive, Hill finally suggests that, since 'Nature, as she enlarges for Mankind one Quality, diminishes another', Garrick may have recovered his sense of hearing, having lost his 'Excellence of Voice'. The petitioner therefore appeals to his sense of hearing, to make one final plea to be heard in the name of 'our National Pronunciation'.

This final accusation echoes earlier comments that had shown how Garrick's foreign descent posed a threat against the integrity of the English language, on and off the stage. Defending the inherent sophistication of the English language, Hill reminds Garrick that

however harshly Foreigners may have spoken of our Language, there is not
in it a Termination so hoarse and barbarous as this URM now introduced by
your Example and Authority; nor one Word that will rhyme with FURM in
all our Dictionaries. (Hill 1759: 13)

As a parting shot, Hill intimates that the French, Garrick's countrymen,
'would rise, if one they employed to entertain them, presumed to alter but
an Accent in their Pronunciation'. 'Certainly', Hill retorts, 'there is as
much Taste in Britain'.

The harshness of Hill's invective against Garrick's social background,
his lack of a classical education and foreign descent must have struck a
chord in Garrick, because he unusually responded to Hill's attack and did
so publicly, by writing a witty short poem called 'Garrick's Reply to *The
Petition I*':

> If 'tis true, as you say, that I've injur'd a letter,
> I'll change my note soon, and I hope for the better;
> May the right use of letters, as well as of men,
> Hereafter be fix'd by the tongue and the pen;
> Most devoutly I wish that they both have their due,
> And that *I* may be never mistaken for *U*.
>
> (Garrick 1785: 490)

Underlying the light, witty tone of this poem, one can sense Garrick's wish
that both 'letters' and 'men' were used rightly. Sadly, though, the barrage
of attacks on Garrick was far from over. As reported in Thaddeus
Fitzpatrick's 'An Enquiry into the Real Merit of a Certain Popular Performer' (1760), Garrick's detractors went on 'scrutinizing every character
personated by him . . . with equal rigour' for years to come (10).

The severity of contemporary attacks on Garrick's acting style did not
prevent him from becoming the most successful actor on the eighteenth-
century stage. Most crucially for the purpose of the second half of this
chapter, Garrick went on to become an influential model for theatre
managers who, taking Garrick's debut at Goodman's Fields as an important
precedent, challenged the ban on spoken drama and for non-professional
and regional actors, who emulated his acting style in fringe theatres, private
venues and 'spouting clubs' all over the country. It is a strange and a happy
coincidence that the two men who most prominently supported these two
movements, were both called John Palmer. The two Palmers, as the rest of
this chapter shows, ensured that Garrick's legacy would continue to grow
after his death in 1779 and well into the nineteenth century.

§

A Tale of Two John Palmers

John Palmer (1742–1818), theatre proprietor and postal reformer, and John Palmer (1744–1798), stage actor and would-be theatre manager, born two years apart from each other in Bath and London, had radically different individual qualities and career trajectories. Aged twenty-six , the older John Palmer secured the first royal patent outside London for his father's theatre in Orchard Street (8 Geo. III c.10, 1768). The licensing of Orchard Street Theatre paved the way for the proliferation of licensed provincial theatres that started in the 1780s (Dobson 2011: 70).[9] Palmer then went on to reform the national postal system and achieved prominent civic roles in Bath and a seat in Parliament in the final years of his life (Buchanan 2004).

By contrast, the slightly younger John Palmer, also known as 'Plausible Jack' after the coxcomb in William Wycherley's *The Plain Dealer*, struggled to remain solvent all his life, dividing his time between Drury Lane in the winter and the Haymarket in the summer, and between London and provincial theatres when he could not get work in the capital. His reputation was tarnished by rumours that he mistreated the wife he had married for money and temporarily abandoned straight after the wedding in order to live with his mistress. He nevertheless gained the respect of his fellow actors and theatre managers, because of his dogged loyalty to the acting profession. He rather memorably died on stage, after collapsing during the fourth act of Benjamin Thompson's *The Stranger*, in which he was playing the lead role (Bull 2004).

Despite their different personalities, life goals and achievements, the two John Palmers played a curiously similar role in the context of mid- to

---

[9] See also Foulkes: 'Although not dating back to 1660, the situation in the provinces had been the subject of successive legislation in Parliament. The 1737 Licensing Act was intended to outlaw all theatrical performances in the provinces, but it was honoured more in the breach than the observance'. Following the granting of a licence for the performance of spoken drama in Edinburgh in 1768, the Lord Chamberlain granted licences to Bath and Norwich the following year, with Bath claiming 'the distinction of being the first-royally-sanctioned provincial theatre in England' by a few days (Blackwell and Blackwell, quoted in Foulkes 2012: 173). Still according to Foulkes, 'in 1769 Tate Wilkinson 'obtained the royal patent for his theatres in York and Hull, again requiring an act of parliament. Others followed: Liverpool 1771, Manchester 1775 and Bristol 1778. In 1788 an act was passed empowering local justices to license players for sixty days at a time. After 1843 the licensing of theatres outside London and places of royal residence was devolved to the jurisdiction of the local authorities. As in the metropolis, therefore, any properly licensed theatre could perform the plays of Shakespeare. In due course this led to a crop of new theatres, ... but as in London this and other changes arising from the 1843 legislation took some time to filter through' (174).

late-eighteenth-century theatrical culture, by developing two related aspects of Garrick's legacy. Besides securing the first royal licence for a provincial theatre, the older John Palmer edited one of the most interesting collections of prologues, epilogues and short extracts from classical and contemporary plays, which became very popular in the second half of the century among amateur or aspiring, semi-professional actors. These collections were commonly known as spouting manuals. Palmer's *The Spouter's Companion* (1770?), first reissued around 1772 and then revised and expanded as *The New Spouter's Companion* ([1781] and 1790?), departed from earlier collections, which were aimed at members of the upper-classes with a penchant for private theatricals. By contrast, Palmer's collection addressed lower-class amateur or semi-professional actors. The latter, often lacking a formal education and theatrical training, would congregate for the sheer pleasure of reciting famous set pieces from the professional stage or in the hope of being talent-spotted and recruited by touring companies as a stepping stone towards a career in the theatre. The actor, whose formidable rise from obscurity via a minor theatrical establishment had served as prime precedent for all aspiring spouters, was, of course, David Garrick.[10] On the back of Garrick's precedent, Palmer's *Companion* explicitly encouraged spouters to challenge the social and acoustic decorum that associated playacting in licensed theatres with elitism and privilege.

Like his namesake, London-born John Palmer actively contributed to the rise of an anti-monopolist movement, which had also been inspired by Garrick's debut at Goodman's Fields and which would eventually lead to the lifting of the ban on spoken drama with the passing of the Theatre Regulation Act in 1843. Palmer's plan to build and manage The Royalty, a new theatre in Well-Close Square in Tower Hamlets, just to the east of the City of London, in the late 1780s, was not successful. However, it

---

[10] Although other actors, including Edmund Kean in the early nineteenth century, inspired amateur and semi-professional dramatics, Garrick has been linked to the rise of this popular phenomenon as early as the mid-eighteenth century. See, for example, Dane Farnsworth Smith in his *Plays about the Theatre in England*: '[t]he exact causes of this remarkable phenomenon appear inexplicable, but Garrick's meteoric rise as an actor and his popularization of Shakespeare surely influenced many a young man to take acting lessons or to join one of the numerous organizations derisively known as "spouting clubs"' (1936, 148). See also, more recently, John Thieme, who has linked the kind of 'hero-worship' enjoyed by Garrick to the rise of spouting clubs in the period (1975: 11), and Leslie Ritchie, who has established that '[m]ore than thirteen percent of spouting companions' content acknowledges Garrick as speaker or author. Leslie adds that, since much of Garrick's repertoire was so well known as to not need attribution, this number would only rise if all of the works known to be identified with Garrick were included'. As Ritchie sums up, 'Garrick's famous roles (Benedick, Lear, Richard, Hamlet), his versatility in comic and tragic roles, and his repute as a "prologue-smith" shaped the spouting repertoire' (2012: 53).

triggered sustained public debate about the legal, social and ethical implications of the ban. Garrick, once again, served as the foremost precedent to
argue that current theatre regulations were unjustly stifling talent and
limiting access to spoken drama to those sections of the population who
could not afford entrance and transportation to the patented theatres in
the West End.

'Split[ting] the Ears of the Groundlings'; Or, the Spouters' Revenge

This line from Hamlet's speech to the players (3.2.10–11) was often
quoted to complain about the uncouth, animal-like quality of the voices
of those who dared to recite Shakespeare and other classical or established
dramatists in spouting clubs up and down the country, from the mid-
eighteenth well into the nineteenth century. Before the publication of
Palmer's *Companion*, spouters were routinely disparaged in satirical plays
and comic satires that mocked this new fad and in collections of dramatic
extracts aimed at upper-class readers with a fondness for amateur dramatics.

A representative early collection published in 1756, whose title I quote
in full below, is ostensibly devoted to 'all lovers' of the theatre and to all
those who wanted to put their own acting skills to the test:

> *Original Prologues, Epilogues, and Other Pieces never before printed. To which
> is added, a collection of such as are celebrated for wit, humour or entertainment,
> spoke at the theatres or at private plays . . . Most humbly inscribed to all lovers of
> theatrical diversion, whether bloods, bucks, joyous spirits, honest fellows, smarts,
> jessamies, jemmies, beaus and fribbles, but more in particular to the Societies of
> Spouters.*

The address 'To the Reader' and the selection of extracts included in this
collection however make it clear that, while seeming to appeal to 'all lovers'
of the theatre, including spouters, the compiler was in fact addressing
upper-class readers, who performed in private theatricals or in benefit
performances staged at the licensed theatres. Among the prologues, the
compiler, for example, includes 'The prologue to Othello, as it was acted at
the theatre in Drury-lane, by persons of distinction for their diversion'
(Anon. 1756: 8).[11] The opening of this prologue openly criticizes professional actors who act for a living:

---

[11] At least one other prologue in this collection is explicitly addressed to 'persons of distinction'; see
'Prologue and Epilogue to the Adelphi, of Terence, which was acted by the Charterhouse

> While mercenary actors tread the stage,
> And hireling scriblers lash or lull the age,
> Ours be the task t'instruct, and entertain,
> Without one thought of glory or of gain.
> Virtue's her own — from no external cause
> She gives, and she demands the self-applause:
> Home to her breast she brings the heart-felt bays,
> Heedless alike of profit, and of praise.
>
>   (Anon. 1756: 8)

This prologue then begs 'the shade of SHAKESPEAR' (1756: 9) to bless the proceedings. Shakespeare here stands for a time '[w]hen Britain with transcendent glory crown'd,/For high atchievements, as for wit [was] renown'd'. This was also a time when, as this prologue continues, Britain '[c]ull'd from each growing grace the purest part,/And cropt the flowers from every blooming art' (1756: 8). Art, in other words, could only be pure when free from any logic of profit.

Spouters are also the target of harsh criticism. An 'Epilogue spoken at a private play' and the address 'To the Reader' prefaced to this collection reveal a profound disapproval for those who have neither the sense, wit, nor taste to act, and yet seem compelled to do so, even when their compulsion to spout jeopardizes their livelihood and mental wellbeing. According to the 'Epilogue spoken at a private play', 'spouting is the devil' because 'it spoils society'. As evidence to prove this viewpoint, the epilogue mentions the following anecdote:

> The other day one would not let me pass,
> But, prithee *Paul* – pfhaw – pox – come – take a glass;
> Agreed – I'll pledge thee – scarce he'd ta'en up a sup,
> But as *Macbeth* when *Banquo*'s ghost come up;
> Like a stuck pig he stares, and trembling stands,
> Down drop the glass, and bottle from his hands:
> The frighted waiter saw his tackle broke,
> As this his attitude – and thus he spoke –
> *Thou canst not say I did it bloody* Banquo!
> *Sir* – cries the waiter – *by my soul I can though.*
>
>   (1756: 6)

As this incident suggests, spouting was not 'to house, or home confin'd' (1756: 6), but was indulged in public, at inappropriate times, and brought disgrace and ridicule to its foolish perpetrators. This epilogue also shows

Scholars, . . . before the Right Rev. the Bishops of Oxford, Chester, Worcester, and Fern, and many other persons of distinction' (1756: 45).

how the spouters are especially ridiculous when they dare to speak Shakespeare's lines:

> *Stentor* roar'd out one day down *Drury-lane*,
> *I'll call thee Father, King, or Royal Dane.*
> A porter blest with impudence and ease,
> Cried – *you be damn'd, sir – call me what you please.*
> (1756: 6)

The address 'To the Reader' similarly reinforces the difference in social status between those 'persons of distinction' who claim ownership over Shakespeare as the patron and protector of the art of acting and those who act for profit or debase Shakespeare by spouting his lines in the streets or in public houses. The address 'To the Reader' includes 'The life of Nomentanus', the son of a 'wealthy farmer in Yorkshire', who relates how he was brought to London to be apprenticed to a 'shopkeeper in the city'. The young man remembers that, when he first moved to London, he was mocked because of the 'modest simplicity in [his] manner', his 'provincial accent', 'a slouch in [his] gait', 'a long lank head of hair', and 'an unfashionable suit of drab coloured cloth' (1756: iv). He also mentions how he had decided to improve 'his speech' (1756: v) and spruce up his wardrobe. He then goes on to explain that he had also started to attend the playhouse in order to learn how to imitate the actors in speech and appearance. As a result, his 'pronunciation' had become more 'feminine' and his speech more 'vicious' (vi). As the young man puts it:

> At the same time, I made considerable advances in swearing; I could pronounce damme with a tolerable air and accent, give the vowel its full sound, and look with confidence in the face of the person to whom I spoke. (1756: vii)

His newly acquired proficiency as a speaker, which he calls a 'distinction', had encouraged him 'to attempt yet greater excellence':

> I learned several feats of mimicry of the under players, could take off known characters, tell a staring story, and humbug with so much skill as sometimes to take in a knowing one. I was so successful in the practice of these arts, to which, indeed, I applied myself with unwearied diligence . . . that I kept my company roaring with applause. (1756: vii)

Nomentanus's unorthodox apprenticeship results not in professional advancement and increased wealth, but in the acquisition of qualities associated with the stock characters mentioned on the title-page of this collection: 'a Jemmy', 'a Jessamy', a 'Smart', a 'Joyous Spirit' and a 'Buck'. Both the extensive paratext and some of the extracts gathered in it make it abundantly clear that this collection, though seemingly addressed to 'all lovers' of the theatre, is in fact consistently intent on praising the natural wit and discretion of those elitist groups who perform Shakespeare 't'instruct and entertain', all the while denigrating those who act for profit or, worse still, those who parrot professional actors in spouting clubs or public spaces.

The abhorrent qualities of the spouter's voice are ridiculed for similar reasons in Henry Dell's *The Spouter: Or, the Double Revenge*, a comic satire in three acts, which was also published in 1756. The spouter in Dell's satire is called Mr Buskin and his defining trait is his 'bullocking voice' (1756: 2). This phrase conjures animal-like qualities – a bullock is a young or a castrated bull (*OED n*1) – and the relentlessness associated with hard physical labour or an overbearing, loud, and pompous preacher (*OED, v*2 and 3). The harshest criticism levelled at Mr Buskin comes from Florimond, who claims that, by 'pretend[ing] so much to the Art of acting', Mr Buskin and his fellow spouters in fact produce a mere cacophony of alarming and unsettling sounds:

> Intoxicated with Plays, [they] neglect their proper Business, [and] make Clubs, where they meet together to rehearse Parts and Speeches of Plays; making such a Noise and Confusion, and breeding such Riots and Disturbance, [that] they often get themselves into the Roundhouse. (1756: 13)

The discordant noises produced by the spouters are suggestive of, and linked to, deeper anxieties about social disorder and unrest.

The transgressive qualities of the spouters' voices are memorably captured by a popular pictorial satire called 'A Slap at the Minors or the Beauties of an Unrestricted Drama' (Fig. 11). As Moody notes,

> the anonymous cartoonist stages the grotesque consequences of plebian Shakespearean production... [where] each of the motley performers is spouting a Shakespearean quotation which ironically exposes the 'trash', rant and 'horrid speech' . . . produced once 'every Vile pretender . . . born in the Metropolis' can spit and roar 'the Noblest of our National Poetry'. (2000: 137)

Shakespeare himself is summoned to denounce the shameful maiming of his lines. Represented this time as a disconcerted ghost, half-hidden among the clouds, Shakespeare refers to the spouters' delivery of his lines as 'Murder most foul and Unnatural'. What upsets Shakespeare, and amuses the viewer, is the combination of the spouters' monstrous physical and vocal attributes: a heavily featured and rotund Juliet mispronounces her line, 'Oh Romeyo vear art thou Romeyo', while a squinting Jacques, who is sawing the air too much with one hand and holding his script with the other, still manages to misquote Shakespeare's half line 'His acts being seven ages' (*As You Like It* 2.7.143) as 'There are Seventy Stages'. This cartoon

8. Shakespearean Innovations. *A Slap at the Minors or the Beauties of an Unrestricted Drama.*

Fig. 11. 'A Slap at the Minors, or the Beauties of an Unrestricted Drama', a pictorial satire, in the Brady Collection. Reproduced with permission of Christ Church Library, University of Oxford caricatures the spouters, but it also functions as a sobering reminder of the acoustic (and social) disorder that 'an Unrestricted Drama' would unleash onto the English stage and in public spaces. Last, but not least, this cartoon conjures the lack of taste and discernment associated with lower-class audiences: as the caption suggests, the 'murder most foul and unnatural' of Shakespeare's lines draws a 'yell of "Bravo" from every Gallery rabble'.

By the mid-eighteenth century, alternative views about who had the right to perform Shakespeare were already starting to emerge. Also in 1756, Garrick's biographer and playwright, Arthur Murphy, made two major contributions to the ongoing debate about the proliferation of spouting clubs in the wake of Garrick's rise to stardom in the 1740s – his farce in two acts, *The Apprentice* (1756), and *The Spouter, or, The Triple Revenge* (Anon. 1756a), which is an open rebuttal of Dell's comic satire discussed above. In the opening sequence of *The Apprentice*, Dick, the title-character, is reported to have run away from in his master Gargle's apothecary shop to join a company of strolling players and to have got himself arrested. However, Murphy's satirical attack is clearly aimed at the crass materialism and benighted ignorance of those who criticize him, including his master and his father, Wingate. When Gargle complains that Dick 'ought to be reading the Dispensatory ... [instead of] constantly poring over Plays, and Farces, and Shakespear', Wingate agrees:

> 'Ay, that damned Shakespear! – I hear the Fellow was nothing but a Deer-stealer in Warwickshire. – Zookers! if they had hanged him out of the Way, he would not now be the Ruin of honest Men's Children. – But what Right had he to read Shakespear? – I never read Shakespear! (1756: 6)

Wingate's lack of familiarity with Shakespeare turns him into the butt of the joke. His ignorance is, for example, exposed and ridiculed when he urges Dick to 'send to [his] Friend *Shakespear* now to bail [him]' (1756: 44). Also telling is the fact that regional and lower-class accents are not used to belittle Dick, but some of his associates, including the Scotchman, who is fond of quoting *Macbeth* (1756: 25), and Simon, Gargle's servant, who speaks in a heavily marked Cockney accent, pronouncing 'him' as 'un' (1756: 2), or 'going' as 'gang' (1756: 15). Dick's voice, on the other hand, is unmarked, which is especially significant considering that he speaks only by quoting from plays, and mostly from plays by Shakespeare.

The Advertisement prefaced to the 1756 edition of *The Apprentice* offers a rare insight into how the farce was originally staged and how its original audience responded to it. Wingate, described in the Dramatis Personae as 'a passionate old Man, particularly fond of Money and

Figures', was played by Mr Yates, who is praised for having 'exhibited the Impotence of the Mind' when playing this role. Apparently Mr Yates had shown how Wingate's 'Ideas extend[ed] very little beyond the multiplication Tables' and how his 'Passions [were] ever in a crazy Conflict', except 'when they all subside[d] into a sordid Love of Gain' (1756: A3). On the contrary, Mr Woodward, who played Dick, had lent this role 'such a Spirit . . . that the *Apprentice* may again elope from his Friends, without any one's desiring him to Return to his Business' (1756: A3). Dick may be forced to return to Gargle's shop by the end of the play, but Murphy's Advertisement suggests that his farce may very well encourage the audience to wish otherwise! The Advertisement is ostensibly at odds with the Prologue written by Garrick and spoken by Mr Woodward, especially when the Prologue explains that the author's aim was to 'check' young 'Heroes' like Dick, 'To bring 'em back to Reason – and their Shop' (1756: A4). However, even this Prologue then hints at Dick's popularity with the audience: 'The Hero is a Youth by Fate design'd / For culling Simples, but whose Stage-struck Mind, / Nor Fate could rule, nor his indentures bind' (1756: A4).

All in all, Murphy's apparent attack on spouting in fact offers a largely sympathetic take on this peculiar theatrical phenomenon: 'rather than blocking the spread of spouting', as Betsy Bolton argues,

> Murphy's *The Apprentice* largely created the fad, greatly hastening its expansion beyond the context of private theatricals in which it seems to have first developed. Rather than 'the spouter's revenge', Murphy's farce may be better described as the spouter's seduction. . . . In fact, Murphy's farce disseminated the possibility of amateur theatricals . . . since the printed script circulated the idea of spouting blubs to the provinces as well as the metropolis. (2014: 47, 50)

I would add that Garrick was not only the main source of inspiration for spouters like Dick but also the real-life model for this character. Stage-struck from an early age, Garrick, like Dick, had turned down the opportunity to become apprenticed to his wine trading uncle in 1729 and his legal studies at Lincoln's Inn straight after enrolment in 1737. Also noteworthy is how Gargle's description of a spouting club, as 'A Meeting of Prentices and Clerks and giddy young Men, intoxicated with Plays', who 'meet in Public Houses to act Speeches' and so 'neglect Business, despise the Advice of their Friends, and think of nothing but to become Actors', evokes Garrick's own early engagement with amateur dramatics and his brother's open and hostile opposition to it. The main difference between Dick and Garrick is the social status of their associates. Samuel Johnson, who had moved from Lichfield to London with Garrick, encouraged him to play the title role in Henry Fielding's *The Mock Doctor* in an amateur production that took place in St John's Gatehouse in Clerkenwell (Thomson 2004a). However, Garrick was also renown among his friends for indulging in less refined forms of theatrical entertainment, including 'mounting [on] table[s] to display those talents for mimicry, for which he [was] much celebrated' (Murphy 1801 1.15). In this respect, Dick can be read as a loose fictive counterpart of the young Garrick.

The same logic of sympathetic endorsement thinly disguised as satire informs Murphy's *The Spouter, or, The Triple Revenge* and the ironic quality of its Prologue. In the Prologue, spouting is described as a 'gen'ral epidemic Rage', and as 'the Phrenzy of this madd'ning Age' (Anon. 1756a: A1v). Yet, Murphy's satire is directed at Garrick's rivals, Theophilus Cibber and John Rich (1692–1761), who are easily identifiable as Squint-Eyed Pistol and Lun. And it is Lun, rather than Slender, the gentleman spouter, who mispronounces '*Othello*' and '*Othallo*' and 'learned' as 'larned'. He even mangles Garrick's name, when he boasts that he could have played 'Richard with Mr. Derrick' (Anon 1756a: 19).

Murphy's sympathetic portrayal of spouters has nevertheless been read as ultimately half-hearted, if not altogether condescending. Among recent scholars, Leslie Ritchie has for example argued that

> Murphy's farce 'does not take account of professional actors' interest in spouting clubs, of the clubs' production of actors for professional play-houses and strolling companies, nor of the range of abilities and repertoire represented in spouting clubs, all of which are vastly under-represented . . . for comic effect'. (2012: 42)

A contemporary account of Murphy's farce however confirms that it is only overtly aimed at spouters. The reviewer notes that, although '[i]n his prologue [Murphy] professes [that] his aim is to reform a number of shoe-blacks, beer-drawers, and city-prentices, who are run "sublimely mad" with tragic-comedy', he can 'only find one slender sketch of such an original, that serves as an awkward usher to introduce the other characters of private persons [that is Cibber and Rich], who are not ridiculed, but reviled with as little decency as humour'. The reviewer concludes that Murphy had written the whole farce 'with a view to gratify the pride of one theatrical manager . . . on whom he depends . . . [Garrick] at the expense of another [Rich]'. The reviewer also wonders whether the impoverished Slender is ultimately sympathetic because possibly autobiographical (Anon. 1756a: 146–7).

Murphy's sympathy for spouters was fairly exceptional at the time. Another, near-contemporary satirical poem, William Woty's 'A Picture of a Spouting Club', or 'The Spouting Club' (1760), reduces the spouters to mere caricatures.[12] In this poem, the spouters have heavily marked accents. Rantwell, for example, whose 'cruel inauspicious Fate/Destin'd [him] to oil [and] to dress the flowing Curl', abandons his shop to 'assume the Port/Of Tyrant Richard', but his voice lets him down: 'His labour'd Speech/Sounds gutt'ral, like the hoarsely-croaking Race,/Upon the Banks of some pellucid Stream' (1760: 91–92). Similarly, 'Hibernia's Son' raves and rants as Bajazet, but his 'roaring Voice' is like the 'harsh Lung-cracking Nois [sic]' commonly heard 'on the Mart/Of fishy Billingsgate' (92). Soccado, the taylor, is vanquished by a lisp, which 'robs each Word of its emphatic due', until 'stamm'ring Welchmen here, and Scotchmen there' (97) bring the evening to an abrupt end.

Only Great Stentor is granted a little sympathy, possibly because he, like Dick in Murphy's *The Apprentice*, bears some resemblance to its author. Like Stentor, Woty, who was well educated but of obscure origins, had begun working as a legal clerk at Lincoln's Inn after moving to London (Fullard 2004). He also had a passion for the theatre, which however remained unfulfilled, and a talent for fine writing, which he was able to develop, becoming a well-respected poet and editor of literary magazines later in life. Woty had vented his frustration as a young clerk, by lamenting that '[h]alf a guinea a week [was] reckoned a prodigious sum for a Clerk who works only ten hours a day, and is obliged to appear like a Gentlemen' ('The Discontented Lawyer's Clerk', quoted in Fullard 2004). Woty's account of his personal experience as a young clerk resonates in lines spoken by Stentor in this poem:

> Him had his Parents sent
> To London, (Seat of Business) there the Laws
> Of Albion's State to learn and exercise.
> For him, a well-experienc'd Don was found...
> But fruitless was this Spouter's Parents Care
> ...   For scarce Two Years had roll'd,
> Since proud Augusta first had bless'd his Eyes,
> E'er the warm Youth in these Expressions broke.
> "Was it for this, that o'er the Classic Sea
> "I sail'd, and landed on Poetic Shores?...
>   Oh, Shakespear! come
> "With all thy Pupils! Fire my glowing Breast,
> "Expand my Genius, and enlarge my Soul!"
>   (1760: 93–4)

---

[12] This poem was first published individually in a pirate edition in 1758; it was then included in Woty's poetic collection, *The Shrubs of Parnassus*, in 1760. This poem was reprinted several times into the nineteenth century.

Unfortunately, Stentor's theatrical ambition is not equal with his talent, and, like the other spouters in Woty's poem, he is let down by his voice. As he starts playing Othello,

> his Voice
> Rises and falls, as Oysterella's soft
> And strong, when ev'ry Street and curving Lane
> Adjacent, echo the testaceous Cry!
>
> (1760: 95)

As it turns out, poor Stentor's voice is better suited to a fish market than the stage.

The publication of Palmer's *Spouter's Companion* around 1770 marked the first significant departure from the condescending attitudes that had informed earlier collections of dramatic extracts and most comic satires about spouters. In Palmer's collection, spouting is regarded as a worthwhile undertaking for the improvement of young minds and the training of new generations of actors. Spouting is also seen as a thoroughly edifying and diverting pastime for 'Readers, Speakers, and Hearers' alike.[13] While earlier collections had reinforced contemporary norms of theatrical and dramatic decorum,[14] Palmer's *Companion* was addressed to '[y]oung Actors ..., in classic schools ne'er taught'. Crucially, in its third edition, it also included a warning against those 'frowning critics', who would 'condemn where *Garrick*'s self would spare' (Palmer 1781: 82).

The first edition of the *Companion* combined 'A Select Collection of the most esteemed Prologues and Epilogues, which [had] been spoken by the most celebrated Performers of both Sexes' along with 'Curious Originals, Written on Purpose for this Work' (title-page). Roughly half of the 'esteemed Prologues and Epilogues' were written and (or) spoken by Garrick, who is clearly identified as the ideal model for the readers targeted by this collection:

---

[13] The full title reads: *The Spouter's Companion; Or, The Theatrical Remembrancer. Containing a select collection of the most esteemed prologues and epilogues, Which Have Been Spoken By the most celebrated Performers of both Sexes. Together with variety of curious originals, written on purpose for this work. Among which are Several Prologues and Epilogues, To be spoken in the Characters of Bloods, Bucks, Choice Spirits, Fribbles, Bravos, &c. Together with a New Prologue on Epilogues, and An Epilogue on Prologues. To which is added, the spouter's medley; containing select parts of the most celebrated comedies and tragedies, contrasted in such a manner as to render their Assemblage extremely diverting to the Reader, Speakers, and Hearers.*

[14] See, for example, *The Essence of Theatrical Wit: Being a Select Collection of the best and most admired Prologues and Epilogues, that have been delivered from the Stage* (1768), or *The Court of Thespis; Being A Collection Of the most admired Prologues and Epilogues That have appeared for many Years; Written by some of the most approved Wits of the Age, viz. Garrick, Coleman, Foote, Murphy, Lloyd, &c.* (1769), where an extract from Robert Lloyd's *The Actor* (1760) sets the tone for the rest of the collection: 'More natural uses to the stage belong / Than tumblers, monsters, pantomime, or song'.

> Bold is his task, in such a critic age,
> Who launches forth upon the British stage,
> To paint the passions critically true,
> And hold great Shakespeare to the public view:
> Attempts most arduous, since they still require
> A Garrick's genius, with a Garrick's fire.
>
> (Anon. 1770?: 11)

Like most of the other 'Curious Originals, Written . . . for this Work', this Prologue invites self-reflection and encourages aspiring actors to learn how to represent 'the passions critically true' from the example set by Garrick:

> All pale and trembling then must we appear,
> With apprehension shock'd, abash'd by fear;
> When we presume stupendous heights to soar,
> And trace those paths which Roscius trod before.
>
> (Anon. 1770?: 12)

The aspiring actors are invited 'Humbly to copy what [they] must admire'. Far from being mocked or accused of mimicking their betters, the aspiring actors are reassured that, 'If but a ray of genius gleans to sight,/Or one small dawn of feeling breaks to light', audiences will reward their efforts with their approval (Anon. 1770?: 12).

Also noteworthy is the emphasis on an actor's need to observe Nature, according to the example set by Garrick. Nature is here seen as an alternative to training in the classical tradition of play-acting, as taught in 'classic schools'. The very first extract, 'The Playhouse Display'd', ends with a manifesto for the new type of acting (and the new type of actor) promoted by this collection:

> Let nature then for ever be the rule,
> In rage, grief, tenderness, and ridicule;
> Nature should give the manager his law,
> From nature players should instruction draw;
> And whether actors laugh, intreat, or storm,
> Nature should each beholder's judgment form.
>
> (Anon. 1770?: 3)

These lines, briefly but incisively, reset the agenda for managers, players and audiences in the context of what was becoming 'a fierce debate about the social allegiances of the national drama' (Dobson 2011: 65) in the period.

The contents in the second edition (1772?) are unchanged, except for the addition of a benign dramatic satire about spouters, called 'The Spouting-Club in an Uproar; Or the Battle of Socks and Buskins'. The cast list reveals the comic vein in which this satire is written. The characters, all Shakespearean, are comically miscast, so Ben Bulky plays Master Slender, while Sam Spidershanks plays Sir John Falstaff. Two spouters fight over who is better qualified to play King Lear, but the dispute ends amicably, with both characters admitting that they sometimes 'spout speeches [they] don't understand' because even 'where the purport is extremely plain,/The tenor sometimes overcomes [their] brain' (Anon. 1772?: 104). Despite their simplicity, the members of this merry crew are perfectly aware of their limitations. They are nevertheless undeterred and thoroughly committed to their harmless pastime. The spouters in this dramatic satire are simple, but not foolish, because they are neither self-deceived nor inappropriately ambitious. They are simply a different type of theatrical breed from the young, unschooled, but gifted actors described in the 'Curious Originals' included in the first edition and reprinted in the second.

The third edition (Palmer 1781) is advertised as being radically revised to suit 'the present Time'. The title page announces the addition of the best specimens of prologues and epilogues spoken on 'other Stages in different Parts of the Kingdom'. Provincial theatres, which, following Palmer's successful bid for a royal license for the Orchard Street Theatre in Bath, had also secured patents to perform spoken drama are here praised for offering their audiences exemplary playacting. The stigma attached to regionally inflected voices, which haunted Garrick throughout his career, is all but absent here. The visibility granted to regional theatres in Palmer's *Companion* is all the more significant in light of the fact that attacks against players who came from the provinces increased in the early nineteenth century, and grew even worse after the Theatres Regulation Act passed in 1843 removed the ban on spoken drama for good.

Telling in this respect is the controversy sparked by the erection of a statue of Shakespeare outside the newly built Theatre Royal in Manchester in 1845. As Antony Taylor reports, '[t]he marble statue was derided for its crudeness, its poor construction, [and] its position outside a haunt of semi-trained and uncouth non-professional actors who mutilated his verses' (2002: 372). A satirical poem, written as if spoken by Shakespeare, laments the debasement of his poetry as delivered by the actors at the Theatre Royal:

> No wonder that I look so white,
> When forced to hear inside each night,
> My verses mouthed, squeaked and frittered
> By ranting knaves, unshaped, unlettered,
> Who spout in bass or treble key,
> Just in proportion to their pay.
>
> (Taylor 2002: 372)

Even tracts and didactic writing aimed at young actors and published outside London reinforced the stigma against regionally marked voices. A representative example is *The Prompter, or Cursory Hints to Young Actors. A Didactic Poem, to which are prefaced Strictures on Theatrical Education*, which was published in Dublin in 1810. In this manual, the author reinforces the notion first introduced by orthoepists in the eighteenth century that the stage should set a standard for correct pronunciation: 'A Nation's language to correctly learn,/Soon to the Stage a watchful ear we turn' (Anon. 1810: 37). But then the author proceeds to warn young actors not to imitate those actors whose voices diverge from a correct, 'classic diction': 'Provincial dialects we sometimes hear,/with grating cadence pain the tuneful ear' (Anon. 1810: 38). These regionally inflected voices do not only offend to sense of hearing in the well-educated, but they also mar the meaning of the lines: 'Such novel accents mock your author's verse,/And tragic scenes descend to downright farce' (Anon. 1810: 38). The author finally urges young actors to seek the advice of 'Some men of taste' who can set them straight, if they are ever in doubt about the correctness of their accents (Anon. 1810: 38).

Attacks against spouters and their accents intensified in the first half of the nineteenth century. Class phobia may well have been responsible for the increasing opposition against the performance of Shakespeare and the national drama by actors whose voices failed to meet prevailing standards of acoustic decorum, because it was at this time that different forms of amateur dramatics started to be more firmly associated with specific social groups. As Dobson explains, 'the upper-class tradition of private theatricals [was] by . . . the 1800s . . . moving down-market into upper-middle-class villas and gentlemen's clubs' (2011: 66). Spouting was also undergoing a 'transmogrification into working-class private theatres of the 'song-and-supper' clubs of the 1820s and 1830s' (Worrall 2006: 246n). The association of different social groups with specific forms of theatrical entertainment therefore hardened just before the abolition of the theatre ban on spoken drama in 1843.

In the 1780s, spouting was still associated with socially diverse groups, who varied both in terms of the social status of their members and the range of their abilities and aspirations. The third edition of Palmer's *Companion* (1781) capitalized on the diversity of its target readers, and, as well as paying homage to the provincial theatres, it included new 'Curious Originals', which praise young actors who aspired to emulate Garrick, while exorcizing the memory of the types of spouters caricatured in earlier collections:

> KIND Sirs, you're welcome to our humble fare,
> Tho' plain, yet honest, from a heart sincere;
> No buskin'd *Hero* treads our little stage,

No *S-r* now roars out his frantic rage;
Dazzled with *Cato's* robe and *Hotspur's* name,
At *Globe-lane* theatre he struts for fame!
Falstaff to *Eastcheap*, *Hal* t'a distant shore,
Both fled, shall torture now your ears no more:
Quitting this scene, they've all took different ways,
On random schemes each sure to win the *bays*.
(Palmer 1781: 81)

The speaker of this prologue stresses how this young company might not include classically educated actors, but its members are nevertheless learning from Garrick's example and from his 'natural' approach to acting:

Young Actors we, in classic schools ne'er taught,
Declaiming numbers, or with language fraught,
Yet dare to-night in tragic scenes to try,
Well pleas'd to spout *beneath good nature's eye*:
No frowning critic sure will enter here,
Or once condemn where Garrick's self would spare:
Candid as just he'd fan our youthful fire,
Nor blame with half the passion as admire!
Like him in you may we protection find,
Each place is free unto a gen'rous mind.
(Palmer 1781: 82; my emphasis)

A 'natural' style of acting suggests here a lack of artifice, both in terms of gesture and modulation of the voice, as recommended in contemporary writing about the theatre aligned with the 'school of Garrick'. In *An Essay upon the Present State of the Theatre in France, England and Italy* (1760), the author had for example pointed out how 'declamation need not be strained much beyond the pitch of common conversation.' 'Proper dignity', he continued, can be given to the verse 'without swelling into a tympany, which has less resemblance to natural elocution as a voice magnified by a speaking trumpet has to the same voice, when unassisted by art' (1760: 183).

Later spouting companions did preserve some of the radicalism introduced by Palmer's collection. Even when later collections included unconditionally vicious attacks on spouting, some other extracts echoed the 'Curious Originals' first published by Palmer. In *The Thespian Oracle; or, A New Key to Theatrical Amusements* (1791), for example, a prologue invokes nature and 'Garrick's ease' as ideal models that the actors' 'infant tongues' should strive to imitate (1791: 40). However, this prologue was spoken 'at a Private Play, performed by some young gentlemen for their diversion' (1791: 40). Palmer's collection therefore remains unique in singling out humble, unschooled but dignified spouters as part of its target readership.

The fourth and final edition of Palmer's *Companion* (1790?) was once again expanded. From the new occasional pieces written or performed on the English stage since the third edition, Palmer selected a new prologue spoken 'at the Opening of the Royalty Theatre' in London in 1878 by John 'Plausible' Palmer. It is quite fitting that the older John Palmer should acknowledge his younger namesake, who had in the meantime become the catalyst for the most important challenge to the duopoly since the Licensing Act of 1737.

§

'The Soil from Which Our Garrick Came':[15]
Marked Voices and the Politics of Place

The last two stanzas in the 'Prologue spoken by [the younger] Mr. Palmer at the Opening of the Royalty Theatre' advance radical arguments that would have appealed to the older John Palmer.[16] Lamenting the opposition that the younger John Palmer had faced in the run-up to the opening of the Royalty Theatre, the prologue denounces the artificial restriction that the Licensing Act of 1737 had imposed on spoken drama:

> Yet some there are who would our scheme annoy;
> 'Tis a monopoly they would enjoy.
> Th' Hay-market, Covent-garden, and old Drury,
> Send forth their edicts "full of sound and fury".
> The jarring states are leagu'd in jealous fit,
> And they, whom wit maintains, wage war on wit.
> But wit, like day-light, nothing should restrain,
> The same in Goodman's-fields and Drury-lane.
> And if the Drama list on virtue's side,
> Say, can the moral be diffus'd too wide?
> If the sun gild yon west with golden ray,
> The east may feel the beams of rising day.
>
> (1790?: 15)

These lines question the viability of regulations that determined the legitimacy or illegitimacy of spoken drama in relation to the physical location of the theatre venues where it was performed. Why should wit

---

[15] Palmer 1790?: 15.
[16] In Anon. 1787a: 60, this prologue is attributed to Arthur Murphy, who, as explained above, had written sympathetically, if humorously, about spouters in the 1750s.

in the form of spoken drama adorn the West End and not the East End of London? The Shakespearean quotation and the reference to Goodman's Fields evoke Garrick as a precedent to criticize the restrictions that prevented spoken drama from thriving on the stage of the so-called Minor theatres. Garrick is linked in the following stanza to the 'soil', or district, in East London, where Palmer built the Royalty – 'The Soil from which our Garrick came'. Garrick is specifically invoked to denounce the unfairness of the double standard imposed by the ban, whereby *place*, rather than the intrinsic quality of the acting, functions as the discriminating factor between high art and unlawful entertainment.

Similarly, Palmer's 'Address ... to the Audience, after the Performance on the First Night of the Opening' reinforced the notion that artistic legitimacy should not be confined to theatres in the West End: '[t]he purpose ..., for which we have this night exerted ourselves, may serve to shew, that a Theatre near Well-Close Square, may be as useful as in Covent Garden, Drury Lane, or the Hay-market' (in Anon. 1787a: 60). Palmer's enterprise, in other words, set out to demonstrate that spoken drama could, and should, be offered to wider audiences outside the West End. The opening of the Royalty was indeed hailed as a major turning point in the debate over the viability and sustainability of the ban. The anonymous author of *A Review of the Present Contest between the Managers of the Winter Theatres, the Little Theatre in the Hay-Market, and the Royalty in Well-Close Square*, for example, hoped that

> the nation will become powerful advocates with its parliamentary representation to obtain authority for a man to establish an undertaking which he has pursued with such deserving activity ... and who will venture to asperse the respectability of the project whence a Garrick rose, and whence, should the present undertaking gain that firm establishment, ... another Garrick may rise'. (Anon. 1787a: 56)

The emphasis is once again on the problematic connection between place and (lack of) legal legitimacy and on the auspicious connection between place and the alternative form of artistic legitimacy bestowed on the Royalty by Garrick's debut in the same neighbourhood in the 1740s.

Palmer had opened the Royalty with a production of *As You Like It*, in which he played Jaques on 20 June 1787, having raised the funding to build the theatre from private sponsors. Palmer had obtained permission from the Lord Lieutenant Governor of the Tower to build in Wellclose Square, which lay within Tower jurisdiction, and a licence from the Tower Hamlets magistrates, as Palmer himself explained in the afterpiece delivered on opening night (Anon. 1787a: 60). However, he lacked a proper licence, which, as the Licensing Act of 1737 stipulated, could only be issued by 'his Majesty, his heirs, successors or predecessors, or by the licence of the lord chamberlain of his Majesty's household' (Pickering 1761: 141). Palmer was therefore obliged to open with a benefit perform-ance in order to circumvent the ban on any 'entertainment of the stage' performed 'for hire, gain, or reward' (Pickering, 1761: 140). Palmer was nevertheless forced to close the Royalty after opening night because he had charged for Garrick's *Miss in Her Teens*, a farce in two acts that followed his production of *As You Like It*. Some of the performers were arrested, and although they were soon released on bail, the Royalty never reopened as a venue for spoken drama, as originally envisaged by Palmer.

Albeit short-lived, Palmer's experiment proved to his critics and to his opponents that spoken drama could be as refined, edifying and enjoyable when performed by companies who may have lacked a royal patent, but were, in all other respects, as well equipped to perform Shakespeare and the national drama as the patent holders. Palmer had gone out of his way to employ actors who would normally play at the patent theatres in the West End in order to expose the arbitrary and exclusionist nature of the ban. He had himself been regularly engaged to perform at Drury Lane, and he managed to secure Mr Quick and Mrs Martyr, two other actors employed by the same company, for his production of *As You Like It*. Palmer's effort to recreate the same material conditions of theatrical production in the East End as audiences were used to expect from the patent theatres in the West End did not go unnoticed. Thomas Harris, who was then managing Covent Garden, reprimanded Mr Quick for failing to abide by the legislation that made him a respectable actor in the West End and a criminal in Tower Hamlets:

> Will you, one of the heads of a profession in itself as liberal as that of law, physic, or any other, degrade, vagabondize, and, as far as you are able, ruin all Theatrical Property, and in most certain consequence, all its dependants? Such must be our inevitable fate, when unprotected by legal monopoply [sic], and Royal and Parliamentary sanction. (Anon., 1787a: 61)

The short distance between Covent Garden in the West End and the Royalty in Tower Hamlets was sufficient, in Harris's view, to deprive playacting of its legitimacy and to turn an actor into a vagrant and a criminal.

Palmer's supporters invoked the same double standard, though, of course, they did so in order to denounce, rather than to support, the ban. Isaac Jackman, in his 'Letter to Phillips Glover, Esq. of Wispington, in Lincolnshire' (1787), pointed out that 'if Garrick was now living, and had been guilty of playing Lear in Wellclose Square, the laws of this country would ... commit him to the house of correction, as a rogue, a wagrant, and a wagabone' (54). In a similar vein, a poem published in *The Theatrical Journal* in September 1787, as part of the larger controversy stirred up by the opening of the Royalty, invited readers to ponder on the absurdity of a legislation according to which, 'Should Garrick's self, with all his powe'rs a-new/Rise on this very spot – where first he grew,/Even He your kind indulgence still must beg,/And sing "Roast Beef," or hop upon one leg' (223). The location and the status of the venue, in other words, rather than Garrick's talent, determined what Garrick would or would not be allowed to perform at the Royalty.

The same argument was made a week after the opening of *As You Like It* about Palmer, who, himself an actor, was clearly being judged differently, according to where, and not to how, he delivered his lines:

> The immorality, the vice, or the profaneness [of Palmer's delivery] does not inhere in the representation – I had almost said, it inheres no where. – Shall we say, it inheres in the *place*? No: Goodman's-fields have been moral, and it is certain, may be moralized again by a legislative process. Does it inhere in Mr. Palmer? No: Mr. Palmer is virtuous or vicious according to Act of Parliament; or rather his moral qualities – properties he has none – are assimilated to the *place* on which he happens to stand – if on holy ground, he is holy; if on profane, he is profane: at Wellclose-square, he is a pest to society and alarms his Majesty's ministers, ever anxious for the morals of the public, to immediate interference – at Drury-lane, he becomes, by virtue of the King's Patent, a public benefit: though equally in both *places*, the father of eight children ... he becomes, by appearing in one, and performing *the very same act* as in the other – a rogue, vagabond, and sturdy beggar! (Anon. 1787b; my emphasis)

The arbitrary nature of the theatrical legislation that regulated the performance of spoken drama was brought into sharp relief by Palmer's strategic attempt to recreate at the Royalty the same conditions of performance associated with the patented theatres.

As well as employing the same actors who would normally work on the stage of the patent theatres in the West End, Palmer had also endeavoured to build a venue that was as impressive, spacious and elegant as the patent venues. A contemporary description of the Royalty Theatre, published in the *London Magazine* in May 1787, just before its opening the next month, emphasized its imposing architectural features:

> The Royalty Theatre, for so it is denominated from the ground on which it is erected being within the precincts of a palace, is constructed of the very best materials, neither expense nor labour having been spared to render it a perfectly complete building. If there be any fault in the architect, it is of the same nature with that imputed to Sir John Vanbrugh, who, in designing

> the Opera-house, carried strength and solidity to such an excess, as if he
> intended his edifice to defy the ravages of time. Mr. John Wilmot, the
> architect, seems to have fallen into the same, if the expression be allowable,
> laudable error; for, contrary to the interest of his profession, he has been the
> fabricator of a building which, from it's [sic] excellent workmanship, will
> occasion the proprietors to incur very little expense in the repairs during the
> continuance of a century. (253–4)

The comparison with Covent Garden in this extract attests to the ambition
of Palmer's project. The Royalty, however, was different from the patent
theatres in the West End in at least one important respect. As reported in
The Gentleman's Magazine, '[t]he galleries at the Royalty Theatre [were]
infinitely superior to any belonging to the various theatres in the kingdom'
and more spacious than in any other theatre 'in the metropolis'. According
to *The London Magazine*, '[t]he upper gallery ... on the most accurate
computation contain six hundred and forty persons' and '[t]he second
gallery ... one thousand' (Anon. 1787d: 536). The galleries were also
constructed to offer unrestricted views of the stage:

> [b]eing of a semicircular form, there is not a situation from which the
> spectators will not have a distinct view of every part of the stage, and from
> the last seat of both galleries, the extremity of the building is conspicuously
> discerned, without stooping, or in any manner varying the natural position
> of the body. (Anon. 1787d: 536)

The galleries at the Royalty were built so that spectators who paid considerably less for admission than they would for a seat in the pit, or the front
or side boxes, would not have to 'stoop' to get a good view of the stage.
Stooping, both literally and metaphorically, was no longer required of the
poorer members of Palmer's audience. Access was clearly Palmer's priority,
given that his galleries seated nearly twice as many people as the pit and the
boxes. As Donohue observes:

> The audience to which Palmer hoped to appeal is evident in the very
> configuration of the Royalty auditorium: some 60 per cent of an overall
> capacity of nearly 2,600 person was devoted to galleries, a far higher
> proportion than in the rehabilitated Drury Lane and Covent Garden of
> half a decade later. (2004: 41)

Palmer's supporters hailed the increased geographical and economic accessibility offered by the Royalty to greater sections of the population as a
daring move on his part. Jackman, in his 'Letter to ... Glover', emphasized
how Palmer's theatre was 'of considerable benefits to every class of people'
(1787: 9). Similarly, the author of *A Review of the Present Contest* (1787a)

pointed out how 'the other places of dramatic representation were at a very considerable distance' from Tower Hamlets, and how the poorer citizens from that district were not be able to 'pay a further tax for conveyance' to the West End, even when they were able to afford admission to the patent theatres.

Despite Palmer's best efforts, he was forced to close down the Royalty after its opening night. The Royalty never reopened as a performance venue for spoken drama. The failure of Palmer's enterprise meant that the dire predictions made by his opponents about the detrimental impact that opening up the performance of spoken drama to venues beyond the West End would have on the quality of theatrical entertainment was never put to the test. In his scathing response to Jackman's 'Letter to . . . Glover', the author of *A Letter to the Author of the Burletta called 'Hero and Leander', in Refutation of what he has advanced in his Dedication to Philips Glover, Esq.* (1787c) had warned his readers that,

> [i]f the laws for regulating the stage should be repealed, every disappointed or ambitious actor, possessing money or abilities, would have his Theatre. *St. Mary-le-bon* would make her curtsy to the legislature, and put in her claim; and *St. Giles* would make his bow and exhibit his pretensions. Every petit town in Great Britain would attempt to maintain her own company, 'til . . . the performers would be divided into factions, theatres would spring up in every quarter, and ribaldry, tumblers, fire-eaters, dancing dogs, learned pigs, and musical ducks would disgrace the stage, the drama would degenerate, and actors, *without* offending the law, would become *rogues* and *vagabonds* from necessity. (18–19)

Palmer's intent had been precisely to show that Tower Hamlets could have, and should have, its own magnificent venue for spoken drama, and that current theatrical regulations, as opposed to the taste and inclinations of the lower-class citizens who inhabited that district, were responsible for limiting the provision of high-quality theatrical entertainment to lower, or minor, dramatic genres. However, the author of *A Letter* reiterated his belief that '[c]opying after Nature, who gives ornament and elegance to the essential qualities of her noblest productions' ought to remain the prerogatives of companies invested by royal approval.

Yet Palmer's attempt did at the very least succeed in exposing the class bias at the heart of the legislation. As Moody puts it, 'the spectre of plebeian audiences watching Shakespear[e] . . . undermined conventional assumptions about the proper relationships between social class and cultural hierarchy' (2000: 133). More generally, Palmer's venture confirmed that, as Moody continues, '[t]he battle for free trade in drama was not only a campaign to overturn a commercial monopoly, but also a deeply political conflict about who should control theatrical culture' (2000: 5). Though only temporarily, Palmer had managed to challenge not only the current theatrical legislation, but also broader assumptions about the conventions regulating the production of spoken drama and who should be granted access to it.

§

After the two John Palmers had effectively, if temporarily, managed to expose the cultural and class bias underlying the ban on spoken drama in the second half of the eighteenth century, critical responses to unconventional voices and accents by and large hardened into even more vehement disapproval in the early nineteenth century. Actors associated with the provinces or amateur or semi-professional actors who performed in private theatres in London were routinely accused of not being able to speak English correctly. The actor who played Rolla in *Pizarro* was, for example, ridiculed for his 'complete ignorance of the English language' (*Rambler*, 22 January 1822); similarly the actor who played Osmond at the Rawstrone Street Theatre early in January of the same year is said to have 'murdered the language most inhumanly' (*Rambler*, 2 January 1822). Later that year, the actor playing Valverds was described as 'beastly ignorant' and was advised to 'learn to speak English' (*Rambler*, 24 October 1822). The following year, the actress who played Emilia in a production of *Othello* was reprimanded for 'marr[ing] her mother tongue' (*Mirror of the Stage*, 1823).

Responses to provincial accents were especially vitriolic. The actor who played the Ghost of Old Hamlet at the Wilson Street Theatre in March 1823 was criticized for sounding like 'a Lancashire loon' (*Mirror of the Stage*, 24 March 1824). More generally, the voices of provincial actors who performed in private theatres in the capital were patronizingly described as beastly.[17] These actors were variously said to roar like wounded bears (*Rambler*, 22 January and 8 March 1822), squeal like hogs (*Rambler*, 20 January 1822), bray like asses (*Rambler*, 27 March 1822), howl like mad dogs (*Rambler*, 11 April, 23 July and 22 October 1822), chatter like baboons (*Mirror of the Stage*, 18 April 1823), or quack like ducks (*The Acting Manager, or, The Minor Spy*, 14 May 1831). Lower-class accents were also consistently critiqued. John Smith, who performed the role of Peregrine in *John Bull* at the

---

[17] This category of actors was routinely compared to animals. See, for example, the review of *Richard III*, as performed at the Rawstrone Place Theatre in April 1822, where the reviewer complains that he is 'tired of seeing this poor tragedy cut up by such animals' (*Rambler*, 18 April 1822), or the review of another production of *Richard III*, this time performed at the Pavillion, in the Old Town in Hoxton, where Mr Green is reported 'to know as much about Shakespeare, as a monkey knows about philosophy' (*The Acting Manager: or, The Minor Spy*, 2 May 1831).

Rawstrone Place Theatre on 5 July 1824, was reported to have come across as a 'consummate blockhead ... who mistook the stage for a milliner's shop' (*Rambler*, 1 August 1824), while the actor who played Pizarro at the Berwick Street Theatre in March 1822 was ridiculed for sounding like a 'Bond-street Lounger' (*Rambler*, 8 March 1822).

By far the strongest criticism was prompted by the temporary engagement of actors normally associated with provincial or minor theatres at the patent theatres. Thomas Cobham (1779/1786–1842), for example, who had played Shylock in an amateur production of *The Merchant of Venice* in Lamb's Conduit Street, then made a name for himself by playing in the provinces. When he returned to London, he became known as 'the Kemble of the minor theatres' (Knight and Cockin, 2004) and received damning reviews, when he was invited to play Richard III at Covent Garden in 1816. His performance was negatively compared to Edmund Kean's very popular Richard III at Drury Lane. Even the most enlightened of reviewers dismissed Cobham as unsuitable to play at a patent theatre. William Hazlitt, for example, stated quite bluntly that Richard III and Cobham were 'quite different things' and that Cobham had shown 'no common sense or decorum' in the way he performed this role (Hazlitt 1818: 274). Interestingly enough, when Kean was invited to play Othello next to Cobham's Iago at the Coburg, where the latter had become popular and firmly established, Kean was hissed by the audience, in a rare but telling instance of lower-class spectators regarding the acting style of a patent theatre actor as out of place in a minor theatre.

Similarly, commenting on a Mr Priest who performed as Shylock at Drury Lane in December 1825, the reviewer in *The Literary Chronicle* argued that, though he 'might pass in a private theatre', he had 'neither the person, features or voice' to be suited to perform in the West End (17 December 1825). Even well-established actors, like Junius Brutus Booth (1796–1852), did not fare well, once they became associated with touring in the provinces, or even on Continental Europe or North America. When he returned to the patent theatres in London, reviewers found him unsuitable for the job. About his Richard III, Hazlitt said that it would be quite appropriate for the provinces but not for London,[18] while *The Literary Chronicle* reviewer dismissed him for having a 'hoarse voice', which America 'had not improved' (15 October 1825).

---

[18] In the *London Examiner*, Hazlitt had insinuated that, although Booth's acting 'may pass at Brighton for *grand, gracious, and magnificent*, even the lowest of the mob will laugh at [it] in London' (quoted in Archer 1992: 3).

Common to all these comments was a deeply rooted anxiety concerning the impact of uncouth voices on the beauty of the English language, and on Shakespeare more specifically. Earlier in the eighteenth century, Woty, writing about the young barber who had become possessed by the desire to perform Shakespearean roles, had lamented that, when '[t]he lofty Tonsor . . . assumes the Port/Of Tyrant Richard', the 'graceful Periods' penned by 'Divine-inspired Shakespear! on his Tongue,/Imperfect die away'. What had concerned Woty and continued to animate the controversy over provincial and lower-class actors in the early nineteenth century was the belief that Shakespeare's divine-inspired poetry would not survive spouting and bad pronunciation. Though 'divine-inspired', Shakespeare's language was deemed to be ultimately vulnerable to marked voices that threatened the legacy of his work and the high literary and artistic status accorded to it. As Taylor puts it,

> For many contemporary critics the performance of Shakespeare's works in unlicensed penny gaffs and the fringe theatres emerging in the provincial centres degraded the plays of the nation's poet. Such crude presentation of Shakespeare's theatre to the masses was regarded as a debased variant of the original works. (2002: 372)

Nearly seventy years after Woty's poem was first published in 1760, a reviewer in *The Literary Chronicle* expressed similar views, first by praising 'dramatic poetry . . . as the cream of every language' and then by connecting the 'genius and taste of a nation' to 'its morals'. Hence this reviewer's sense that 'a coarse, mouthing, blustering actor . . . [had] an operative effect upon something more than the mere manners of his audience and spectators' (21 April 1827).

Garrick, first, and then the two John Palmers, inspired by Garrick, ushered in a short-lived, but radical period of change in the production and reception of Shakespeare and spoken drama, which contributed to the eventual dismantlement of the monopoly first introduced by Charles II in 1660. However, Garrick's 'natural' style of acting and the two John Palmers' interventions also revealed a deeply rooted aversion for voices that challenged acoustic correctness, and, by extension, theatrical to social decorum. Despite the lifting of the ban that followed the Theatre Regulation Act of 1843, the criticism levelled at Garrick and the two John Palmers in the second half of the eighteenth century became ingrained in elitist attitudes towards the ownership of Shakespeare and spoken drama in the nineteenth century. These attitudes survived into the late nineteenth and early twentieth centuries, when, as explained in Chapter 2, RP reigned supreme on the English stage.

Symptomatic of the acoustic uniformity that dominated the Shakespearean stage from the mid-nineteenth to the mid-twentieth century is the
critical appraisal of Henry Irving's idiosyncratic diction. Despite being the
first British actor to receive a knighthood in 1895, Irving was often
criticized for failing to conform to StP. Irving, who had grown up in a
mining village near St Ives in Cornwall, was schooled in London at the
City Commercial School led by Dr Pinches, who believed in the need to
impart elocution lessons to all his pupils. After watching Samuel Phelps
play Hamlet at Sadler's Wells, Irving decided to restart elocution classes to
train his voice and fulfil his childhood ambition to become a professional
actor (Davies 2008). Even while working as a clerk, he seems to have
encouraged his fellow workers to use StP as a marker of social distinction.
As Irving biographer Jeffrey Richards reports, 'he drew up a list of fines to
be imposed on other clerks to improve their English, eliminating cockneyisms, ungrammatical expressions and redundant aspirates' (2005: 23–24).
Still according to Richards, Irving regarded 'accent and bearing' as the
'outward and visible signs of gentlemanliness' and worked hard to improve
both his voice and his demeanour throughout his life (2005: 24). Irving
went as far as changing his real name, John Henry Brodribb, when he
started acting, in order to distance his professional persona as one of the
most successful actors of his generation as much as possible from his lowly
upbringing in Cornwall. In this respect, Irving anticipated Richard
Burton, who, as mentioned at greater length in Chapter 1, was born
Richard Walter Jenkins in a mining community in South Wales but went
on to adopt the surname of his English teacher, Philip Burton, who had
trained his memory and his voice after spotting his talent for acting while
Richard was still in school.[19]

Despite his efforts, Irving's contemporaries continued to find faults with
his pronunciation, even when he performed the Shakespearean roles for
which he became most famous and was most admired. Thanks to the
timely invention of the Edison's phonograph, we can still hear Irving
pronounce 'this sun of York' as 'this sun of Yark' from the opening
soliloquy in *Richard III*,[20] as he delivered it at the Lyceum Theatre in
1877, which is possibly among the acoustic idiosyncrasies in Irving's
delivery that struck his contemporaries as indecorous, if not downright
aberrant. Henry James was among those who found Irving's pronunciation
unfamiliar and challenging:

---

[19] For more details, see p. 55. [20] Irving's audio recording is included in Various Artists 2000.

> Mr Irving's peculiarities and eccentricities of speech are so strange, so numerous, so personal to himself, his views of pronunciation, of modulation, of elocution so highly developed, the tricks he plays with the divine mother-tongue so audacious and fantastic, that the spectator who desires to be in sympathy with him finds himself confronted with a bristling hedge of difficulties. (Foulkes 2008: 29)

Irving's efforts to improve his pronunciation may have got rid of recognizable regional variations, but his speech still struck even a North American speaker like James as constructed, artificial and too 'personal' to Irving himself.

James's response to Irving's idiosyncratic accent is especially interesting in light of the fact that North American actors who performed on the late nineteenth-century London stage were subjected to particularly harsh censure, if any phonetic variation in their pronunciation betrayed their origins. Edwin Booth, for example, who, like Irving, enjoyed popular and critical acclaim as one of the most accomplished actors at the time, was similarly critiqued for sounding North American. The critic for *Bell's Life in London*, writing about his performance in the title role in *Richelieu*, for example, cautioned him 'on some American accents which offend English ears'. Among them, he mentions Booth's pronunciation of 'commend' and 'gallant', stressing how the accent should fall on the second and first syllable respectively (Bloom 2013: 57). Similarly condescending are the remarks by the critic for *The Literary Gazette*, who found his performance inconsistent, because one moment he made his character look 'physically infirm, all but moribund' and the next he rose to 'rant and stagger and rave in a voice that would do credit to a Thames waterman' (Bloom 2013: 57).

Telling in these two responses to Irving's and Booth's accents is the association of regional, as well as foreign and lower-class variations, with sounds that were deemed as equally incongruous on the London stage and that would continue to be singled out for indignant disapproval well into the twentieth and, occasionally, the twenty-first century, as shown in Chapters 1 and 2.

CHAPTER 4

'Usual Speech' and 'Barbarous Dialects' on the Early Modern Stage

The alignment of Shakespeare with the speech of elitism began when the theatres reopened in London in 1660 and gathered pace after the emergence of StP in the eighteenth century and the rise of RP in the nineteenth century, as shown in Chapter 3. The widespread assumption that early modern actors spoke in a variety of accents because no accent had as yet acquired prestige status and because there was no expectation that they should conform to any fixed acoustic norm or standard pronunciation is however a misleading commonplace. This chapter argues that actors in Shakespeare's time did in fact use an emerging standard of pronunciation, then known as 'usual speech',[1] and that national and regional English accents – i.e. Scots, Hiberno-English, Welsh, Cornish and North and Southern dialects within Anglo-English – were effectively, if sparingly used in simplified stage versions to modulate characterization and to achieve sophisticated dramatic effects.[2] While the first half of this chapter considers the cultural connotations associated by Shakespeare's contemporaries with this emerging standard of pronunciation, the second half focuses on two case studies about the use of accents that deviated from this emerging standard in *The Merry Wives of Windsor* and *King Lear*. These case studies and this chapter as a whole show how a better understanding of how Shakespeare was spoken on the early modern stage can shed light on how Shakespeare sounded to his contemporaries and how differently some of his characters and plays were interpreted by their original audiences.

§

---

[1] This phrase occurs in a frequently quoted passage from George Puttenham's *The Arte of English Poesie* (1589, STC 20519), where 'vsuall speach' is defined as the 'speach of the Court, and that of London and the shires lying about London within lx. myles, and not much aboue' (R3r).

[2] For a discussion of the alternative view that early modern English accents were 'non-realist symbols of identity', see 'Introduction', pp. 7–14.

'Sweetness of Words, Fitness of Epithets'[3]

The sporadic occurrence of dialect in early modern drama, and in Renaissance literature more generally, reflects the gradual emergence of London English (or Chancery English) as the written standard used at court and in parliament in the late fifteenth century. Later known as the 'King's English',[4] this emerging standard was disseminated through the new medium of print across the country, thus severely limiting the use of other dialects for official and literary purposes. As Paula Blank explains, '[i]t is not surprising, ... [given] the centralization of power heralded by the Tudor accession, ... the importance of court patronage and the localization of the publishing industry in London, ... that regional literature, mapping out an autonomous imaginative space outside the capital, finds few representatives in the canon of Renaissance works' (1996: 71).

Pronunciation, on the other hand, did not become standardized until well into the eighteenth and nineteenth centuries, as shown in Chapter 3. Therefore, variation was not only a marker of regional speech but also intrinsic to how early modern English was spoken. As a result, it is often quite difficult to distinguish regional from phonetic variation more generally. As Russ McDonald points out,

> [Early modern English] was undergoing the process known to linguists as 'The Great Vowel Shift', in which pronunciation of English was moving from its Middle English habits to something approaching its modern forms. When Shakespeare counted he probably pronounced the number 'one' as something like 'own' or the first syllable in 'only'. He probably rhymed the noun 'sea' not with 'bee' but with 'lay'. And he regularly rhymed the noun 'wind' (as in 'weather') with the long-vowelled 'kind'. None of these forms was exclusive, however: Shakespeare's rhymes indicate that certain words could legitimately be pronounced in more than one way. (2001: 22–3)

Equally crucial, though, was the gradual privileging of the spoken English used at Court and by the well educated in London, where, according to spelling reformer John Hart, 'the flower of the English tongue [was] vsed' (1569: A3v). The accent associated with the Court, otherwise known as 'usual speech', was not a firmly established, non-geographical sociolect, as recent scholars have rightly stressed.[5] This emergent standard nevertheless fed into a growing ambition to compete with other European nations both

---

[3] Gosson 1582: E1r.   [4] This phrase was first used in Wilson 1553: 86r.
[5] See, for example, Hope 2010: 133.

in terms of boosting the prestige of English as a literary language and in terms of maritime, commercial and cultural expansionism and international influence.[6]

Evidence drawn from supporters and detractors of Shakespeare's theatre shows that 'usual speech' was the accent most commonly spoken on the early modern stage. The combined efforts of early modern playwrights and the acting companies who performed their work were praised by those who regarded the theatre as a privileged site for the forging of English as a literary language. As briefly mentioned in Chapter 2, Thomas Heywood proudly observed that

> our *English* tongue, which hath ben the most harsh, vneuen, and broken language of the world ... is now by this secondary meanes of playing, continually refined, ... so that ... from the most rude and vnpolisht tongue, it is growne to a most perfect and composed language. (1612: F3)

Conversely, the use of 'usual speech' on the early modern stage was regarded by detractors of the theatre, like Stephen Gosson, as symptomatic of the more generally deceptive and therefore corrupting qualities of playacting. In his *Playes Confuted in Five Actions* (1582, STC 12095), he explains that

> [a]ction, pronuntiation, apparel, agility, musicke, seuerally considered are the good blessings of God, ... yet being bound vp together in a bundle, to set out the pompe, the plaies, [are] the inuentions of the Diuell (C6v).

Later in the same tract, Gosson reinforces the same notion that 'euery man must show him selfe outwardly to be such as in deed he is', and since 'outward signes consist eyther in words or gestures, to declare our selues by wordes or by gestures to be otherwise then we are', he concludes, 'is an act executed where it should not, therefore a lye' (E5r).

As Gosson explains here, actors who routinely donned not only the precious garments discarded by their betters but also their accents were perceived, both visually and acoustically, as transgressive upstarts and were

---

[6] Representative of the power attributed to the refined acoustic qualities of English as a spoken language are Samuel Daniel's well-known verses from his *Poeticall Essayes* (1599; STC 6261): 'And who in time knowes whither we may vent/The treasure of our tongue, to what strange shores/This gaine of our best glorie shal be sent,/T'inrich vnknowing Nations with our stores?/VVhat worlds in th'yet vnformed Occident/May come refin'd with th'accents that are ours? ... O that the Ocean did not bound our stile/VVithin these strict and narrow limits so:/But that the melodie of our sweete Ile, Might now be heard to *Tyber*, *Arne*, and *Po*:/That they might know how far *Thames* doth out-go/The Musique of declined Italie' (F2v 9–14; A3v 9–14).

accordingly attacked not only for looking like their betters, but also for sounding like them. The use of 'usual speech' on the Shakespearean stage was not an uncontested marker of literary and social status; it was rather a daring and controversial bid to secure it for an emergent art form and for those who practised it.

Particularly striking in this respect is the use of the same elevated register and imagery in lines attributed to high and low status characters in Shakespeare, which in turn suggests that these characters would also have sounded similarly well spoken, despite belonging to different social groups. The Gardener's lines in *Richard II* (1597, STC 22307), for example, are arranged in polished and regular verse and are as rich in imagery and allusions as the rest of the language spoken by the king and the nobility in the most poetical and metrically regular of Shakespeare's history plays. Particularly well-known are the Gardner's references to the orderly harmony that is lost in the realm but carefully maintained in his garden, where 'young dangling Aphricokes' are bound up when, 'like vnruly children', they 'make their sire, / Stoope with oppression of their prodigall weight' (1597: G3, 3–5). One might argue that gardeners at courts throughout early modern Europe in the period were likely to be skilled and educated professionals (see, for example, Eklund 2017). However, First Man speaks in just as elevated a register as the Gardner:

> Why should we in the compas of a pale,
> Keepe law and forme, and due proportion,
> Shewing as in a modle our firme estate,
> When our sea-walled garden the whole land
> Is full of weedes, her fairest flowers choakt vp,
> Her fruit trees all vnprunde, her hedges ruinde,
> Her knots disordered, and her holsome hearbs
> Swarming with caterpillers.
>
> (1597: G3, 14–21)

First Man's reference to England as a 'sea-walled garden' echoes John of Gaunt's famous eulogy of England as a 'little world, / This precious stone set in the siluer sea, / Which serues it in the office of a wall...' (1597: C3v, 28–30). First Man describes what has become of England after the fall brought about by Richard's misrule, but the imagery, the register, and the ample rhythm of the verse recall Gaunt's speech. In short, both the Gardener and First Man are allowed to sound like the highest figure of (symbolic, if not institutional) authority in the play.

The elevated language associated with dreams and the imagination is similarly never the exclusive domain of high-ranking characters in

Shakespeare. And one doesn't need to wait for Caliban,[7] or even for Bottom the Weaver,[8] to come across the most unlikely of dreamers of all, Christopher Sly, who sounds quite unlike himself, albeit briefly, in the Induction that prefaces *The Taming of the Shrew* (1623a, STC 22273). 'Translated' out of his poor garments (and idiolect), Sly wonders:

> Am I not *Christopher Slie*, old Slies sonne of Burton-heath, by birth a Pedlar, by education a Cardmaker, by transmutation a Beare-heard, and now by present profession a Tinker. (1623a: TLN 170–3)

Barton-on-the-heath and Wincot, which Sly mentions in the next line (1623a: TLN 174), are the closest fictive locations to Shakespeare's home-town in the entire canon. These two villages, a few miles from Stratford-upon-Avon, could have prompted Shakespeare to mark Sly's speech with linguistic features associated with the Midlands, if the Inductions in *A Shrew* were indeed penned or revised by Shakespeare.[9] Instead of reflecting regional variation, Sly's speech, which is initially marked by the odd dialectal word – 'ILe pheeze you [fix you] infaith' (1623a: TLN 4) or 'I am your good-man [husband]' (1623a: TLN 259) – quickly switches to a different register, as the Lord and his servants persuade him that he is also a lord:

> Am I a Lord, and haue I such a Ladie?
> Or do I dreame? Or haue I dream'd till now?
> I do not sleepe: I see, I heare, I speake:
> I smel sweet sauours, and I feele soft things:
> Vpon my life I am a Lord indeede.
> (1623a: TLN 220–4)

What is notable about these lines is that Sly *can* switch from prose to verse, and that he can 'see', 'heare' *and* 'speake' in a different register, like a lord, if only temporarily. The quality of Sly's speech here makes him more than a mere caricature. For a moment, even Christopher Sly is given to *sound* other than he is. More generally, as Hope has observed, 'when characters [in Shakespeare] comment on language . . . it is almost always to remark on [its] surprisingly high status . . . . In fact', as Hope adds, 'Shakespeare's characters are constantly amazed by how well people speak' (2010: 108).

---

[7] 'Sometimes a thousand twangling Instruments / Will hum about mine eares; and sometime voices, / That if I then had wak'd after long sleepe / will make me sleepe againe'. (*The Tempest*, STC 22273, 1623a: TLN 1494–7)

[8] 'I haue had a dreame, past the wit of man, to say; what dreame it was'. (*A Midsummer Night's Dream*, STC 22302, 1600: G1v 28–9)

[9] For a recent account of the authorship debate in relation to *A Shrew*, see Kidnie 2006: 1–4.

Detractors of the theatre, like Gosson, were understandably nervous about the fact that actors used accents and registers that made them (and the characters they personated) sound socially above the lowly status accorded to their profession. Theatre historians have so far focused mostly on the controversy generated by cross-dressing as a distinctive practice of the Shakespearean stage,[10] but not enough attention has been paid to other aspects of playacting, which the anti-theatricalists regarded as equally deceptive and idolatrous. It is therefore important to stress that Gosson was not alone in denouncing the risks associated with allowing lowly actors and fictional characters to sound like the educated elite.

One of the most explicit and damning invectives against actors who sounded like their social superiors can be found in John Davies's poem, *Microcosmos* (1603, STC 6333):

> But that which grates my *Galle*, and mads my *Muse*,
> *Is* (ah that ever such iust cause should *Bee*)
> To see a *Player* at the put-downe *stewes*
> Put vp his *Peacockes* Taile for al to see,
> And for his hellish voice, as prowde as *hee*;
> What *Peacocke* art thou prowd? Wherfore? because
> Thou *Parrat*-like canst speake what is taught thee:
> A *Poet* must teach thee from clause to clause,
> Or thou wilt breake *Pronunciations* Lawes.
>
> (1603: Ff3v)

The voice of the actor who dons the accent of his betters is 'hellish' because he parrots accents that do not naturally belong to him, who can only 'vse [his] Tongue / To speake as [he is] taught, or right or wrong'. (1603: Ff4v)

Imitating someone else's voice, whether marked or unmarked by national, regional, or social features, was of course deemed dangerous enough in its own right to warrant accusations of 'idolatrie', as Gosson had intimated in his *Playes Confuted in Fiue Actions* (1582: C6v). I. G., another staunch anti-theatricalist, expressed the same concern about the intrinsically deceitfulness of words and deed in theatrical representation:

> The action is two-fould, in word, and in deede. The action in word is lasciuious speches, idle and vaine scoffing, ieasting, and foolery, and cosenage, knauery, flattery, and what soeuer els, set forth in their coullors, phrases, and tearmes, and with the grace, elegancy, and lustre of the tongue. The action in deede is the setting forth of all enormities, and exorbitances, with the personating of the doers of them; with false representations, lying

---

[10] See, for example, Levine 1994.

shewes, killing, stabbing, hanging, and fighting; actiue demonstration of cosenage, whorish enticeing, all kinde of villany, and hypocrisie; with embracing, clipping, culling, dandling kissing; all manner wanton gestures, and the like. (1615, H1v)

The most worrying aspect of the players' actions, or playacting, which comprised voice and gestures, words and deeds, was their ability to reproduce any mode of speech and to dress their words with 'the grace, elegancy, and lustre of the tongue', even though they naturally possessed none, because of their lowly professional and social status.

Anti-theatricalists disapproved of playacting as a 'fictive art' practised by the players to appear and sound other than who they were.[11] They condemned the players for parroting their superiors as vehemently as they lambasted them for cross-dressing. Reinforcing his disapproval of the player's ability to mimic the elevated speech associated with his social superiors, Gosson condemns him for divorcing his 'person' from his 'speach', and for turning himself into a 'cypher', because he 'must stand as his parte fals, sometime for a Prince, sometime for a peasant' (1582, A8v). The player's personation of 'a Prince', in the original meaning of *per-sonare* as sounding-through (Smith 1999: 280), is perceived as an act of acoustic and social trespassing, which threatens the orderly functioning of the public body of the state.

In a passage that draws from Aesop's 'Fable of the Belly' (and which anticipates Shakespeare's use of the same parable in the opening scene in *Coriolanus*), Gosson first stresses the players' problematic lack of social status. 'Most of the Players', he laments, 'haue bene eyther men of occupations, which they haue forsaken to lyue by playing, or common minstrels, or trayned vp from theire childehoode to this abhominable exercise & haue now no other way to gete theire liuinge' (1582, G6v). The players' lack of an honest vocation is particularly problematic in light of the fact that the state is conceived as a body, 'whose heade is the prince':

> if any part be idle, by participation the damage redoundeth to the whole, if any refuse to doe theire duetie, though they be base, as the guttes, the gall, the bladder, howe daungerous it is both to the bodie, and to the heade, euerie man is able to coniecture. (1582, G6v)

---

[11] I. G. defines playacting as a 'fictive art', juxtaposing it to rhetoric, which he describes as a 'liberal science', because rhetoric, unlike playacting, enhanced the speaker's ability to convey genuine emotions, motives and intentions (1615, C2v).

Players are all the more dangerous, because they are not only 'idle' in not
having an honest vocation, or in refusing to get one, but also because they
look and sound other than they are, thus refusing to occupy the position
and perform the role that best befit their lowly status:

> If we grudge at the wisedome of our maker, and disdaine the calling he hath
> placed vs in, aspyring somewhat higher then we shoulde, as in the body;
> when the feete woulde be armes, the armes would be eyes; the guttes would
> be veines, the veines would be nerues; the muscles would be flesh, the flesh
> would be spirit, this confusion of order weakens the head: So in a com-
> monweale, if priuat men be suffered to forsake theire calling because they
> desire to walke gentleman like in sattine & veluet, w^t a buckler at theire
> heeles, proportion is so broken, vnitie dissolued, . . . that the whole body
> must be dismembred and the prince or the head cannot chuse but sicken.
> (1582, G7r–G7v)

In this context, the acoustic pretensions of the players amounted to
veritable acts of political insubordination.

Gosson's anxiety also resonates in contemporary writings about the
problematic relationship between appearances and inward dispositions,
about seeming and being, especially when they focus on the voice as a
potential agent of dissimulation. D. T., for example, warns the readers of
his *Essaies Politicke, and Morall* (1608; STC 24396) that, while '[t]he sillie
Sheepe can neuer change his naturall voyce, . . . man can alter, and fashion
his, to as many seuerall, and sundry Dialects, as he please, till such time as
his Ambition haue attain'd to that, which it desired' (Q4). The voice is
seen as particularly dangerous because of its 'flexible and pliable' nature,
which deceives by pretending to convey genuine emotions from the heart,
as Thomas Wright explains in his tract on *The Passions of the Minde* (1604:
STC 26040):

> the passion passeth not onely thorow the eyes, but also pierceth the eare,
> and thereby the heart; for a flexible and pliable voice, accommodated in
> manner correspondent to the matter whereof a person intreateth, conueyeth
> the passion most aptly, pathetically, and almost harmonically, and *euery
> accent, exclamation, admiration, increpation, indignation, commiseration,
> abhomination, exanimation, exultation, fitly (that is distinctly, at time and
> place, with gesture correspondent, and flexibilitie of voice proportionat)
> deliuered,* is either a flash of fire to incense a passion, or a bason of water
> to quench a passion incensed. . . . A man therefore furnished himselfe with
> the passion or affection he wisheth in his auditors, shewing it with voice and
> action, although his reasons be not so potent, hath no doubt a most potent
> meane to persuade what he list. (1604: M8, my emphasis)

The potency of the voice – its ability to penetrate the ear and thereby reach the heart – and its pliability – all its modulations, covering the entire spectrum of human emotions – make it possible for a man to 'furnish' himself with the passion he wishes to convey to his 'auditors' (which is not necessarily a genuine passion) and to 'persuade' them in whichever way 'he list', whether 'his reasons' are solid and justified ('potent') or not.

Wright's understanding of the potency of the voice is echoed in a very popular sermon, Robert Wilkinson's *The Ievvell for the Eare* (1602: STC 25652.7), which was reprinted six times in just over twenty years, between 1602 and 1625. In this sermon, Wilkinson first explains that '[t]he holy Ghoast discended vppon the Apostles not in the shape of heads, that they should onely vnderstand the word, nor of harts that they shuld onely loue the word, but like toongs that they should preach the word' (1602: A5). Wilkinson therefore proceeds to exhort his congregation to 'Take heed how you heare', because, as he goes on to add:

> there is ... an arte of hearinge as well as of speaking. These two are fitly compared to a locke and a key, for as the key openeth the lock and maketh entrance in at the doore, so the tongue of the minister shoulde open the eare of the hearer, that the spirit of knowledge and vnderstanding might passe into the heart. (1602: A4v)

According to Wilkinson, our sense of hearing is a divine gift given to man to admire 'the creation of the world'. The sense of hearing is here taken to be more potent than the sense of sight, because the knowledge that we gain through our eyes is deemed 'vnperfect as the glimmering of a light' (1602: A8), whereas the knowledge that we gain through our ears is 'more specially and expressely ... the knowledge of Gods reuealed will' (1602: A8). Hence Wilkinson's conclusion that 'God neuer commeth so néere a mans soule as when he entreth in by the doore of the eare' (1602: A8), and his warning:

> Wee must not think our eares are giuen vs for worldly vses onely, to harken after our profit, to listen to him that can teach vs a Gospell of gold, that can tickle our eares with musicke, or our mindes with vnhonest mirth. (1602: A5v)

Towards the end of his sermon Wilkinson denounces the 'vnhonest mirth' derived from having one's ears 'tickled at a play' and condemns playhouses as 'tabernacle[s] of wickednesse' (1602: C4v), as opposed to the churches, which are the 'house of god', where the congregation listens to the preacher's words.

In keeping with Wilkinson's distinction between having one's ears tickled by a preacher or by a player is a more general attempt among contemporary detractors of the theatre to separate theatrical performance from legitimate oratory aimed at teaching, converting and persuading the listeners to embrace virtue and theological truth. William Prynne, for example, drew a distinction in *Histrio-Mastix* (1633, STC 20464a) between 'Orators', who 'speak onely to the eare' and whose job it is to 'expresse, to describe the things they speake of in an elegant flexanimous phrase, and grave elocution' and 'Roscius the Actor', who 'represent[s] things to the eye' (6C3v). However, Prynne (perhaps inadvertently) used the same term – 'flexanimous', which is defined in Thomas Blount's 1656 *Glossographia* (B3334) as 'easily bent or turned', thus harking back to Wright's notion of the human voice as 'flexible and pliable' – to describe both the orator and 'that flexanimous rhetoricall Stage-elocution', that is 'that lively action and representation of the Players ... which .. pierce deeply into the Spectators eyes, their eares and lewde affections' (1633: 6C3v).

Stage players in Shakespeare's time may have retained some level of geographical and social variation, as currently assumed, but anti-theatricalist tracts suggest that their speech generally came across as elevated and peacock-like, because of their tendency to sound like their betters. The controversial and bitterly censured use of 'usual speech' on the early modern stage therefore makes the occurrence of deviations from it all the more noteworthy. The next section of this chapter accordingly focuses on the cultural connotations that Shakespeare's contemporaries attached to national, regional and class variations and how they were used on the early modern stage.

§

'Dark Words':[12] National and Regional Phonetic Variation on the Shakespearean Stage

The most prominent and debated aspect of the English language in Shakespeare's time was its variability. Among others, historian and antiquarian John Stow commented on variation in terms that encompass

[12] Quoted from Philemon Holland's 1603 translation of Plutarch, *Moralia* (STC 20063): 'take heed rather, & see whether Plato hath not covertly under these dark words lisped and signified somewhat that is pertinent and proper unto you' (3S6).

wonder and frustration in equal measure: 'it is a thing very rare and maruellous, that in one Iland there should be such varietie of speeches' (1580, A3v). Variety, not problematic per se, often struck Shakespeare's contemporaries as a barrier to common understanding: writing about 'the fourth and last part of Brytaine named *Cornwal*', Stow explains how the different parts of Britain are simultaneously bound and divided by the languages spoken by their inhabitants:

> Their tong is far dissonant from English, but it is much like to the Walsh tong, bicause they haue many words common to both tongs: yet this difference there is betwéen them, when a Walsh man speaketh, the Cornish man rather vnderstandeth manie words spoken by the Walshman, than the whole tale he telleth, whereby it is manifest, that those thrée people doe vnderstand one another, in like maner as ye Southern Scots doe perceiue and vnderstand the Northern. (1580: A3v)

The boundaries between the languages spoken in the different parts of Britain, as surveyed by Stow, were fluid and produced variations within English itself. Each English national variation carried specific connotations, which changed rapidly during the early modern period because of England's shifting relations with its neighbours.

Regional variation added to the 'rare and maruellous' linguistic diversity discussed by Stow. In line with Stow's efforts to map out the main linguistic areas in early modern Britain, several of his contemporaries surveyed and classified the main dialects spoken in England. John Bullokar, for example, defined 'dialect' as 'a difference of some words, or pronunciation in any language: as in England the *Dialect* or manner of speech in the North, is different from that in the South, and the Western Dialect differing from both' (1616: E8v–F1). Similarly, clergyman and author Richard Rogers notes how 'we Englishmen, namely southerne and northward, differ much one from another in our dialect or manner of pronouncing, though we all speake one language' (1615: 3G2v). Rogers, like Bullokar, refrained from commenting on the respective qualities of the 'southerne' or 'nortward' dialects. Conversely, Alexander Gil, who classified English dialects as 'Communis [the general], Borealium [the Northern], Australium [the Southern], Orientalium [the Eastern], Occidentalium [the Western], and Poetica [the Poetic]' (1619: 102), wrote openly in favour of the general and the poetic dialects as representative of the standard spoken by the learned elite. Gil branded the other dialects as barbarous because he felt that they lacked in clarity, elegance and sophistication, both in terms of their vocabulary and, crucially, their pronunciation.

A similar, socially inflected bias emerges in Richard Carew's writings, especially when the latter writes about the 'English speach' spoken in Cornwall. Carew describes it as 'good and pure' when spoken as 'receyu [ed] . . . from the best hands of [the] Gentry, and the Easterne Marchants'. He however adds that local speakers

> disgrace it, in part, with a broad and rude accent, and eclipsing (somewhat like the Somersetshire men) specially in pronouncing the names: as Thomas they call *Tummas & Tubby*: Mathew, *Mathaw*: Nicholas, *Nichlaaz*: Reignald, *Reinold*: Dauid, *Daaui*: Mary, *Maari*: Frauncis, *Frowncis*. (1602: P4)

Speakers from the South West of England were indeed notorious for their broad regional accent. Well known is John Aubrey's reference to Sir Walter Ralegh's West Country burr: 'Old Sir Thomas Malett', as Aubrey explains, 'knew Sir Walter and I heard him say, that notwithstanding his great Mastership in style, and his conversation with the learnedest and politest persons, yet he spoke broad Devonshire to his dyeing day' (Buchanan-Brown 2000: 270).

Worth stressing is the distinction that Aubrey draws between *what* Ralegh says and *how* he sounds. Ralegh's 'Mastership in style' is often remarked upon in contemporary accounts of his life: in *Fragmenta Regalia*, Robert Naunton describes Ralegh as possessing 'a strong naturall wit, and a better judgement, with a bold and plausible tongue' (1870 [1653]:48) and then reports how Ralegh impressed Elizabeth I, when he was summoned by the Privy Council to settle a 'variance' with Thomas Grey of Wilton, Lord Deputy of Ireland:

> (what advantage he had in the cause I know not) but he had much better in the telling of his tale; and so much, that the Queen and the Lords took no slight mark of the man, and his parts; for from thence . . . the Queen . . . began to be taken with his elocution, and loved to hear his reasons to her demands: and the truth is, she took him for a kind of Oracle. (1870 [1653]: 49)

These contemporary references to Ralegh's distinctive idiolect show that, while his 'style' and 'elocution' gave him an edge over his adversaries, his Devonshire accent still marked him off as an outlier.

The link between regional accents and notions of 'strangeness' and 'peregrinity' is powerfully evoked in Robert Ashley's translation of Louis Le Roy's *Of the Interchangeable Course, or Variety of Things in the Whole World*, where Le Roy comments on the changeable quality of languages, both over time and among contemporary speakers of the same language:

> But howbeit they change vncessantly, and that in the same Countrey and language, there appeareth in short time a difference both in speaking, and pronouncing: yet euery where there are somethat speake finer, and purer then the rest. (1594: E6)

The 'finer' speakers are not only learned but also metropolitan. 'It is certaine', Le Roy adds, 'that in Athens there was but one language, and . . . yet the speach of the common people was not so pure, as that of men of calling, and the ciuiler sort'. However, Le Roy then goes on to note that, as reported by Tully in the third book of his *Orator*, even when 'the learning of the Athenians was lost in Athens . . . an vnlearned Athenian [still] excelled the most learned of Asia, not in words but in sound of the voice; and not so much in speaking wel, as in pronouncing sweetly' (1594: E6). The more remote regions are from the metropolitan centre, where learned speakers share a common dialect, or 'usual speech', the more their pronunciation is deemed to be extravagant and barbarous.

The same paradigm applied to early modern London. George Puttenham, as mentioned above, described 'usual speech' as the 'speach of the Court, and that of London and the shires lying about London within lx. myles, and not much aboue' (1589: R3r). However, Puttenham was also starting to sound socially biased, as he condemned 'the speech of a craftes man or carter', because, even when 'inhabitant or bred in the best towne and Citie in this Realme', 'the inferiour sort . . . abuse[d] good speeches by strange accents or ill shapen soundes, and false ortographie' (1589: R2v). Similarly, he regarded the English spoken by gentlemen throughout the country as less than 'natural' and 'pure', not because he doubted that 'in euery shyre of England there be gentlemen and others that speake but specially write as good Southerne as we of Middlesex and Surrey do', but because even 'the gentlemen and also their learned clarkes do for the most part condescend' to the English spoken by the 'common people' who live there (R3r). Although not firmly and exclusively associated with social prestige nor taken to stand for the standard pronunciation that every speaker should aim to acquire, 'usual speech' was nevertheless singled out as more 'natural' and 'pure' than other variations, which denoted vulgarity and eccentricity.

Having established the prominence accorded to 'usual speech' on the early modern stage and the widening of the gap between this emerging standard and the lower status attributed to other regional variations, I now want to turn to the sophisticated, if occasional, deployment of stage versions of national, regional and class variations in contemporary drama. Playwrights were alert to the cultural connotations carried by (stage) dialects and phonetic variation and, as the rest of this chapter will show, used them to achieve varied and nuanced dramatic effects. The relative neglect of the role played by phonetic variation in early modern drama is at least partly due to its perceived sparseness. As mentioned above, its relatively low frequency is undoubtedly linked to the gradual emergence of written and spoken standards. Also worth noting is the extent to which print can be expected to reproduce aural aspects of theatrical performance, including phonetic variation. Early modern theatre historians and performance studies scholars now tend to agree with Stephen Orgel that, if the play is a book, it is not a play (2006: 13–54). Orgel has, in other words, quite rightly stressed the distance between text and performance, between what we can reasonably assume happened on stage and what was eventually reproduced on the page of early modern playbooks. It seems therefore reasonable to assume that regional variation may not have been systematically recorded by composing playwrights or scribes and that the printed texts reproduce a minimal level of notation, which may not reflect the extent to which the actor's voice conveyed regional variation on stage.[13] It is however certainly the case that characters in early modern plays *use* and *hear* variation and accents, and respond to them, even when the text of the dialogue as reproduced in the early modern playbook registers none.[14]

A notable exception is the so-called Irish scene in *The Life and Death of Captain Thomas Stukeley* (Anon. 1605a, STC 23405). This scene survives as two variant versions, one written in English (D2v–D3) and the other in Irish dialect (D3–D4). The dialogue spoken outside Dundalk by the Irish insurgents – Shane O'Neill, O'Hanlon, and Neil McKenna, O'Neill's secretary – is different in the two versions, but the overlaps effectively highlight differences between the early modern standard English used throughout the play (and in the English version of this scene) and its Hiberno-English variant.

---

[13] See also Dillon 1994.

[14] An interesting example occurs in the Folio version of *The Merry Wives of Windsor* (1623a: STC 22273; henceforth F1), where Falstaff laments his humiliation at the hands of a 'Welsh Fairy' at TLN 2564. The spelling preserved in the Folio does not alert the reader to the fact that the fairy is in fact Sir Hugh Evans in disguise: 'Wher's *Bede*? Go you, and, where you find a maid/That ere she sleepe has thrice her prayers said,/Raise vp the Organs of her fantasie,/Sleepe she as sound as carelesse infancie,/But those as sleepe, and thinke not on their sins,/Pinch them armes, legs, backes, shoulders, sides, & shins. . . . Pray you lock hand in hand: your selues in order [set;]/And twenty glow-wormes shall our Lanthornes bee/To guide our Measure round about the Tree./But stay, I smell a man of middle earth' (TLN 2532–7, 2560–3). The shorter version of this exchange in the Quarto version (1602: STC 22299; henceforth Q1) signals phonetic variation – '*Pead*' for '*Bede*' and 'plew' for 'blue' in a line on G2v that corresponds roughly to TLN 2537. See also footnote 18 and footnote 22, for more details about the theory of 'scribal regularization . . . in the theatrical manuscript that was transcribed to be used as printer's copy for F1' (Wells and Taylor 1987: 342).

When, for example, the insurgents report hearing 'One [that] coughs within', McKenna mocks the English and the weakness of their constitution and diet: 'These English churles die if they lacke there bed, / and bread and beere porrage and powdred beefe' (Anon. 1605a: D3). The Irish version is slightly shorter, but displays recognizable stage-Irish forms, as 'dees' for dies' and 'lee' for 'lie': 'The English churle dees if he get not bread and porrage and a hose to lee in' (Anon. 1605a: D3v). Similarly, in the English version O'Hanlon suspects that they will not be able to surprise the English and enter the city, because their 'spies within' are not giving them the agreed signal to advance: 'Our labour lost, for we can see no signe / of any white that hangeth ouer the wall' (Anon. 1605a: D2v). This time the Irish version is a bit longer and more elaborate: 'The siegne is a paire Of feete trouzes, or a feete shurt, or some feete blankead, To be hang oote ober the valles, fan we sall be let in At the lettle Booygh dore by the abbay' (Anon. 1605a: D3v). Once again, the forms of the Irish dialect used here are easily recognizable: 'feete' for 'white'; 'valles' for 'wall'; and 'ober' for 'over'. The inclusion of this scene in two versions in the first quarto of 1605 attests to potentially deliberate changes in the staging of this scene and to readerly interest in the Irish dialect, even in its imprecise rendition in a stage play.

The survival in print of the two versions of this scene is all the more significant in light of the fact that Hiberno-English is generally among the most sparsely recorded variation and the most openly condescended by English speakers who comment on it. Quite crass is, for example, the treatment of the Irish dialect in Thomas Dekker's *Old Fortunatus* (1600, STC 6517). In this play, a Scottish and a French lord, Montrose and Longaville, whose speech is unmarked by foreign or regional inflections, are conned by Fortunatus's reckless son, Andelocia, and by Shadow, his servant, when, disguised as 'Irish coster-mongers', they sell them 'féene Tamasco peepeins' (1600: I1). Agripyne, King Athelstane's daughter, is alarmed by their accent and warns the other courtiers: 'These Irishmen, / Some say, are great dissemblers, and I feare, / These two the badge of their owne countrie weare' (1600: I1v). She is nevertheless tricked by Andelocia and Shadow, and, like Montrose and Longaville, she buys their fine apples for their assumed miraculous powers. The Scottish and the French lords are mocked for their vanity – Montrose buys an apple believing that it will give him a 'sweet and strong countenance' because he wants to 'conquer men by strength and women by love' (1600: I2), while Longaville wishes to become 'wondrous wise' (1600: I2) – but their speech remains unmarked throughout. The Irish accent is instead heavily marked, as shown by Andelocia's response to Agripyne's slanderous remark about the Irish:

> By my trat, and by Saint Patrickes hand, and as Créez saue me la, tis no
> dissembler: de Irish man now and den cut di countrie-mans throate, but yet
> in fayt hee loue di countrie-man, tis no dissembler: dis féene Tamasco apple
> can make di swéete countenance, but I can take no lesse but thrée crownes
> for one, I weare out my naked legs and my footes, and my tods, and run
> hidder and didder to Tamasco for dem. (1600: I1v)

Most forms – 'Créez' for 'Christ'; 'hee' for 'he'; 'féene' for 'fine; and 'dis' /
'de' for 'this' / 'the' – represent the Hiberno-English spoken by English
speakers from Ireland only approximately, but are in keeping with how the
Irish dialect was represented in other plays from the period, whether it is
spoken by Irish speakers or put on by non-Irish speakers.

   That the Irish dialect spoken on the early modern stage is the least
varied and nuanced out of the other English dialects under consideration
was most likely due to the strained relations between England and Ireland
at a time when rampant English colonial expansionism was met by
sustained and belligerent resistance on Irish soil. While Blank's conclu-
sions that Irish is very nearly absent from Renaissance English literature
has been effectively queried,[15] her corollary according to which the Irish
dialect is marginalized or reduced to caricature seems closer to the
mark. An important and well-known exception is the role played by
speakers of Hiberno-English in Ben Jonson's *Irish Masque at Court*
(1616, STC 14751).

   The bumbling Irish footmen – Dennis, Dermock, Donnell and
Patrick – speak in a heavily inflected variation that suggests simplicity
and lack of education, if not downright abjection. Although seemingly
harmless, the footmen's comic dispute as to who 'ish te vesht man of hish
tongue' (1616: 2P4) effectively delays the beginning of the dance at the
heart of the masque. Also worth noting is that the footmen share their
marked speech with the Irish citizen who speaks just before them. Like
Andelocia and Shadow in *Old Fortunatus*, this character introduces himself
as a costermonger: 'me name is *Dennish,* I sherve ti Mayesties owne
cashtermonger, be me trote; and cry peep'sh, and pomwater'sh i'th
Mayesties shervice, tis five year now' (1616: 2P4). As Helen Burke

---

[15] Cf. for example, Palmer 2001: 'It is hardly an exaggeration to say that the Elizabethan texts make
Irish-speakers mute. But what remains when speech is denied is not necessarily silence. The mute
are not noiseless and these texts are full of strange, disturbing sounds: cries, yelps, groans,
strangulated shots, whispers. ... The Elizabethans responded to their lack of understanding by
evacuating language of its semantic component. They registered only sounds divorced from sense in
an ideologically charged manœuvre that transformed speech into a clatter on nonsense syllables. For
there can be no doubt that what are called "cries", with its implication of pre-linguistic
vocalizations, are, in fact, utterances fully shaped in language'. (64–5)

explains, '[f]ruit vending was . . . one of the typical occupations of the poor Irish in London at the time' and the character of the citizen 'anticipat[es] anxieties about the growing numbers of Irish immigrant communities seeking employment in the capital' (2011: 32–3).

The footmen's tardiness in clearing the stage for the masquers and the coarseness conveyed by the heavily marked speech they share with the Irish citizen are complicated by the fact that other Irish characters in the masque, namely the bard and 'the civil gentleman of the [Irish] nation' who leads the delegation of Irish ambassadors-masquers, are, as James Knowles has recently pointed out, 'notably loyal . . . and not simply the barbarian other' (2015: 80). Furthermore, as James M. Smith has argued, the footmen's unruliness and their heavily marked language align them with the Old English settlers, who were Catholic and resembled the native Irish in their customs, manners and speech (1998: 302). The Old English settlers, as much as the native Irish, resisted the settlement of the New English colonial administration. Tensions between the Old English and the New English settlers came to a head when the former obstructed the proceedings of Parliament in Dublin on 18 May 1613, a few months before Jonson's masque was staged at White Hall, as part of the celebrations for the wedding of Frances Howard and James's favourite, Robert Carr, on 29 December 1613. According to David Lindley, the footmen therefore embody the 'disorderly Parliamentary proceeding[s]' in Dublin that then led a delegation of Old English settlers to travel to London to petition James (1986: 355). By the time Jonson's masque was staged, members of this delegation had been arrested (Smith 1998: 303). So when the 'civil Gentleman' banishes the footmen at the end of the antimasque, Jonson is paying homage to James and the rule of the New English administration in Ireland. But the complexity of Jonson's treatment of Hiberno-English in this play reveals contemporary anxieties about ongoing events, which were to affect Anglo-Irish relations more than a decade after the end of the Nine-Year War had marked a crushing defeat for the Irish insurgents. More generally, Jonson's complex representation of Irishness in this masque shows how subtly marked and unmarked speech could be used to suggest the interplay between civility and barbarism across contested national borders.

The importance of context in evaluating the use of Hiberno-English in Jonson's masque suggests that the exceptional level of attention paid to this variation in *Captain Thomas Stukeley* may also be due to the fact that the play was originally performed in the mid-1590s and then revised around 1599, at the height of the Nine-Year War led by Irish chieftains like Hugh

O'Neill. Whatever set of circumstances led to the performance and publication of both versions of the Irish scene in *Captain Thomas Stukeley* and of Jonson's *Irish Masque*, they attest to the significance that even a marginalized and caricatured national variation like Hiberno-English could carry on the early modern stage, when deployed to represent complex national relations at times of military conflict or great diplomatic tension.

The two case studies that follow in the second half of this chapter similarly highlight a nuanced use of nationally and regionally marked voices. As with the Hiberno-English variation discussed above, these case studies show how another national variation, Anglo-Welsh, and a regional variation, Southern English, were used to fine-tune characterization or to add layers of complexity or irony to the dramatic situation. These case studies focus on the characterization of Sir Hugh Evans in *The Merry Wives of Windsor* and Edgar's use of a Southern English dialect in *King Lear* in order to show how stage versions of national and regional variations were deployed to achieve specific effects. Phonetic variation in these two plays, and in other contemporary plays which I compare and contrast with them in each case study, sets some speakers apart from other characters, thus creating a layered acoustic context within which individual voices take on specific, local connotations. These connotations, in turn, give us a point of access into how marked voices were heard within the fictive world of these plays and by their original audiences.

§

'Good Worts? Good Cabidge': The Butt of the Joke in *The Merry Wives of Windsor*

The Anglo-Welsh dialect was first extensively used in Shakespeare in *The Merry Wives of Windsor* and *Henry V*.[16] While Captain Fluellen has attracted sympathetic and subtle re-interpretations, as exceeding an 'ethnic stereotype' (Maley and Schwyzer 2010: 4) and standing for 'Harry's historical conscience' (Blank 1996: 139), Sir Hugh Evans in *The*

---

[16] Huw Griffiths, querying Gary Taylor's claim that 'Shakespeare was the first Elizabethan dramatist to attempt a Welsh accent', mentions, but only in passing, earlier plays, including George Peele's *Edward I* (1593), Thomas Dekker's *The Welsh Ambassador* (1597 [sic]) and *The Patient Grissill* (1600), and *Sir John Oldcastle* (c.1599), which include fragments of Welsh dialect, where Welshness is represented 'either through the mispronunciations of "Welsh" characters or by a particular affinity between Welshness, music and poetry' (2010: 113).

Merry Wives of Windsor needs careful reconsideration. Even critics who detect a 'degree of cultural hybridity' in the play (Shrank 2012: 583) tend to associate Evans primarily with Doctor Caius, the French physician, as comically marked and linguistically incompetent non-English speakers.[17] However, the play draws an important distinction between Evans's control and understanding of the English language and Caius's lack thereof: although both characters *sound* different and their speech is uniquely marked by orthographic variation, Evans is mocked for how he sounds while Caius is ridiculed both for how he sounds and for what he says (or fails to say or grasp). Caius, in other words, is indeed linguistically incompetent; Evans, on the other hand, is aware of his accent and can also turn it to his own advantage. Even more crucially, he is not only tolerated by his English neighbours, but joins them in punishing those who threaten the social cohesion *and* the linguistic decorum of their community. All in all, phonetic variation in Evans's role shows how effectively nuanced the stage use of the Anglo-Welsh accent and dialect was from its very inception on the Shakespearean stage.

Anglo-Welsh was far less caricatured on the early modern stage than generally assumed, and certainly less so than other national variations.[18] As well as offering a re-reading of Evans and his role in *The Merry Wives of*

---

[17] See also Tudeau-Clayton 2010. Similarly Griffiths, who argues that the clown Robert Armin, rather than Shakespeare, may be the sole originator of the Welsh accent as represented on the Shakespearean stage, associates the performance of Welshness with comic caricature, as it is indeed the case in Armin's own play, *The Two Maids of Moore-clacke* (1609, STC 773). However, Griffiths acknowledges that the current dating of *Merry Wives* precludes Armin's involvement (2010: 113).

[18] As explained earlier, Hiberno-English dialects and accents were mostly negatively connotated or caricatured, due to the vexed quality of Anglo-Irish relations in the period. Scottish dialects and accents, on the other hand, while generally mocked as broad and uncouth in late Elizabethan plays, like *The Reign of King Edward III* (see also Introduction, p. 1), were more positively represented, when it became clear that James VI of Scotland was likely to succeed Elizabeth I. Sympathetic Scots from late Elizabethan drama include Captain Jamy in Shakespeare's *Henry V*, or Jockie, Mistress Shore's loyal footman in Thomas Heywood's *1* and *2 Edward IV* (1599, STC 13341). Incidentally, *1 & 2 Edward IV* proved very popular among early modern audiences and readers, as suggested by the fact that the first quarto edition of 1599 was reprinted four times during James's reign. Its popularity therefore challenges the theory that the use of Scottish dialect was systematically removed from the stage and from printed playbooks from the turn of the century onwards as a form of respect towards the future king. See, for example, Blank: 'the disappearance of Scots from English literature during James's rule suggests that the portrayal of dialect itself was considered a sort of slander' (1996: 161). More helpfully, Lauren Mary Stewart lists occasional lines in Scottish dialect in Thomas Middleton's manuscript play *The Witch* (c. 1616) and in John Fletcher, Francis Beaumont, and Philip Massinger's *Thierry and Theodoret* (1621, STC 11074) (2011: 49–55). All in all, while the harsh measures taken against the authors of *Eastward Ho!* (1605, STC 4970) for referring to the Scots as 'no greater friends to English men and *England*, [than] when they are out an't' (E3v) confirm Blank's views, one should entertain the possibility that (self)censorship may not lie behind the omission of Captain Jamy from the quarto editions of Shakespeare's *Henry V*, since

Windsor, this case study considers other instances of stage Welsh in order to show how the specificity of Anglo-Welsh relations in the late medieval and early modern periods had a direct impact on the status accorded to Welsh in contemporary (theatrical) culture. The first Act of Union of 1536 had enforced the use of English for administrative and legal purposes throughout Wales, but Elizabeth I had authorized a Welsh translation of the Bible in 1563. Equally crucial was the claim that Tudor and Stuart monarchs shared Welsh ancestors and lines of descent from the ancient, unassimilated Britons who had resisted the Roman and the Saxon invasions. Besides, the relatively peaceful and settled quality of the political and cultural relations between England and Wales had made the Acts of Union of 1536 and 1542 seem at least ostensibly more like integration than annexation or colonial conquest.[19] Despite the suppression of Welsh as the official language of government in Wales, Welsh continued to be spoken not only in Wales, but also in London. Following the Acts of the Union, 'there was hardly one sphere of activity into which Welshmen did not penetrate,' giving rise to what historians have described as the 'Welsh colonization of English professions' (Dyfnallt Owen, quoted in Wilson 2010: 262).[20] Unsurprisingly, therefore, Welsh characters, whose speech is marked by distinctive features, including *b*, *d*, and *g* for *p*, *t* and *k* (as in 'pridge' for 'bridge'), *f* for *v* (as in 'falorous' for 'valorous'), or *sh* for *j* (as in 'Shesu' for 'Jesus'), are often comic, but they are not necessarily the butt of the joke, nor are they simply patronized.

Evans is the best example of the complex status and social standing accorded to Welsh characters in the period. Far from being denigrated and ostracized, Evans is firmly part of his local community, whose cohesion is cemented by the ritual expulsion (and re-integration) of Sir John Falstaff, when the latter threatens it. Evans does not only take part in the 'ferry

this brief but memorable role in the longer version of the play eventually published in the First Folio of 1623 (STC 22273) is positively flattering.

[19] As John Kerrigan explains, 'Henry VIII's incorporation of Wales had the paradoxical effect of producing, for the first time, a coherent Welsh domain ... Locally controlled by a Council in the Marches based at Ludlow, Wales was also peculiarly subject to the crown, because Henry VIII preserved powers to govern it without legislation passing through the Westminster parliament' (2008: 117).

[20] Because Welsh, even more than other English dialects, was commonly spoken in London, both actors and their audiences can safely be assumed to have included Welsh speakers among them or to have at the very least been able to reproduce and to understand the Welsh dialect (Lloyd 2010). The orthographic traces that Welsh (and other dialects) left on the printed pages of early modern plays may therefore constitute a woefully inadequate counterpart of what early modern audiences heard in the theatre.

honest knaveries' (TLN 2208)[21] that lead to Falstaff's third and final humiliation at Hern's Oak in Windsor Park at the hands of the merry wives; from the very opening of the play, Evans has in fact his own reasons for wanting to disgrace Falstaff, as the only character who is openly uncooperative and confrontational in his exchanges with him. Fastaff, for example, mocks Evans even when Evans agrees that Justice Shallow should not bring his grievances to the attention of the Star Chamber. Evans's line – '*Pauca verba*, (Sir John) good worts' (TLN 116) – is mocked by Falstaff – 'Good worts? good Cabidge' (TLN 117)[22] – and routinely misread by critics who rather oddly assume that Evans, the tutor who teaches William Page Latin in 4.1, mistranslates the Latin phrase he has just used.[23] Evans is in fact praising Falstaff for *concisely* summing up the very same point of view which he had expressed earlier in the same scene: Falstaff's ironic remark, "Twere better for you if it were known in councell: you'll be laugh'd at' (TLN 114–15) matches Evans's advice: 'It is not meet the Councell heare a Riot' (TLN 37–8).[24] Falstaff however refuses to acknowledge Evans's willingness to help him pacify Shallow.

Conversely, when Evans interacts with the other characters in this scene, his pronunciation is seamlessly integrated into witty repartees that acknowledge Evans's status as a competent speaker. In the opening exchange with Shallow and his nephew, Master Abraham Slender, Evans encourages skilful word play. When, for example, Slender mentions 'the dozen white Luces in

---

[21] Variants from Q1 (1602) are recorded in footnotes, when Q1 includes a counterpart to the Folio lines under consideration. Q1 variants are only discussed in detail when they preserve alternative spellings that heighten or qualify the phonetic spelling used in F1 to mark Evans's inflected speech.

[22] Here Q1 reads: '*Sir Hu.* Good vrdes sir *Iohn*, good vrdes. / *Fal.* Good vrdes, good Cabidge'. (A3v) As in F1, Falstaff's pun depends on the double meaning of 'worts' / 'vrdes' as 'worts', that is vegetables of the cabbage family (*OED, n*2), and 'words', pronounced as 'worts' in stage Anglo-Welsh by Evans.

[23] See, for example, Craik 83. The same sort of warped logic is applied to readings of Evans's apparent failure to recognize a Biblical allusion in Pistol's line, 'He hears with ears' (TLN 138). See, for example, Melchiori 1999: 134. However, it makes more sense for a parson like Evans to take offence at Pistol's clearly blasphemous use of the Scriptures and for him to allude to the proverbial commonplace that 'the devil can cite Scripture for his purpose', as Antonio puts it in *The Merchant of Venice* (1.3.90). Evans's remark, 'The Teuill and his Tam: what phrase is this? he heares with eare? why, it is affectations' (TLN 139–40), seems a perfectly apt response, especially in light of the fact that 'affectation', which generally meant 'the putting on of airs' (*OED n*2a), was also used, in a religious context, to suggest 'the pretended or counterfeit assumption of some characteristic idea' and therefore 'simulation or pretence' (*OED n*2b). See, for example, Thomas Norton's translation of Calvin's *The Institution of the Christian Religion*: 'In all ages that irreligious affectation of religion ... hath shewed and yet dothe shewe fourthe it selfe, that menne do alwaye delyte to inuente a waye to obtayne ryghteousnesse bysyde the woorde of God'. (1561: 46v)

[24] '*Fal.* Twere better for you twere knowne in (counsell, / Youle be laught at'. (B3v); there is no counterpart to Evans's advice as phrased at TLN 37–8 in Q1.

their Coate [of arms]', and Shallow adds, 'It is an olde Coate', Evans puns on the double meanings activated by his accent: 'The dozen white Lowses doe become an old Coat well' (TLN 21–2). Evans's pun here depends on the fact that 'Coat' is also the Welsh pronunciation of 'Coad', or 'cod', a salt-water fish, which he juxtaposes to 'luce', which, in its heraldic designation, from the French, means 'pike', a fresh-water fish.[25] Far from cutting him off or mocking him, as Falstaff does later in this scene, Shallow redundantly explicates the pun: 'The Luse is the fresh-fish, the salt fish, is an old Coate' (TLN 24–5). The punning here is a collaborative linguistic endeavour that requires wit on the part of speakers like Evans, at the expense of other speakers like Slender. The punning produces pleasure for the listeners as decoders of the multiple meanings supported by Evans's inflected pronunciation. In the very next exchange, Slender's suggestion that he 'may quarter' (TLN 26) the coat of arms is once again taken up by Shallow, who rejoins, 'You may, by marrying' (TLN 27). When Evans, sensing the opportunity for another pun, says, 'It is marring indeed, if he quarter it' (TLN 28), and Shallow is not quick enough to grasp or sustain the pun, Evans is not put off by the latter's literal-minded reply, 'Not a whit' (TLN 29), and proceeds instead to explain it to him: 'Yes, per-lady: if he ha's a quarter of your coat, there is but three Skirts for your selfe, in my simple coniectures' (TLN 30–2). Evans's conjectures are in fact far from simple: Evans may pronounce his 't's as 'd's and his 'b's as 'p's and vice versa, but he also deploys his Welsh accent in order to generate word play that depends on it to work.

Variation in the opening scene is therefore used to increase the potential for punning and wordplay, which would simply not be possible among English speakers. Variation does not limit but enhances Evans's competence as an *English* speaker. What makes Falstaff a threat to Evans's sense of belonging to his English-speaking community is precisely the former's unwillingness to acknowledge Evans's mastery of the English language. Ironically, all those critics and directors who regard Evans's marked speech as a mere caricature unwittingly endorse Falstaff's contempt for Evans. This critical blind-spot in readings of Evans is all the more ironic, since Falstaff is harshly punished not only for attempting to seduce the merry

---

[25] Editors conjecture scribal regularization here, so F's 'Coat' probably read 'Coad' in the theatrical manuscript that was transcribed to be used as printer's copy for F1. See, for example, the Oxford Shakespeare editors: 'it is widely agreed the humour [here] depends on Evans mispronouncing 'coat' with a '-d' sound' (Wells and Taylor 1987: 342). While the 1986 Oxford Shakespeare edition read 'coad', the 2016 edition has reversed to F, but a commentary note alerts readers that 'Evans's Welsh accent pronounces this word as if it had a '-d' ending, causing Shallow to respond as if Evans said 'cod', a class of fish including the luce' (1.1.15n). See also footnotes 12 and 18 above.

wives but also for slandering Evans's command of the English language. As mentioned above, Falstaff singles out the humiliation he suffers in the final scene at the hands of a 'Welsh Fairy' (TLN 2564) as the lowest point of his comic fall. Falstaff's line, 'Ignorance it selfe is a plummet ore me' (TLN 2649–50), though ultimately obscure, can be taken to mean that Falstaff, who now feels even more worthless than Evans ('Ignorance itself'), continues to overlook the fact that Evans' neighbours do not in fact regard him as 'ignorant' at all.

There are of course other characters in the play who accuse other speakers, including Evans, of maiming the English language. And some of these accusations are not unfounded, although the English spoken by these characters is not unmarked either. Mistress Quickly, for example, rightly predicts that, should her master, Doctor Caius, return home and find Simple, Slender's man, in his house, there would be 'an old abusing of Gods patience, and the Kings English' (TLN 403–4). Doctor Caius, unlike Evans, has only a limited control over the English language. The phonological features of his French-inflected speech are not the only markers that set him apart from native English speakers at Windsor: unlike Evans, he regularly lapses into French, because his English vocabulary is too limited to convey his meaning, as shown by his exchange with the Host of the Garter in 2.3, when the latter dupes him into believing that 'Mock-water' means 'Valour' (TLN 1121) and that to 'Clapper-claw' means to 'make . . . amends' (TLN 1126, 1128). However, even Mistress Quickly's comment on Dr Caius's 'abusing of . . . the Kings English' is qualified by the fact that her English is not flawless either: she notoriously mars words – she uses 'Allicholy' for 'melancholy' (TLN 538) – and even fails to realize that the Latin spoken by Evans and William Page in 4.1 is not English – hence her bawdy mistranslations of '*caret*' as 'a good roote' (TLN 1870–1871), the '*Genitiue case*' as 'Ginyes case' (TLN 1875–1876), or '*horum*' as 'whore' (TLN 1877, 1879). Also worth stressing is the fact that Mistress Quickly never comments on Evans's Welsh inflection, despite her readiness to pass judgment on Caius's linguistic competence.

The Host of the Garter, on the other hand, erroneously paints Evans and Caius with the same brush. When, having agreed to 'measure' their weapons in preparation for the duel, the Host in fact proceeds to direct Evans and Caius to meet in different locations outside Windsor, he glibly concludes: 'let them keepe their limbs whole, and hack our English' (TLN 1225–6). Once again, as with Mistress Quickly, it is important to note that the Host is far from the proficient speaker he believes himself to be.

The main feature of the Host's unique idiolect is affectation. He often peppers his sentences with foreign words to show off his presumed mastery and knowledge of foreign languages, which is however extremely basic at the best of times. He, for example, correctly uses 'cavaliere', the Italian for 'knight', in relation to Falstaff (as in 'my Knight? my guest-Caualeire', TLN 742–3) but incorrectly in relation to Justice Shallow and Slender, when he calls them 'Caualeiro *Slender*' (TLN 1134) and 'Caualeiro Iustice' (TLN 727,731). Like Falstaff, the Host gets his comeuppance at the hands of the 'injured parties', Caius and Evans. The latter unsurprisingly takes the lead: 'Let us knog our prains together' (TLN 1262–3). The stratagem devised by Caius and Evans is perfectly fitting. They let the Host believe that there are German gentlemen who need to hire his horses to pay homage to a German Duke who is visiting the English court at Windsor. Having established that the German gentlemen speak English and relying on his conviction that the '*Germanes* are honest men' (TLN 2290), the Host is conned and has his horses stolen from him. While the citizens promise to make amends to Falstaff, the Host never gets his horses back, thus suggesting a harsh penalty for his linguistic pretensions and his sense of superiority over Caius and Evans.

All in all, though, Falstaff is the harshest critic of Evans's accent. Even after he has been thoroughly humiliated at Hern's Oak, Falstaff slurs Evans: 'Haue I liu'd to stand at the taunt of one that makes Fritters of English?' (TLN 2628–9). As mentioned above, Falstaff's response to Evans's accent is generally taken to reflect a prevailing bias shared by the other characters in the play, when in fact, this bias is confined to speakers, whose use of English is far from normative. Also generally unnoticed is the fact that, while Falstaff is presumably cured of his predatory urges to seduce the wives, he is not cured of his linguistic prejudice against Evans and that his speech is also marked by what the Host memorably describes 'Anthropophaginian' excess. When Simple arrives at the Garter Inn to talk to Falstaff, the Host warns him that 'hee'l speake like an Anthropophaginian vnto [him]' (TLN 2229–30). Speaking 'like an Anthropophaginian' involves reducing speakers or their speech metaphorically to edible matter. When Falstaff recollects being thrown into the Thames while hidden inside Mistress Ford's buck-basket under 'stinking Cloathes, that fretted in their owne grease', he accordingly describes himself as 'subiect to heate as butter; a man of continuall dissolution, and thaw' (TLN 1781–4). The same qualities that Falstaff attributes to Evans – fritters are portions of batter, sometimes containing apple or meat (*OED n*1) – actually apply to Falstaff's inflated, hyperbolic idiolect. Also significant is the fact that another character who remarks on Evans's accent is Pistol, Falstaff's associate, when, in the opening scene, he refers to the parson as a 'mountaine Forreygner' (TLN 149). Ironically, Falstaff's own use of English marks him out as a threat to the community, within which Evans himself is instead perfectly integrated.[26]

One other type of speaker is singled out for ridicule in the play. Master Page, talking about Nim, memorably says that the latter 'frights English out of its wits' (TLN 678). Nim's speech is crucially not marked by regional variation. What belittles Nim, as much as Slender and his man, Simple, is not dialect or regional accent but his limited control over the English language *as* an English language speaker. In the opening scene Bardolph insinuates that Slender cannot possibly remember who stole his chain, because he had 'drunke himselfe out of his fiue sentences' (TLN 162). Slender, Nim and Simple are poor speakers because they have a narrow vocabulary and fail to detect puns and double-meanings when they interact with other speakers. For example, Slender fails to understand Anne's formulaic question, 'What is your will?', which prompts him to reply: 'I ne're made my Will yet (I thanke Heauen:) I am not such a sickely creature' (TLN 1624, 1626–7). Ironically enough, the one character who corrects Slender when he 'misplaces' is none other than Evans, who also feels compelled to correct Bardolph's comic variation of the proverbial phrase 'to be frightened (scared) out of one's wits (five wits or seven senses)' (Tilley W583). From much vilified 'corrupter of words', Evans, on closer inspection, can be seen to act as a custodian of the 'King's English', warts/worts and all!

Shakespeare does refer to some well-known stereotypes about the Welsh, which may in turn have encouraged readings of Evans as a stage type or ethnic caricature. Evans, for example, having dispatched Simple to Doctor Caius's house in 1.2, then hastens back to dine at Master Page's house, because 'ther's Pippins and Cheese to come' (TLN 297–8). The predilection of the Welsh for cheese – baked, roasted, toasted or otherwise – was proverbial in Shakespeare's time (Eschenbaum and Correll 2016: 26). Similarly, Evans is bound to prompt uproarious laughter, when he sings a few lines from Christopher Marlowe's very popular poem, 'A Passionate Shepherd to his Love', in order to keep calm, as he waits for his opponent, Doctor Caius, in 3.1: '*To shallow Ruiers* [sic] *to whose falls:*

---

[26] Tudeau-Clayton has also pointed out how 'Falstaff ... is ... an enemy to good language' (2010: 109).

melodious Birds sings Madrigalls: There will we make our Peds of Roses . . .'
(TLN 1174–6). However, interpreting (and performing) Evans as a witty,
linguistically competent, and socially integrated member of his community
will only become possible when the character is no longer reduced to the
comic caricature which scholars and directors alike still associate with his
stage dialect.

The general tendency among Shakespeareans and early modern drama
scholars is still, by and large, to regard the annotation of Welsh and other
dialects and accents in early modern plays like *The Merry Wives of Windsor*
as sporadic, inconsistent and condescending towards those who speak
them. It is therefore important to contextualize this re-reading of Evans
by considering other characters who speak with a distinctly Welsh accent
in later plays. Scholars who have discussed Welsh speakers in Jacobean and
Stuart drama have generally dismissed them as 'parroting' the stage dialect
first used by Shakespeare in *The Merry Wives of Windsor* and *Henry V*
(Maley and Schwyzer 2010: 4). However, these characters, like Evans,
exceed caricature. Among them, the title characters in *The Valiant
Welshman* (1615; STC 16) and *The Welsh Ambassador* (c. 1623) reveal a
similarly complex and nuanced use of the Welsh dialect.

In *The Valiant Welshman*, the title-character, Caradoc, which is based
on the historical Caradoc the Great, has no Welsh accent. His nobility is
matched by the terse, elevated, and unmarked quality of his speech
throughout the play. His cousin, the loyal, bold, good-natured Lord
Morgan, Earl of Anglesey, is the only character in the play whose speech
is inflected, as signalled by orthographic features in his first speech, which
also establishes his Welshness by means of recognizable culinary
stereotypes:

> As for the Rebell *Monmouth*, I kanow very well what I will do with her.
> I will make Martlemas beefe on her flesh, and false dice on her pones
> for euery Conicatcher: I warrant her for Case bobby and Metheglin:
> I will make her pate ring noone for all her resurrections and rebellions.
> (1615: B2 7–12)

Morgan pronounces 'bones' as 'pones' and uses 'her' as a generic pronoun
that applies indifferently to a variety of numbers, persons, and cases.
'Resurrection' for 'insurrections' is a fairly isolated instance of linguistic
incompetence, which adds to the comic quality of this character. Generally, though, Morgan enjoys indulging in puns and wordplay and is
benignly humoured by the other characters in the play, as shown by the
following exchange with Caradoc:

MORGAN	Cousin *Caradoc*, well, in all these pribble prabbles,

MORGAN   Cousin *Caradoc*, well, in all these pribble prabbles,
            I pray you, how dooth our vncle *Cadallan*? bee Cad,
            I heard he had got a knocke: if it bee so, I pray you
            looke that the leane Caniball, what doe you call him
            that / eate vp *Iulius Cesars* and *Pompeyes*: a saucy knaue,
            that cares no more for Kings, then lowsie beggers &
            Chimney-sweepers.
CARADOC   Why, death, man.
MORGAN   I, I, Death, a poxe on her: as Cad shudge mee, hee will
            eate more Emperours and Kings at one meale, then
            some Taylors halfepenny loaues, or Vsurers decayed
            shentlemen in a whole yeare: therefore I pray you
            Cousin, haue a care of her vncle.
CARADOC   He is in heauen already.
MORGAN   In heauen! why did you let her goe thither?
CARADOC   It is a place of rest, and Angels blisse.
MORGAN   Angells! Cots blue-hood: I warrant her, there is ne're a
            Lawyer in the whole orld, but had rather haue eleuen
            shillings, then the best Anshell in heauen.
                                        (1615: B3 32–5, B3v 1–15)

Having struggled to remember the English word for 'death', Morgan then gets carried away by his penchant for punning and quips that lawyers prefer shillings to angels, hinting at the double meaning of the word 'angel' ('ministering spirit or divine messenger', *OED*, *n.*1.; and 'an old English gold coin, ... having as its device the archangel Michael standing upon, and piercing the dragon', *OED*, *n.6*). At least on one occasion, though, the light relief provided by Morgan's tendency to indulge in broad linguistic humour backfires and exposes his dialect as 'barbarous' in its original, etymological sense of '"not Latin nor Greek" and therefore "pertaining to those outside the Roman empire" ... hence "uncivilized, uncultured"' (*OED*, *adj.* 1–3). In the following exchange, Morgan comes across as 'barbarous' because Gallicus, a Roman emissary, fails to understand him:

MORGAN   ... I pray you, from whence come her?
MARCUS   From Rome.
MORGAN   From Rome! And I pray you, what a poxe ayles her, that
            you cannot keepe her at home? haue you any Waspes in
            her tayles? or liue Eeles in her pelly, you cannot keepe
            her at home? Harke you me: I pray you, how toth
            M. *Cesar*? toth he neede era parbour? Looke you now: let
            him come to Wales, and her Cousin *Caradoc* shall trim
            his crownes, I warrant her.
MARCUS   I vnderstand you not.

MORGAN   Cads nayles? Cood people, doth Morgan speake
              Hebrewes or no? Vnderstand her not?
CARADOC   Now, Romane, for thy habit speaks thee so:
              Is it to vs thy message is directed?

                                            (1615: F3v 19–32)

Morgan's marked speech cuts him off from the exchange of official
messages with the Romans, who, as in Shakespeare's *Cymbeline*, threaten
to invade when Britain refuses to pay its tribute to Rome.

On the whole, though, Morgan's speech does not denote lowly social
standing. The '*company of Rustickes*' in 4.3, who, echoing the gravediggers
in *Hamlet*, attempt to establish whether a 'man that has hangde himselfe,
be accessary to his own death or no' (G2v 24–6), have no distinctive
inflection. Similarly, dialect is not a marker of lack of wit, as shown by the
fact that Morgan's foolish son, Morioso, does not speak with a Welsh
accent. Besides, Morgan is loyal to Caradoc even when his own people
betray him. The Welsh dialect therefore seems to be a generational and
cultural marker, denoting an ancient type of loyalty and moral stature, as
well as coarsely expressed but genuine feelings of familial and national
allegiance. In this respect, there is definitely a 'touch' of Fluellen to
Morgan, who fits quite well the king's description of the Welsh captain in
Henry V: 'Though it appeare a little out of fashion, / There is much care
and valour in the Welchman' (1623: TLN 1933). The ancient Britain
represented in the fictive world of this play shows a communion of
language and intent between the English and the Welsh characters, especially as they close ranks against the threat of a foreign invasion. The
Welshness embodied by Morgan becomes the vehicle for the inclusive
ideal of Britishness promoted by King James, which in turn looked back,
nostalgically, to ancient Britain, thus bypassing the more recent history of
the English conquest of Wales under King Edward I in the thirteenth
century and annexation and centralization under the Tudors in the
sixteenth century.

The Welsh Embassador is also set in ancient Britain. This manuscript
play, generally attributed to Thomas Dekker and John Ford (c. 1623),
focuses on the English court of king Athelstane. The king, who already has
a wife, Armante, the Duke of Colchester's daughter, and a son, needs to be
cured of his infatuation for Penda's virtuous wife, Carintha. The king
arranges for Penda to be killed on the battlefield by his captain, Voltimar.
The latter, however, warns Penda and the king's brothers, Edmond and
Eldred, who decide to feign their deaths and return to the English court in
disguise – Penda as the title-character, Eldred as a gentleman from Wales

and Edmond as an Irish footman. Penda refers to their plan, aimed at exposing Athelstane, as 'a Comedy of disguises'. There is undoubtedly an element of parody in the way in which these English noblemen don their fake Welsh and Irish identities. The coarseness of the Welsh-inflected English spoken by Penda and Eldred and Eldred's fiery temper are predictably stereotypical: Eldred proves easily offended when he thinks that Voltimar is laughing at him and Penda apologizes for his lack of sophistication as a speaker:

> [I]n wales (oh magnanimious kinge Athelstanes) wee haue noe vniversities to tawge in vplandish greekes & lattins, wee are not so full of rethoriques as you are heere, & therefore yor greate & masesticall eares was not to looke for fyled oratories & pig high stiles. (c. 1623: fol. 10a)[27]

Having established the credibility of the three noblemen's disguises through ethnic and linguistic stereotypes, the play then goes on to show that the English noblemen in fact share fundamental national traits and qualities with the Welsh and Irish gentlemen they personate. When King Athelstane asks the Duke of Conrwall to tell him what sort of a man the Welsh ambassador is, Conrwall replies:

> ... [T]roath sir a goodly gentleman
> take that rough barke awaie his cuntry gives him
> (yett growes hee straight & smooth) yor self would sweare
> natu[r]e had spent some Curiosity
> ⟨w[hen]⟩ shee made him...
>
>   (c. 1623: fol. 9b)

The ambassador's Welshness is merely the 'bark' that his country of origins gives him, that is an outer layer of roughness that can be stripped away to reveal a 'straight & smooth' core underneath. The core identity that lies beneath the ambassador's outer Welsh roughness is in turn understood as originating in a shared British ancestry. Similarly, when Eldred is asked to identify himself, he reveals his assumed Welsh name, but then he goes on to explain, once again, that what sets him apart from the English noblemen and their king is merely a difference in manners and customs:

> tis Reese ap meridith, ap shon, ap lewellin, ap morris yet noe dancers for awle you are english lords, you are made of noe petter wole then a welse man is, a little finer spunne & petter carded thats awle; o[u]r pludd is as well dyed, & o[u]r spirrits as good a napp vppon her. (c. 1623: fol. 10b)

---

[27] All references are to Dekker 1920 [1921].

The English might be better 'spun' and 'carded' than the Welsh, but they are both made of the same 'wool' and their bloods are as 'well dyed'. The reference to blood here clearly works as a marker of shared origins and national identity, which is further reinforced by the king's admission, at the end of this exchange, that 'wee . . . in nothinge differ butt in tongue' (c. 1623: fol. 10b).

Even the Welsh 'tongue', when understood both as language and dialect, is not an absolute marker of difference: Penda and Eldred predictably praise the 'welse tongue' while in disguise as a 'lofty tongue' spoken by 'praue sentill men as are in the vrld' (c. 1623: fol. 10b); but they also pretend to reminisce about meeting Penda and Eldred on the battle field, about how the English noblemen drank 'metheglin' (a spiced drink associated with Wales) and how they 'loue[d] to gabble a little welse too' (c. 1623: fol. 10b). While an impenetrable linguistic barrier makes communication between the English and the Welsh impervious at Glendower's court in Shakespeare's *1 Henry IV*, the English noblemen in this play enjoying 'gabbling' in Welsh. 'Gabbling' may not amount to being fluent in a language that is granted equal status to the English spoken at the English court. However, drinks and words are shared and enjoyed in a convivial atmosphere, which seems more genuine and inclusive than the communality of land and blood invoked by Shakespeare's Henry V, as he appeals to his army as a 'band of brothers' (1623: TLN 2303).

The brotherhood celebrated in *The Welsh Embassador* is also notable because it stems from a careful rewriting of the historical past. The clown's prophecy (c. 1623: fol. 18a) mentions dates ranging from 1217 to the present day of the play's date of composition, thus suggesting that the fictive world of the play predates the English conquest. However, the Welsh ambassador is visiting the English court because the date when the yearly tribute that Wales owes to the English king is fast approaching. Penda, disguised as the Welsh ambassador, anachronistically calls King Athelstane 'landlord of wales' and professes the unconditional allegiance of his people to the English throne:

> [A]wle the sentillmen of wales send Comendations to you awle & sweare w
> [i]th true welse harts, & longe welse hooke, to fyde vppon yor side when
> they can stand, till o[u]r *Bardhes* play on twincklinge . . . harpes the praverys
> of your victories. (fol. 10a)

Penda's pledge of allegiance clashes with the historical timeframe of the clown's prophecy. Not only was Wales still independent at the time when the action of the play takes place, but that time was also a period of open and fierce hostility between the English and the Welsh. In fact, by asking 'the reason that wee english men when the Cuckoe is vppon entrance saie the welsh embassador is Cominge' (fol. 13a), the Clown evokes a darker subtext that gives the title of this festive and ideologically pro-union history play a very different connotation. The past evoked by the Clown's question and by Eldred's answer quoted below summons memories of brutal bloodshed rather than consanguinity and shared origins that go beyond geographical borders:

> but I now can tell you, for manie summers agoe o[u]r valliant, Comragues & feirce prittons about Cuckoe tymes, Come & wth welse hooke hack & hoff & mawle yo[u]r english porderers, & so fright the ymen that they to still theire wrawlinge bastards cry out, husht the welsh embassador comes. (fol. 13a)

The Welsh ambassador is not only a temporary disguise, the rough bark that can be shed, to reveal an underlying shared British identity; it also revives troubling memories of a distant and brutal past that still haunts the present conviviality between the English and their Welsh neighbours. It seems therefore all the more important to appreciate the extent to which the sharing of a language, variants and all, is activated in this play to exorcise those memories.

All the plays under discussion in this section illustrate how Anglo-Welsh was used to add complexity, local dramatic specificity and wider cultural and historical resonance to characters whose speech is marked by phonetic variants conventionally associated with it. Whether these variants, as voiced on stage or reproduced in print (or manuscript), fell short of representing how Anglo-Welsh was actually spoken at the time is less important in the context of this study than the connotations that these plays associate with it. These connotations carried social and political meanings which, no matter how tenuously or how closely related they might have been to how Anglo-Welsh was heard and decoded by English speakers at the time, signified in highly specific, local ways within the fictive world of the plays. As this section has shown, the specificity of the situations within which Anglo-Welsh is used suggests that audiences were expected to be able to recognize and respond to the range of connotations and related social and political meanings that the plays ascribed to it.

§

'Anger Hath a Privilege': Rusticity and Compassion in *King Lear*

The final section in this chapter shows how regional variations were also used, albeit mostly as simplified stage dialects, in order to achieve a variety of dramatic effects. Out of all the main regional variations recorded in early modern play books, the Southern dialects and Southern accents seem to have been used most creatively.[28] A closer look at how the use of Southern dialects and Southern accents evolved from their emergence in mid-six-teenth-century interludes to their sophisticated deployment in a variety of dramatic genres in the first half of the seventeenth century can clarify the significance of its best known occurrence in *King Lear*, when Edgar suddenly starts speaking with a distinctive Southern burr during his confrontation with Oswald in 4.6.

Edgar had earlier in the play already disguised himself as Poor Tom by swapping his courtier fineries for a mere loincloth. He had smeared his face with mud and had spoken the haunting language of deranged vagrant beggars. When, at the beginning of Act 4, he agrees to escort Gloucester to Dover Cliff, he lapses back into his usual, elevated register, prompting Gloucester to remark 'Me thinks thy voyce is altered, and thou speakest / With better phrase and matter then thou didst' (1608: I2v, 1–2).[29] Edgar continues to hide his identity from his blind father and denies that his speech sounds more refined: 'Y'ar much deceaued' (1608: I2v, 3). When, later in Act 4, Oswald threatens to kill Gloucester, Edgar switches to using a distinctively Southern dialect:

> STEWARD VVherefore bould pesant durst thou support a publisht
>   traytor, hence least the infection of his fortune take like
>   hold on thee, let goe his arme?
> EDGAR   Chill not let goe sir without cagion.
> STEWART Let goe slaue, or thou diest.

---

[28] For recent work on Northern dialects and Northern accents in early modern literature and drama, see, for example, Blank 2006: 100–25; especially noteworthy is the level of attention devoted to the use of Northern English dialects in Richard Brome's plays in *Richard Brome Online* at www.hrionline.ac.uk/brome/.

[29] All references are to the first quarto edition of 1608 (STC 22292); the quarto passages where Edgar's speeches are marked by Southern variations do not vary substantively from the version preserved in the Folio edition of 1623, although, as Hope observes, the Folio version is even 'richer in its depiction of dialect features than the Quarto' (2010: 113). I am less interested in how accurately or inaccurately actual Southern dialects are represented here than in establishing what meanings this stage dialect conveys here; I am therefore using the Quarto rather than the Folio text, because it is chronologically closer to other plays where the same stage dialect is used to achieve similar effects.

EDGAR   Good Gentleman goe your gate, let poore voke passe,
           and chud haue beene swaggar'd out of my life, it would
           not haue beene so long by a fortnight, nay come not
           neare the old man, keepe out, che uore ye, or ile trie
           whether your coster or my battero be the harder, ile be
           plaine with you.
STEWART   Out dunghill.
           they fight.
EDGAR   Chill pick your teeth sir, come, no matter
           for your foyns.
STEWART   Slaue thou hast slaine me,

                                        (1608: K1, 8–22)

Oswald's death marks the end of Edgar's momentary slip into this
regional variation.[30] His next speech is unmarked – 'I know thee well, a
seruiceable villaine, / As dutious to the vices of thy mistresas badnes would
desire.' (1608: K1, 27–8).

The dominant view according to which Southern and South Western
accents and dialects were simply used as shorthand for rustic simplicity
(Kökeritz 99) has puzzled critics and editors, who have tried to account for
Edgar's sudden lapse into this regional variation under far from comic
circumstances. Readings of this baffling exchange tend to offer plot-driven
explanations. Katie Wales, for example, observes:

> Given that Edgar slays Oswald, Shakespeare is hardly using the dialect here
> to poke fun at West Country peasants. Along with his disguise as Tom the
> Bedlam beggar, the dialect serves to prevent Edgar's discovery, both to his
> father and to Oswald himself, and keeps him on the margins, as it were.
> (2001: 195)

Assuming that this dialect could only have had comic connotations forces
Wales to interpret Edgar's use of dialect as a generic disguise. One might
however wonder why he would not revert back to his assumed identity as
Poor Tom, were the need to continue to disguise his identity the only
reason for Edgar's marked speech in this exchange. More ingeniously, Sara
Pons-Sanz suggests that 'Edgar presented himself as a provincial, low-class
man (and, by implication, not trained to fight) because he knew that
Oswald was a coward . . . and would only pick up a fight with someone he
thought he could beat' (2014: 212). Alternatively, Edgar's brief use of a

[30] While most forms are recognizably Southern, the word 'gate' used to mean 'way' reflects a Northern
rather than a Southern dialect (Culpeper 2001: 212). Also, as Hope explains, 'the voicing of fricatives
indicated by "Zir", and "vurther" is a feature of south-western accents, but the "chud" and "chill" are
features normally associated with south-eastern dialects such as Kentish' (2010: 116).

Southern accent has been read as neither ideologically nor linguistically significant because faked by a courtier (Blank 1996: 93) or as related to literary antecedents, as opposed to actual regional variations (Hope 2010: 116–17). Hope uses the term '"Kentich" to designate the literary dialect and to differentiate it from actual "Kentish"' and traces Shakespeare's use of this dialect to one of Shakespeare's most influential classical sources, Arthur Golding's 1565 translation of Ovid's *Metamorphoses*, where Mercury disguises himself as a shepherd to test the wily herdsman, Battus (2010:218). While I agree with Hope that 'there is no serious attempt to represent an actual dialect ... just as there is no attempt at dialect realism' (2010: 117), I am going to show how Edgar's momentary lapse into a Southern stage dialect connects him to other characters who constitute a distinctive type in plays that are generically linked to *King Lear* and offered the original audience a context within which Edgar's use of this stage dialect makes theatrical sense.

One of the earliest dramatic examples of this Southern stage dialect occurs in the anonymous morality play, *Wit and Science*, which survives only in manuscript (BL Add MS 15233, c. 1550). In the following passage, Ignorance, who cannot even pronounce his own name and continues to fail to do so, despite Idleness's best efforts, displays some features commonly associated with this dialect, including 'chwas' for 'I was' and 'I bore' for 'born':

IDELLNES	... wher was thou borne
INGNORANCE	chwas I bore in ingland mother sed
IDLENES	in ingland
INGNORANCE	yea
IDLENES	& whats half inglande
	heers ing & heers land whats tys
INGNORANCE	whats tys
IDELLNES	whats tys horeson whats tys
	heers ing & heers land whats tys
INGNORANCE	tys my th[umb]
IDELLNES	thy th[umb] ing horeson ing ing
INGNORANCE	yng yng yng yng
IDELLNES	Foorth shal I bete thy narse now
INGNORANCE	vmmm
IDELLNES	shall I not bete thy narse now
INGNORANCE	Vmmm
IDELLNES	say no foole say no
INGNORANCE	noo noo noo noo noo
IDLENES	go to put together ing
INGNORANCE	yng
IDELLNES	no
INGNORANCE	noo

IDELLNES	forth now what sayth the dog
INGNORANS	dog barke
IDLENES	dog barke dog ran horeson dog ran
INGNORANCE	dog ran horeson dog ran dog ran
IDELLNES	put together ing
INGNORANCE	yng
IDELLNES	no
INGNORANCE	noo
IDELLNES	ran
INGNORANCE	ran

(Anon. c. 1550: fr–fv)

As Blank has argued, in this instance 'southern English is the dialect of the unlettered, a language of ignorance' (1996: 82–3). However, in a later Tudor interlude, whose date of original production can be dated quite specifically to February 1601 (just a few years prior to the earliest recorded performance of *King Lear* in 1605–1606), the use of this dialect can no longer be assumed to signal straightforward comic rusticity.

In *The Contention between Liberality and Prodigality* (Anon. 1602, STC 5593), Tenacity speaks with a distinctive South and Southwestern burr. After Tenacity has been murdered by Prodigality, Virtue appoints Equity to oversee Prodigality's trial. The trial scene provides the earliest and most extensive 'representation of the whole procedure of the criminal law from discovery of the commission of the crime to sentence of the murderer' (Dean 1977: 59). Similarly precise and detailed is the indictment read out by one of the clerks, who informs the court that 'one Tenacity of the parish of Pancridge [St Pancras]' was attacked, robbed and murdered by Prodigality on 'the fourth day of February, in the three & fortie yeere of the prosperous raigne of Elizabeth our dread Soueraigne' (Anon. 1602: F3, 27–8; 32–3). The judge extracts a confession from Prodigality, whose last resort is to beg the princely character of Vertue for mercy. The judge's response is interestingly sympathetic:

> Prodigalitie, I not mislike your wailefull disposition,
> And therefore, for you to the Prince, there shall be made Petition,
> That though your punishment be not fully remitted,
> Yet in some part, it may be qualified.
>
> (Anon. 1602: F4, 6–9)

The Epilogue that follows shortly thereafter is addressed to the 'most mightie Queene' and conventionally asks for Elizabeth's approval for all the labour that has gone into the production of this interlude as a form of service and a token of her subjects' loyalty:

> Here prostrate, lo, before your Princely grace,
> I shew my selfe, such as I ought to be,
> Your humble vassall, subiect to your will,
> With feare and loue, your Grace to reuerence still.
>
> (Anon. 1602: F4, 16–19)

Recent scholars have pointed out how the ending shifts the focus from the allegorical character of Virtue to Elizabeth and to the events surrounding the Earl of Essex's rebellion, which had taken place on 8 February 1601 and would lead to Essex's trial on 19 February and his swift execution on 25 February.[31] Though Essex refused to beg for mercy, Elizabeth, unlike the character of Virtue in this interlude, had made it clear that she would refuse Essex an audience (Hammer 2008).

In this highly political (and strategically timed) interlude, Tenacity makes for an interestingly layered character, who exceeds the bounds of its allegorical vice, avarice. Money does indeed lament being imprisoned, fattened and put to no good use by Tenacity, who is therefore depicted like a stereotypical miser:

> He would neuer let me abroad to goe,
> But lockt me vp in coffers, or in bags bound me fast,
> That like a Bore in a stie, he fed me at last.
> Thus Tenacitie did spoile me, for want of exercise.
>
> (Anon. 1602: F2, 18–21)

Tenacity is certainly guilty of refusing to use Money to reward the virtuous, assist the needy, or support good causes, as Liberality, Virtue's chief steward, urges him to do throughout the play. Even Vanity, Prodigality's chief servant, gets the moral upper hand over Tenacity, when he asks him what he would do with Money, were his mother, Fortune, to hand Money over to him:

VANITY	What wouldst thou doe with it?
TENACITY	Chud chud, chud, chud.
VANITY	Chud, chud, what chud?
TENACITY	Chud doe no harme at all.
VANITY	No, nor much good (I thinke) to great nor small.

(Anon. 1602: D4v, 11–15)

Tenacity is nevertheless not simply a miser and does not sit idly, once fickle Fortune hands Money over to him. Tenacity is primarily associated with farming. St Pancras was at this time a rural district, and the

---

[31] See, for example, Partridge 2013.

orthographic features displayed by Tenacity's heavily inflected speech place him firmly within the social type of the rustic clown. But Tenacity, as his name suggests, is not a clown: Tenacity is doggedly hardworking and produces wealth, as opposed to squandering it, like Prodigality. Although he then selfishly proceeds to store it away, Tenacity is a model of good husbandry. Comparing himself to Prodigality, he explains:

> VVHilst thou dost spend with friend and foe,
> At home che hold the plough by'th taile:
> Che dig, che delue, che zet, che zow,
> Che mow, che reape, che ply my flaile.
> A paire of dice is thy delight,
> Thou liu'st for most part by the spoile:
> I truely labour day and night,
> To get my liuing by my toile:
> (Anon. 1602: C2v, 29–30; C3, 1–6)

There is nothing comic or condescending about these lines, despite the fact that Tenacity is disagreeing not only with Prodigality, but also with Equity and Liberality.[32] The choice of Tenacity's name confirms that his character cannot be reduced to the allegorical vice of avarice associated with him. Similarly, the dialect he speaks does not belittle the good qualities that co-exist alongside this character's shortcomings.

If the use of Southern dialects in mid-sixteenth century and late Tudor interludes suggests a shift from comic types to more complex characters, plays that are not only temporally but also generically closer to *King Lear* show how Edgar's Southern burr would have evoked a set of values that enhance and clarify Edgar's role in this scene. The best correlation of this dialect with the set of values Edgar champions in this scene comes from the Shakespearean stage, if not from the Shakespearean canon *per se*. *The London Prodigal* (Anon. 1605b, STC 22333), which was staged by the King's Men, then attributed to Shakespeare on the title page of the 1605 quarto edition and finally included in the third Folio edition of 1663–4, is generally regarded as apocryphal. However, as Jonathan Bate and Eric Rasmussen have recently argued, a broader understanding of collaboration should encourage us to regard as 'Shakespearean' plays like

---

[32] Blank reached the opposite conclusion that '[t]he awkward repetitiveness of the dialectal *che*, a variant of *ich*, creates an impression of plodding dullness' in this passage. More generally, she argued that '[l]inguistic "tenacity" turns the southern dialect into a mere stutter, incapable of liberal expression' (1996: 84). In this respect I agree with Hope that this dialect, though initially associated with rustic simplicity, later denoted neither ignorance nor foolishness or simplicity (2010: 119).

The London Prodigal, which Shakespeare 'as a key member of the company ... explicitly or implicitly signed ... off for performance' (2013: 11). If not by Shakespeare, *The London Prodigal* was staged by the King's Men 'at the height of their fame' (2013: 30), and only one or two years before *King Lear* was first performed in 1605–6. The use of Southern dialect in this play is therefore worth closer consideration than it has been granted so far, because it belonged to the same company who went on to stage *King Lear* shortly thereafter. Far from being puzzling, Edgar's use of Southern dialect in *King Lear* makes perfect sense when viewed in relation to a play that shares with it other important generic features.

Sir Lancelot Spurcock, the father of three daughters of marriageable age, disowns Luce for wanting to remain loyal to Flowerdale even though Sir Lancelot had forced her to marry him and despite Flowerdale's arrest for debt straight after the celebration of their wedding. Albeit firmly rooted in a domestic setting, Luce's banishment anticipates Cordelia's:

> Huswife, you heare how you and I am wrongd,
> And if you will redresse it yet you may:
> But if you stand on tearmes to follow him,
> Neuer come neere my sight nor looke on me,
> Call me not father, looke not for a groat,
> For all thy portion *I* wil this day giue
> Vnto thy syster *Frances*.
>
> (Anon. 1605b: E1v 2–8)

Frances, who is as shallow and vain as Cordelia's elder sisters, though not as smart or malicious, welcomes the unexpected turn of events, as she tells her husband-to-be, Master Tom Civet: 'How say you to that *Tom, I* shall haue a good deale' (Anon. 1605b: E1v 9). Sir Arthur Greenshield, an honourable, Kent-like figure, tries to assuage Sir Lancelot's rage and to help him reconsider his rash decision to banish and disown Luce: 'But syr, that she is wronged, you are the chiefest cause. / Therefore tis reason, you redresse her wrong.' (Anon. 1605b: E4 27–8) Sir Lancelot proves just as headstrong and unreasonable as Lear: 'Must? who can compell me ... ? / I hope I may doe what I list.' (Anon. 1605b: E4 30–1). Then another character, Oliver, a Devonshire clothier, speaks in Luce's defence. His speech displays the morphological and phonetic features most commonly associated with the Southern stage dialect under discussion here:

> Nay, but and you be well euisen, it were not good
> By this vrampolnesse, and vrowardnesse, to cast away

As pretty adowssabell, as am chould chance to see
In a Sommers day, chil tell you what chall doe,
Chil goe spye vp and downe the towne, and see if I
Can heare any tale or dy dings of her,
And take her away from thick a messell, vor cham
Ashured, heele but bring her to the spoile,
And so var you well, we shall meete at your sonne.

(Anon. 1605b: E4, 33–5; E4v, 1–6)

Oliver's accent does not prevent Sir Lancelot from taking him seriously. Sir Lancelot is in fact moved by his offer to try and find Luce. Sir Arthur chimes in and offers to help too. Flowerdale is the only character who fails to appreciate that Oliver is more than a simple-minded country pumpkin. His invective against Oliver evokes familiar stereotypical traits of this stock character:

A plague goe with you for a karsie rascall:
This Deuenshyre man I think is made all of porke,
His hands made onely, for to heue vp packs:
His hart as fat and big as his face,
As differing far from all braue gallant minds
As I to serue the hogges, and drinke with hindes,
As I am very neere now.

(Anon. 1605b: F1v, 19–25)

Flowerdale's prejudiced attitude towards Oliver's accent is a significant flaw and more generally symptomatic of this character's potentially tragic shortcomings. Flowerdale's moral shortsightedness affects Frances too, who fails to recognize her sister Luce, when she approaches her, disguised as a 'Dutch frow [maid]' (Anon. 1605b: F1v, 29). Only Delia, Sir Lancelot's third daughter, who refuses to marry in order to avoid 'the care and crosses of a wife' and '[t]he trouble ... that children bring' (Anon. 1605b: G4v, 26–7), sees through Luce's disguise and put-on Dutch accent: 'Sister Luce', she warns her, "tis not your broken language, / Nor this same habit, can disguise your face / From I that know you' (Anon. 1605b: F2v, 19–21).

The final scene turns a potential domestic tragedy into a tragicomedy: Flowerdale's long-suffering father, who is believed dead but has actually secretly monitored his son's misdemeanours while disguised as Christopher, a 'sailor come from Venice', reveals himself and shames Flowerdale into repentance. The ending draws on a familiar tragicomic device, which was made popular by other so-called 'disguised ruler' plays, where figures of authority – such as, Duke Vincentio in *Measure for Measure*

(1623a, STC 22273), Malevole in *The Malcontent* (Marston 1604, STC 17479), Hercules in *The Fawn* (Sharpam 1606, STC 17483), or the Prince in *The Phoenix* (Middleton 1607, STC 17892) – take it upon themselves to check and reform the sins of their subjects by concealing their identities until the final scene, when they reveal themselves, thus ensuring a generic happy ending. This device makes Oliver's further intervention redundant. However, Oliver continues to model an appropriately sympathetic response for other characters, who are not as willing to forgive the repentant Flowerdale. When Sir Lancelot, unconvinced by Flowerdale's sudden change of heart, is about to disown him again as his son-in-law (and his daughter with him) – 'Out Hypocrite, I charge thee trust him not.' (Anon. 1605b: G3, 20) – Oliver is the first among the onlookers to pity Flowerdale:

> Ywood che were so well ydoussed as was euer white cloth in a tocking mill, and chea ha not made me weepe. . . . I would che were ysplit now, but che beleue him'. (Anon. 1605b: G3, 25–6; 36)

Oliver's heavily marked speech does not detract from his ability to move others. In fact, his compassion at the piteous sight of Flowerdale's fall shows that his dialect is not at odds with, but rather a model for, Edgar's moral outrage. Before anybody else offers to assist Flowerdale, Oliver is willing to part with a considerable amount of money to help him start a new life with Luce:

> Well che vorye he is changed· and M. *Flowerdale,* in hope you been so, hold theres pound toward your zetting vp: what bee not ashamed, vang it man, vang it, bee a good husband, louen your wife· and you shall not want for vortie more, vor thee. (Anon. 1605b: G3v, 2–6)

Oliver then disarmingly adds, '*I* hope your vuder and your vncle here wil vollow my zamples' (Anon. 1605b: G3v, 18–19).

Although the fictive world of *The London Prodigal* is firmly rooted in domestic tragicomedy, we should not forget that Shakespeare's main source for *King Lear*, the historical romance *The True Chronicle History of King Leir*, which, like *The London Prodigal*, was published in 1605 (STC 15343), shared with it a comic ending, with the miraculous restoration of the king's virtuous and unjustly banished daughter, Cordella. The treatment of Southern accents and dialects on the Shakespearean stage makes Edgar's temporary, put-on accent in *King Lear* seem like a natural choice, rather than an aberration, well within the potential range of audience expectations produced by earlier plays like *The Contention between Liberality and Prodigality* and *The London Prodigal.*

The use of this Southern stage dialect later in the seventeenth century confirms that the connotations associated with it support this reading of Edgar's temporary slip into this variation in *King Lear*. Most useful is a quick survey of how Southern dialects were used in Jonsonian comedy dating from the early seventeenth century to the early 1630s. In *The Alchemist* (1612, STC 14755), for example, Kastril, 'the Angry Boy' (A4), is, as it is often the case with Jonson's characters, suitably named not only after a small hawk, or 'kestrel', but also after the secondary meaning of this word, as in 'a lowly, base fellow', or 'coistrel' (*OED n2*). Kastril's association with the country and his unsophisticated naïveté make him a prime prey for the formidable trio of coney-catchers, Face, Subtle and Doll Common. Kastril's speech is only slightly marked by his habit of referring to his sister, Dame Pliant, as 'suster'. Of course, his speech may have been marked in performance in ways that have left no record on the page, but, given the lack of any other phonetic marker in the play as a whole, one may safely assume that Jonson meant Kastril to have just the slightest hint of a rustic accent.

More marked and varied are the voices heard during the 'Game of Vapours' in Jonson's *Bartholomew Fair* (1631; STC 14753.5). The 'Game of Vapours', as Jonson's stage direction explains, requires *'Euery man to oppose the last man that spoke: whethe[r] it concern'd him, or no'* (1631: I2 alongside 6–11). The Game epitomizes the sense of topsy-turvy confusion evoked by Jonson through the carnivalesque world of the fair, but it also places special emphasis on the pleasure of producing and listening to speech as a nonsensical cacophony of sounds and not for its meaning. Some of the voices in the game are regionally marked, and at least some of the speakers are introduced beforehand to ensure that their accents are recognizable to the audience as stage regional. In 4.3, the cutpurse, Ezekiel Edgeworth prepares to steal Bartholomew Cokes's marriage licence, which is carefully guarded by Cokes's old servant, Humphrey Wasp (also called Numps). As part of his plan, he invites Winwife, who has charged him with stealing the licence, to go and watch the vapours. Edgeworth is confident that he can steal the box where Numps keeps the licence, while Numps is watching 'the Vapours'. As he prepares to steal the marriage licence, he introduces 'the Vapours' to Winwife as follows:

> Yonder he is, your man with the boxe falne into the finest company, and so transported with vapours, they ha' got in a Northren Clothier, and one *Puppy*, a Westerne man, that's come to wrastle before my Lord *Maior,*

anone, and Captaine *Whit,* and one *Val Cutting,* that helpes Captaine *Iordan* to roare, a circling boy: with whom your *Numps,* is so taken, that you may strip him of his cloathes, if you will. I'le vndertake to geld him for you; if you had but a Surgeon, ready, to seare him. (1631: I1, 40–7)

Captain Whit, an Irish bawd, is not explicitly introduced to the audience, possibly because his speech is more heavily marked and may have been more immediately recognizable as such. English accents and dialects are interspersed with sociolects 'tied . . . to profession' (Gossett 2000: 13), as with Knockem, the horse-courser:

KNOCKEM	*VVHit,* bid *Vall Cutting* continue the vapours for a lift, *Whit,* for a lift.
NORTHERN CLOTHIER	Il'e ne mare, Il'e ne mare, the eale's too meeghty.
KNOCKEM	How now! my *Galloway* Nag, the staggers? ha! *Whit,* gi'him a slit i'the fore-head. Cheare vp, man, a needle, and threed to stitch his eares. I'ld cure him now an'I had it, with a little butter, and garlike, long-pepper, and graines. Where's my horne? I'le gi'him a mash, presently, shall take away this dizzinesse.
PUPPY	Why, where are you zurs? doe you vlinch, and leaue vs i'the zuds, now?
NORTHERN CLOTHIER	I'le ne mare, I'is e'en as vull as a Paipers bag, by my troth, I.
PUPPY	Doe my Northerne cloth zhrinke i'the wetting? ha?
KNOCKEM	Why, well said, old Flea-bitten, thou'lt neuer tyre, I see.

(1631: I1v, 5–19)

Knockem's speech is thoroughly marked by his profession: he refers to the Clothier, who is feeling exhausted and is about to surrender to his opponents, as an old horse affected by the 'staggers', a term 'used . . . for various diseases affecting domestic animals, of which a staggering gait is a symptom' (*OED, n.* 2a); then he proposes to cure his 'dizzinesse' by giving him a 'mash', that is a 'bran meal, or the like, mixed with hot water and given as a warm food to animals, or a feed of this' (*OED, n*1). As Gail Kern Paster has observed, the 'vapours' are both 'an idiosyncratic feature of [any] one character's language' and 'the redolent steam rising from the fair' (238); the vapours are, in other words, thick with the materiality of the smell of roasted pig and ale, which are consumed in great amounts at the fair, and the heavily marked sounds of the various stage regional dialects spoken by those involved in 'the Game'.

By far the most sustained use of a more genuinely regional dialect in Jonson occurs in his late comedy, *A Tale of a Tub* (1641a, STC 14754). In *A Tale of a Tub*, the language spoken by Jonson's characters reflects not only social status and erudition but also the local inflection of a specific regional dialect, namely the Middlesex dialect spoken in rural areas just outside London, including Finsbury, Paddington and St Pancras, where this comedy is set. As Derek Britton has pointed out, far from being 'an inaccurate authorial fabrication, loosely modelled on the conventional stage "south-western" dialect of the Tudor and Jacobean periods,' the inflected speech spoken mostly by Tobie Turfe, High Constable of Kentish Town, and by his family and associates, is 'in its essentials at least, an authentic representation of the speech of the county' (26–7). Britton then goes on to argue that 'as a Londoner ... [Jonson] must have been very familiar with the Middlesex dialect' and that '[i]t seems inconceivable that he should have tried to pass off as the speech of an area just outside London a garbled and unreal concoction that he knew to be false and which would have been recognized as such by the majority of his audience' (1993: 27). A closer look at a few key exchanges in the play shows that Jonson did not only take the trouble to signal features that his audience would recognize as belonging to rural Middlesex, but that he also allowed his characters to switch in and out of dialect, depending on the context of their interaction and the social standing of their interlocutors.

Jonson's characters in this comedy can elevate or lower their speech register by varying their use of dialect. Basket-Hilts, Squire Tub's 'Man and Governor', speaks in broad Middlesex dialect, as he first enters the stage:

> It i'no sand? nor Butter-milk? If't be,
> Ich'am no zive, or watring pot, to draw
> Knots i'your 'casions. If you trust me, zo:
> If not, praforme it your zelves.'Cham no mans wife,
> But resolute *Hilts:* you'll vind me i'the Buttry.
>
> (1641a: I3v, 37–41)

The high frequency of distinctive features – 'Ich'am' for 'I am', 'Zive' for 'sieve', and recurrent words or saying, including 'praform' for 'perform', and 'Cham no Man's Wife' – help Jonson establish Hilts's character, as summed up by Tub in his exchange with Sir Hugh, the 'Vicar of Pancrass': 'A testie Clowne: but a tender Clowne, as wooll: / And melting as the

Weather in a Thaw: / ... But he'll roar you, / Like middle March afore'
(I3v 42–5). And yet, when Hilts enters in 2.2, disguised as a Captain,
'*bearded, booted and spurr'd*', he addresses Tobie Turfe, high constable of
Kentish Town, and his party using a lofty register and avoiding any
dialectal marker or inflection:

HILTS   Well over-taken, *Gentlemen*! I pray you,
              Which is the Queens High Constable among you?
PUPPY   The tallest man: who should be else, do you thinke?
HILTS   It is no matter what I thinke, young Clowne:
              Your answer savours of the Cart.
PUPPY   How? Cart?
              And Clowne? Do you know whose teame you speake to?
HILTS   No: nor I care not: VVhose Jade may you be?
PUPPY   Jade? Cart? and Clowne? O for a lash of whip-cord!
              Three-knotted coard!
HILTS   Doe you mutter? Sir, snorle this way;
              That I may heare, and answer what you say.
                                 (1641a: K4, 45–6; K4v, 1–8)

Hilts even passes judgment on the language used by Bull Puppy, Turfe's
man – '[it] savours of the Cart' – and uses derogatory terms to describe his
linguistic mannerisms – 'snorle this way'. Similarly, when the vicar
addresses Turfe, the latter deferentially refrains from using the dialectal
features that heavily mark his speech elsewhere in the play:

SIR HUGH Why doe you dally, you damn'd russet coat,
             You Peasant, nay you Clowne, you Constable;
             See that you bring forth the suspected partie,
             Or by mine honour (which I won in field)
             Ile make you pay for it, afore the Justice.
TURFE   Fie, fie; O wife, I'm now in a fine pickle.
             He that was most suspected is not found;
             And which now makes me thinke, he did the deed,
             He thus absents him, and dares not be seene.
             Captaine, my innocence will plead for me.
             Wife, I must goe, needs, whom the Divell drives:
             Pray for me wife, and daughter; pray for me.
                                (1641a: N2v, 22–33)

Jonson's attention to linguistic markers that lend a specific, aurally
localized, identity to his characters extends to those whose speech is
normally unmarked, including Squire Tub. Although generally unmarked,
Squire Tub's speech is occasionally modulated to reveal his social affectations and nowhere more ridiculously so than when he woes Audrey Turfe

in 2.4. When the latter is either too amused or too confused by Tub's ridiculous grandiloquence to reply, Tub wonders whether she is unwell because of the cold weather:

> Shee not speakes:
> Hath the proud Tiran, Frost, usurp'd the seate
> Of former beauty in my Loves fair cheek;
> Staining the roseat tincture of her blood,
> With the dull die of blew congealing cold?
> (1641a: L3v, 14–18)

The farcically inflated rhetorical register in these lines gives way to a lightly marked Southern accent, when he addresses the 'mechanicals' who have set up a masque to celebrate him, 'His Father [who] was a Knight' and 'his Lady *Tub*, the Mother':

TUB	And, who the rest?
HILTS	The wisest heads o'the hundred.
	Medlay the *Ioyner*, Head-borough of *Islington*,
	Pan of *Belsize*, and *Clench* the Leach of *Hamsted*.
	The High Constables Counsell, here of *Finsbury*,
TUB	Prezent me to 'em, *Hilts*, Squire *Tub* of *Totten*.
HILTS	Wise men of *Finsbury*: make place for a Squire,
	I bring to your acquaintance, *Tub* of *Totten*.
	Squire *Tub*, my Master, loves all men of vertue.
	And longs (az one would zay) till he be one on you.
CLENCH	His worship's wel'cun to our Company:
	. . .
TUB	I long (as my man *Hilts* said, and my Governour)
	To be adopt in your society.
	(1641a: P1v, 10–24)

The switch between varying combination of dialect and 'usual speech' even in lines spoken by the same character in different situations and contexts shows that Jonson carefully calibrated the use of Southern accents in order to achieve an unprecedented level of acoustic specificity. Even when editors suspect that the level of variation in the speech features of specific characters may be at least partly due to the vagaries of textual transmission rather than to authorial ingenuity,[33] the overall impression

---

[33] Cf., for example, Happé 2012: 'Sometimes the rural characters speak politely, and, conversely, the language of the educated characters is occasionally infected with rural speech. Such inconsistency may have been created by Jonson himself, by inadequate revision by him, or by copyists or the printers'. However, as Happé goes on to explain, 'they [the rural elements] do offer a distinctive theatrical aspect which might be incorporated in performance' (548–9).

produced by Jonson's use of the Middlesex dialect in this comedy shows how regional variation could produce sophisticated character effects. Edgar's temporary slip into a stage Southern dialect, although less specifically marked than in late Jonsonian comedy, attests to a similar mastery of accents, or what Hope refers to as a 'Mercurial facility with language' (2010: 121). However, Tenacity and Oliver seem to be closer counterparts to Edgar than Mercury, both temporally and generically speaking. Edgar, in turn, anticipates the linguistic nimbleness displayed by later Jonsonian characters, who can best be understood as belonging to a theatrical, rather than more generically literary, tradition of their own.

The occurrence of Southern and South-Western dialects and accents in earlier and later plays from the period suggests that Edgar's put-on Southern accent in *King Lear* was used to enhance traits in Edgar's character that effectively juxtapose him to Oswald. The sudden switch to a Southern accent, brief as it is, gave the original audience a chance to connect Edgar's outrage to Tenacity's husbandry and frugality and to Oliver's compassion and firm moral compass, all values that, by being associated with the country, make Oswald's courtly vices seem all the more conspicuous. Edgar's momentary use of a Southern accent seems also a fitting stratagem in a play where characters deliberately choose whether to speak like themselves or to modify their speech. When banished, Kent, like Edgar, conceals his identity by 'raz[ing]' his 'likenes' and by borrowining 'other accents' that can '[his] speech defuse' (1608: C3, 38; C3v, 1–2). Even Lear, who had asked Cordelia to 'mend [her] speech a little' (1608: B2, 22) during the love-test sequence, when faced by the impending demise he has brought upon himself, wonders whether he still sounds like himself: 'Doth any here know mee? why this is not *Lear*, doth *Lear* walke thus? *speake thus?*' (1608: D1v, 25–6; my emphasis).

The actor who originally played Edgar may or may not have been able to reproduce the phonetic features used by actual Southern speakers, but, as this section has shown, there was a sufficiently strong stage tradition, with other characters that had used the same regional variation in plays that clustered around the early to mid-1600s, for audiences to recognize its acoustic specificity as a stage dialect and the cultural connotations associated with it. This chapter as a whole has shown that we tend not only to underestimate the versatility of English accents and dialects as they were deployed by Shakespeare and his contemporaries on the early modern stage, but that we also tend to underestimate the extent to which inflected voices carried social and cultural meanings. Commercial drama was still a relatively new form of entertainment, and accents played an important role

both to claim social and literary status for it, through the actors' controversial use of 'usual speech', the dialect of Southern educated elites, and to
add complexity and specificity to characters and dramatic situations. Far
from being generically varied, the sound of Shakespeare on the early
modern stage powerfully conveyed, on the one hand, the social ambition
of a young industry and, on the other hand, the acoustic ingenuity of those
who used and of those who decoded stage dialects that reflected, to varying
degrees, national, regional and class variation.

Conclusion

Scholarly and artistic interest in the role of the voice in theatre and performance has grown considerably since I first started working on this book. Among the most exciting recent developments is the realization that 'the embracing of ... non-generic voices is a reminder not only of the complex relationship between bodies and voices in performance but also of the assumptions and expectations audiences can impart on those bodies and voices' (Thomaidis 2017: 50). This book has accordingly investigated 'non-generic voices' on the Shakespearean stage, focusing on key moments in the history of the theatrical reception of Shakespeare, when NSE accents have challenged audiences to reconsider how national, class and ethnic identities are constantly (re)constituted through and in (Shakespearean) performance.

This book has also identified and discussed a significant rise in the range of accents used in contemporary Shakespearean performance. This increase in acoustic diversity is linked to two new specific ways of thinking about the voice. First, the voice now tends to be understood as 'multiply constructed and performative' (Thomaidis 2017: 73). Reinforcing this understanding of the voice as performing, rather than simply revealing, the speaker's identity, Konstantinos Thomaidis explains how a curatorial approach to voices in performance can in turn expose 'the making of voice as a *process* involving both listeners and voicers, their ideological habits, sensory modalities and aesthetic agendas' (my emphasis, 74). In other words, the de-naturalization of the voice in performance can encourage both speakers and listeners to 'rethink *voice* not as given or fixed but as the plural, in-between, challenging and generative practice of *voicing*' (74). My book has proposed a similar understanding of nationally, regionally and socially inflected voices, not as natural determinants of subjectivity, but as a powerful a politically charged acts of self-(re)fashioning.

A second, important development in contemporary theatrical theory and practice is the recognition that the conventional 'expectation to hear voice as non-ethnic, class-unspecific and de-racialized . . . eradicate[s] the body that originates it and silence its diverse origins' (Thomaidis 2017: 50). My work has accordingly exposed the political agents, civic authorities and policy makers, the orthoepists and historical linguists, and, of course, the theatre artists, who have attempted to eradicate acoustic diversity, along with the bodies that originated it, since Shakespeare and spoken drama became aligned with the speech of social and cultural elitism.

This recent shift from thinking about voice as a stable, neutral and functional channel for the production and decoding of identity categories to thinking about voice as an active process of voicing, through which such categories are constantly (re)negotiated, should in turn encourage us to reconsider aspects of current theatrical practice that have become anachronistic as a result. The exciting, but occasional, curation of marked voices on the (Shakespearean) stage and the mostly conventional, if not openly antagonistic, responses that NSE accents continue to elicit suggest how urgently we need to develop not only an 'emancipated' or 're-activated' spectator, or, rather, an 'emancipated' or 're-activated' listener, but also an 'emancipated' or 're-activated' performer.[1] A good starting point would be to think of traditional voice training not as an opportunity for actors to find their 'natural' voice within, that is a voice unencumbered by personal, class or regional inflections, but as an opportunity to perfect a range of accents, including their own, as well as StP.

The 'natural' voice that trainers help actors acquire while at drama school is in fact far too often what audiences at different times have recognized and accepted as a desirable standard of acoustic decorum. This standard, as this book has shown, has accrued social prestige and an impressive pedigree on the Shakespearean and the classical stage since at least the middle of the eighteenth century. Performers still need to master this accent in order to get roles in mainstream classical theatre, including Shakespeare. However, traditional voice training should emphatically not be thought of as a cleansing of vocal features that compromise clarity of delivery and established aesthetic standards of acoustic decorum. Clarity and acoustic decorum are themselves cultural constructs. Audiences bring to performance a very specific and 'culturally constituted horizon of [acoustic] expectations',[2] which in turn lead audiences to hear and reject

---

[1] The notions of 'emancipated' and 're-activated' spectators are drawn from recent work by Jacques Rancière and Nicholas Ridout; see, for example, Rancière 2011 and Ridout 2009.

[2] The notion of a 'culturally constituted horizon of expectations', as currently used in audience reception studies, comes from Bennett 1997.

NSE accents as unclear or uncouth. But the 'horizon of [acoustic] expect-ations' that audiences bring to performance can be changed, and one way of changing them involves training new generations of performers to master and use multiple accents.

A recent production of *Hamlet*, directed in 2016 by Simon Godwin for the RSC, is worth considering in detail to illustrate the need to foster acoustic diversity on the (Shakespearean) stage and a new level of acoustic tolerance and sensitivity in contemporary theatre audiences. The largely black ensemble cast to play all major roles in this production signalled a radical and exciting updating of the play's original setting: a new opening sequence showed Paapa Essiedu's Hamlet receive his degree from the University of Wittenberg in Ohio, USA. Essiedu's Hamlet then returned to Ghana to attend his father's funeral, where the action of the Shakespear-ean version resumed substantially unaltered, except for the fact that only the characters connected to the time Hamlet had spent studying overseas, including Rosencrantz and Guildenstern, were played by white actors. The relocation and updating of the play was positively received. For a start, this production made theatrical history by casting the first black actor to play the role of Hamlet on the stage of the RSC. Godwin's concept for this production also lent depth and poignancy to Hamlet's predicament, as Dominic Cavendish pointed out: 'the brief establishing scene ... rams home the point that the death of his father shatters his overseas education'; similarly, 'after coming face to face with his dead father', Cavendish detected 'stronger intimations of an identity crisis' than in productions that retain the play's original setting (Cavendish 2016). And yet, both Essiedu and Cavendish, as performer and spectator, registered their frus-tration at the fact that the new concept that Godwin brought to the play was not followed through to encompass all aspects of this production.

Cavendish, for example, found that the relocation to Ghana was in some ways half-hearted: 'the production needs more heat and more African dust if it's to enter the annals in its own terms' (2016). Cavendish's comment is highly suggestive but does not single out any specific aspect of production that could have imparted a more African quality to the pro-duction. A clue as to what aspects of this production still felt a little conventional, or too generic and unlocalized, emerges from interviews with Essiedu. When questioned about what he brings to major roles like Hamlet, Essiedu often mentions instead what he sadly needs to leave behind in order to conform with directorial and audience expectations. Essiedu, who is of Ghanian origins but was raised in East London, talks critically about his training at the Guildhall School of Speech and Drama:

So much of [the] training [is] about your own confidence, there's something intangible about what's being taught. Or there's something potentially primitive about what's being taught, because it's so much about what
part of yourself you can bring to work. . . . The syllabus is dominated by
white men in terms of the people that are directing, teaching, creating . . .
it's immediately alienating . . . [and] in the long term it's potentially a
damaging experience. (Minamore 2018)

The symbolic violence Essiedu associates with current training methods is
just as pervasive in the British theatre industry and in current expectations
about how classically trained actors should sound. In another review of the
production, as it went on tour in the early months of 2018, Cavendish
commented on Essiedu's impeccable delivery: '[Essiedu] is softly spoken,
and well-spoken too'. When off-stage, though, Essiedu allows other modulations in his voice to emerge: in his interview for *The Guardian*, Bridget
Minamore reported that 'the Walthamstow in his voice . . . quickly
becomes apparent' (2018). In the same interview, Essiedu talks explicitly
about his frustration, when traces of his Ghanian accent fall on deaf or
unreceptive ears:

> 'The conditioning [of my upbringing in London] does mean that I say [my
> first name] in an English accent. Pa-pa.' He scrunches up his face, before
> repeating the word, this time stretching out the first vowel: 'Paa-pa.' He
> smiles. 'It makes you feel dumb. All those years of people being like: "What
> what what?", not understanding the cadence that's involved. The musicality
> of Twi . . ., a language [he] grew up hearing from [his] mother, . . . is
> completely different'. (Minamore 2018)

Essiedu, who is proud of his dual heritage and thinks of himself as a
Ghanian-British, as opposed to British-Ghanian man, feels that he cannot
bring this 'part of [his own self] to work'. Rather than more 'African dust',
this production needed more marked voices to reflect the complex identities of characters like the young African prince, who, after studying
overseas, returns home to face a reality that has become remote and
unfathomable because of the death of his father *and* because his own sense
of dislocation. This *Hamlet*, for all its clarity in visually relocating the play
to Ghana, was acoustically still fairly conventional and failed to tap on the
vocal range and accents normally spoken by the actors who performed in
it, most notably Essiedu himself.[3]

---

[3] See also Refskou 2019, who notes how 'the heavy accents' used by the guards at Old Hamlet's
funeral in the establishing sequence 'sounded somewhat explicit in comparison with the
predominance of RP . . . in the rest of the show'. Refskou also points out how '[a]ccents only

The pressure to speak and the expectation to hear StP on the (Shake-spearean) stage are still strong and they prevent the urgent, acoustic emancipation or re-activation of both performer and spectator, voicer and listener. Hence my assessment of this otherwise successful and popular production as a missed opportunity: while the relocation and the uncon-ventional casting proved effective and were well received, the production remained too mono-tonal in acoustic terms, thus failing to register a crucial type of diversity. Shifting the emphasis from training actors to sound naturally clear to encouraging actors to use a range of accents, native and acquired, conventional and non-standard, could lead to a more satisfying, less alienating, experience for performers and listeners alike, because both performers and listeners will finally be able to produce and recognize the kind of acoustic diversity that permeates the world around them.

Regrettably, though, Godwin's approach to Shakespeare since 2016 sug-gests that even imaginative directors who are not averse to updating the play's original setting are not focusing consistently enough on voices. Godwin's 2018 production of *Antony and Cleopatra*, his first Shakespear-ean production as Associate Artistic Director at the NT, once again modernized the play and, by casting Sophie Okonedo as Cleopatra, brought 'a valuable ethnic "otherness" to the part [as played] at the National Theatre, [which had been] taken in the past by Judi Dench in 1987 and Helen Mirren in 1998' (Cavendish 2018a). However, in terms of enunciation and verse delivery, this production was even more conven-tional than Godwin's 2016 *Hamlet*.[4] Both productions implied a willing-ness on the part of the performer and the spectator alike to ignore how voice modulates identity. While colour-blind casting is slowly being replaced by approaches that do not rely on the audience's ability or willingness to be blind to race (Thompson 2006: 10–11), the artificially uniform voicing of character (and of the performer's identity) in (Shake-spearean) performance suggests the power and persistence of the larger cultural forces discussed in this book.

---

came back in the gravedigger scene; this time in the form of slightly out-of-place Calypso or Caribbean-inflected intonation. ... The use of pseudo-localized accents for characters of lower social status, while RP was reserved for those with a higher status, ... was in danger of implying RP as the preferred *lingua franca* adopted by those materially able to live in a modern (Western-influenced) world' (210).

[4] Godwin's 2018 *Antony and Cleopatra* did include some NSE accents. Tunji Kasim, for example, who played Octavius Caesar, was encouraged to retain the slight inflection he acquired from being born in Aberdeen, Scotland, and being raised in Nigeria up to the age of twelve, when his family moved back to Aberdeen. However, while Ghanian accents were heard, though sporadically, in Godwin's 2016 *Hamlet*, Kasim's slight accent was tolerated rather than curated in any meaningful way.

And yet, the steady increase in the range of accents used in the recent productions of Shakespeare explored in Chapter 1 reveals an appetite for change. However, experiments by individual theatre artists may not be sufficiently momentous to ensure that pioneering work with marked voices on the (Shakespearean) stage amounts to more than isolated, one-off forays into exciting new soundscapes. A closer look at how contemporary (Shakespearean) performance is funded sheds light on what mechanisms determine who is given the means to produce Shakespeare and, in turn, who has access to it. A fundamental next step needs to be taken to consider not only how (Shakespearean) performance is produced and how it is decoded, in both visual and aural terms, but also, and crucially, who gets the public funding, and the institutional endorsement that comes with public funding, to produce Shakespeare and for whom.

The public funding allocated by the Arts Council England (henceforth ACE) to National Portfolio Organizations (henceforth NPOs) for the period 2018–2022 shows a mismatch between the priorities that inform policy and the type of theatre organizations and work into which resources are being channelled. Data about funding allocation is framed by a series of documents, or 'narratives', through which the ACE presents the rationale that has informed the award process. In its 'Our National Portfolio, 2018–2022: Diversity Narrative', the ACE announces a major investment in bringing diversity into mainstream art forms and organizations:

> The arts can hold a mirror up to our world. They can also be beacons to inspire change. In any case, their long-term viability depends on their relevance – how they represent and speak to a diverse, contemporary society. Over the years there have been numerous initiatives to ensure that relevance, and to increase the diversity of the arts and cultural workforce, work and audiences. These efforts kept diversity high up on the agenda, but was seen as the main responsibility of a specialized group of organizations operating outside the mainstream. Our response has been to embed diversity into the mainstream, recognizing that it must be integral to the thinking and planning of all organisations that we invest in, not an afterthought or the responsibility of others. (ACE 2018)

The vision that emerges from this statement is not borne out by the range of productions, activities and creative outputs that are currently being offered by the main organisations historically tasked with producing Shakespeare for 'the mainstream'. Besides, a conscious effort to foster diversity in 'the mainstream' has meant that significant investment has gone to organisations that have traditionally received large amounts of funding. Mainstream organizations also tend to be concentrated in

London and the South East, so, once again, public funding is dispropor-
tionately high in areas where provision and access are already significantly
higher than in the rest of the country.

The total funding allocated to *all* major theatre organisations outside
London, excluding the RSC, amounts to ca £65 million, and is slightly
lower than the funding received by the NT alone (ca £67 million) and
quite significantly lower than the funding received by London-based
companies (ca £88 million).[5] The total funding allocated to *all* major
theatre organisations outside London is only slightly higher than the
funding allocated to the RSC (ca £60 million). An interactive map of
England on the ACE website shows the high concentration of the theatrical organisations in receipt of the largest awards in London and the South
of England, with only eight other organisations scattered across the rest of
the country.[6]

The Shakespearean productions offered by the major London-based
NPOs in the first year of the current funding period show the limited
impact of the diversity strategies promoted by the ACE. While all London-
based NPOs offer wide-ranging outreach activities, target traditional
minority audiences, and encourage diversity in new work, their Shakespearean provision remains, on the whole, thoroughly conventional in
terms of acoustic diversity. Besides Godwin's 2018 production of *Antony
& Cleopatra*, the NT is currently touring Rufus Norris's production of
Macbeth. In funding terms, this production belongs to an earlier stage of
programming under the artistic directorship of Rufus Norris. It however
shows continuity with Godwin's more recent Shakespearean offering at the
NT in terms of the overall lack of a curatorial approach to voices. In
Norris's *Macbeth*, for example, Rory Kinnear, who played the title role,
spoke his lines with hints of light Estuary English. However, while Kinnear
had used Estuary English to great dramatic effect in the NT production
of *Othello* discussed in Chapter 1, his choice to use the same accent to
play Macbeth did not pay off, because it was not integrated within a
production that lacked clarity and coherence, both visually and

---

[5] The data concerning ACE funding of NPOs discussed here can be found online at www.artscouncil
.org.uk/search/NPO%20successful%202018. Last accessed: 8 November 2018.
[6] These organizations are the Birmingham Repertory Theatre, the Leicester Theatre Trust, the
Nottingham Playhouse, the Sheffield Theatre Trust, the Manchester Royal Exchange, the Leeds
Theatre Trust, the Newcastle Northern Stage and Theatrical Productions and the Liverpool and
Merseyside Theatre Trust. The two organizations outside London in the South of England are the
Salisbury Arts Theatre and the Chichester Festival Theatre.

acoustically. As Natasha Tripney put it, the production, for all its grim, post-apocalyptic aesthetics, left some key questions, including 'where are we exactly, what sort of society is this, and how did people end up here?', regrettably unanswered (Morgan 2018).

The same lack of coherence and local specificity affected another production of *Macbeth*, directed in 2018 by Polly Findlay for the RSC. The role of Macbeth was played by Christopher Eccleston, who is renowned for the distinctive Northern inflection that he has brought to all his major roles for film and television. In the run up to the opening of this production in Stratford-upon-Avon, he made some incendiary remarks about the endemic cultural attitudes to accent that he felt had prevented him from securing major roles in the theatre. In an interview for the BBC, conducted by Arts Correspondent Rebecca Jones, Eccleston talked about 'a perception in the industry that "people like me can't be classical"'. As Jones explains, Eccleston, who was 'born into a working class family on a council estate in Salford in Lancashire in 1964', had never been offered a major Shakespeare role. Even his role as Macbeth was not offered to him; apparently he had to ask for it. 'I should have been offered more [Shakespeare] but I didn't go to the right university or the public schools'. Eccleston protests that this level of discrimination, based on class, access to education, and voice, needs to stop: 'I loathe it', he admits, and then adds, 'I've had a passionate love of Shakespeare since I was 17, but in a way, it's like the love that dare not mention its name' (Jones 2018).

Eccleston did retain his Northern accent when he played Macbeth in this production, but the lack of an overall strategy for the curation of voice prevented a more radical deployment of his trademark accent. Billington's comments in *The Guardian*, on the other hand, confirmed how embedded acoustic normativity still is: 'his speaking of verse', he decided, 'lack[ed] irony or light or shade' (2018a). Even Cavendish, who is normally more attuned to marked voices, observed, rather condescendingly, that Eccleston gave his lines 'the gruff Northern treatment' (2018b). In all fairness to the reviewers, it was probably the lack of coherence and localization in this production, rather than the expectations that they brought to it, which precluded a more constructive engagement with Eccleston's marked voice: his professional persona remained visible underneath his character, but was never put into dialogue with other aspects of this production. However, when compared to Kinnear's Macbeth, Eccleston fared even worse. In his review for *The New York Times*, Matt Wolf, for example, remarked:

there [isn't] much luxuriance in the language spoken by . . . Eccleston in the title role . . . He . . . changes through Macbeth's various set pieces with a flat and unvarying vocal attack . . . and would be happier taking on Jake LaMotta in 'Raging Bull' than ruminating over matters of conscience. (Wolf 2018)

Wolf's reference to film and popular culture confirms Eccleston's sense that cultural prejudice against his regional accent has made it difficult for him to build a career as a stage actor, which apparently was his original aspiration. Possibly unable to hear the tonal differences between StP and Estuary English, which are less marked than the difference between StP and Eccleston's Northern accent, Wolf, who was overall critical of Norris's production, was instead full of praise for Kinnear, whom he describes as 'ravishingly spoken' (2018).

The only other major Shakespearean production recently staged at one of the most generously subsidized theatre organisations based in London was a musical adaptation of *Twelfth Night* by Shaina Taub. This production, originally staged by Public Works at the Delacorte Theatre, in New York City, in 2016, was 'Londonised' by Kwame Kwei-Armah, Artistic Director at the Young Vic, and Oskar Eustis, who co-directed it. Under Kwei-Armah's artistic directorship, the Young Vic has placed unprecedented emphasis on reaching out to its local communities. The theatre will schedule performances of some of its productions at local venues and this production of *Twelfth Night*, which is set in a vibrant and colourful stage version of Notting Hill, includes a thirty-plus community chorus from the local London Boroughs of Southward and Lambeth. The overall feel of the production was one of fun, accessibility and inclusiveness. In *The Guardian*, Billington complained that, in order to achieve his aim of making the theatre 'a fun place for everyone to hang out' (Szalwinska 2018), meant that the co-directors had to jettison all the melancholic and rueful moments in the Shakespearean version (Billington 2018b). Cavendish shared no such qualms and wondered whether Kwei-Armah might be 'the man to give British Theatre a vital multi-cultural shot in the arm' (2018c).

As usual more attentive to sound, Cavendish however noted how it was best 'not to probe the concept too hard', adding that Kwei-Armah 'had underplayed his roots' (2018c). Kwei-Armah, born Ian Roberts in Hillingdon, London, from parents who were born in Grenada, in the West Indies, changed his name after he traced the origins of his family back to Ghana. Cavendish therefore regretted the fact that 'scene-setting reggae, steel drums, pounding bass and jagged grime [were] glaringly absent from the score' of this production (2018c), mindful not only of Kwei-Armah's background but also of the settling of West Indian communities in Notting Hill, following the 1948 British Nationality Act, and the strong association of this area with its Caribbean Carnival and with Afro-Caribbean music and food cultures. Cavendish also wondered why black British and London-born actress Gabrielle Brooks, who played Viola/Cesario, should 'speak with a London accent, but sing with an American one' (2018c). The 'Londonization' of a musical adaptation that originated in New York City offered a unique opportunity to allow local voices and accents to emerge and to lend acoustic resonance to the locale visually evoked by Robert Jones's set design. However, once again, the concept for this production was not thoroughly thought through, at the expense of acoustic depth, localization and coherence.

To sum up, the Shakespeare produced by the RSC and by the most heavily subsidized theatre organisations in London, who have received more than double the amount of funding allocated to *all* other major theatre organisations across the country, shows very little evidence that the diversity strategy championed by the ACE is actually fostering greater acoustic diversity in mainstream organisations. The output by other major theatre organisations outside London, who are in receipt of large grants in excess of £5 million, has so far proved to be just as disappointing. These organisations, who engage regional communities across the country and should therefore be better placed, geographically and historically, to embed (acoustic) diversity in their Shakespearean offerings, have so far produced hardly any Shakespeare at all. A few of them, including the Lyceum Theatre in Sheffield, are preparing to host Norris's NT touring production of *Macbeth*, while others, the Salisbury Playhouse among them, will showcase the NT Live cinecasts of Godwin's *Antony and Cleopatra* and the Almeida *Richard II*, directed by Joe Hill-Gibbins and starring Simon Russell Beale. Apart from a touring production of *Twelfth Night*, directed by Kelly Hunter and presented to Continental European and British audiences on the European Festival circuit, and due to open at the Festival Theatre in Chichester in early 2019, major theatrical organisations across the country offer very little locally produced Shakespeare, if any at all.

The only two notable exceptions are a production of *Much Ado About Nothing* by Northern Broadsides, whose work I have discussed in more detail in Chapter 1, and a production of *Hamlet*, directed by Amy Leach at the Leeds Playhouse. This production is due to open in 2019, and, if Leach's production of *Romeo and Juliet* for the same venue in 2017 is anything to go by, it might very well be the most significant Shakespearean offering in 2019 to capitalize on regional accents. Promising is the casting of Tessa Parr, the actress who played Juliet in 2017, in the title role. Back in 2017, Parr was able to use her native Northern accent, because Leach relocated *Romeo and Juliet* in a Northern, urban setting, where the Capulets run a boxing gym. Reviewers were generally impressed by the updating. Unsurprisingly, though, the variety of accents spoken in this production struck some reviewers as less than clear, and at times confusing.[7] Also regrettable was the fact that the Nurse spoke in the strongest local accent, thus reinforcing a traditional association between regional accents and comic and/or lower-class characters in mainstream productions of Shakespeare. Overall, though, this production was visually and aurally innovative and coherent.

A survey of the Shakespearean offerings at mainstream theatrical venues in the Capital and at major regional venues across the country shows that marked voices still constitute, by and large, a neglected aspect of performance and an obstacle towards achieving greater (acoustic) diversity, both in terms of the work that receives large amounts of public funding and in terms of the type of audience that this work can be expected to develop. It is finally worth considering whether greater (acoustic) diversity in Shakespearean performance is to be found in the work supported by smaller theatre venues or through one-off projects delivered by non-NPOs. The Arts Council National Lottery Project Grants Awards made between 1 April and 30 September 2018 show that theatre projects account for over one third of the overall National Lottery funding allocated to all art forms, but that Shakespeare-related projects represent only around 2 per cent of all funded theatre projects. Although individual Shakespeare-related projects secured on average higher amounts of funding (ca £25,000) than all other theatre projects (ca £15,000), their small number suggests that Shakespeare may not be viewed as a prime site for independent and innovative theatrical work or that Shakespeare is still seen as falling within the remit of large, well-established companies, like the NT or the RSC. Though statistically insignificant, independent Shakespeare-related projects seem to offer a more diverse output than NPOs. In turn, the work currently staged by non-NPOs illustrates the benefits of allowing marked voices to play a greater role on the Shakespearean stage.

A good example is *The Moors*, a show written by Tonderai Munyevu and directed by Arne Pohlmeier, two of the founding members of TwoGents,

---

[7] See, for example, Graham Rickson, writing for *The Arts Desk*: 'there are a few minor quibbles: diction is not always clear, and the range of regional accents can confuse' (Rickson 2017).

the London-based company whose work I discuss at length in Chapter 1.[8] Pohlmeier was awarded a £14,989 Arts Council National Lottery Project Grant to stage *The Moors* at Tara Arts, in West London, in late 2018 and to take the show on tour in early 2019. Earlier productions by this company – *Vakomana Vaviri Ve Zimbabwe* (*Two Gentlemen of Verona*, 2008, revived during the Globe to Globe Festival in 2012) and *Kupenga kwa Hamlet* (*Hamlet*, 2010) – had proved popular and thought-provoking. As explained in Chapter 1, TwoGents managed to put Shakespeare into a productive conversation with South African theatrical traditions and offered a refreshing point of entry into both Shakespeare and the host culture, seeing neither as a source of authenticity or stable identities. *The Moors* represents an exciting development in the Shakespearean output by this company since its inception in 2008, because it invites its audience to reconsider not only familiar characters, how they speak and what they say, but also the economic and cultural forces that shape the theatre industry and Shakespeare within it.

In this five-act play, Tonde (short for Tonderai Munyevu) and TJ (Tunji Lucas), two actors of Zimbabwean and Nigerian origins, who trained in the UK and whose visas expired as work started to dry up, remain in the country illegally and live in a tent, sharing a few earthly possessions, which include an iPad and a cookie jar. One day, they hear Sir Thomas Cowbury-Smith, better known as 'Sir Tom', Artistic Director at Shakespeare's Globe, say on the news that 'Shakespeare is Alive and Kicking' and that he is organizing a gala performance to prove it. Tonde decides that the gala performance is the opportunity that they have been waiting for to try and get work and to get their visas renewed. As part of their plan, Tonde and TJ turn up at the Globe pretending to be 'fresh-off-the-boat' African men and that they are looking for Shakespeare. They are greeted by Barbara at the box office, who proceeds to inform them that Shakespeare has actually been dead for just over four hundred years. Tonde and TJ break down and cry inconsolably: taken aback by their spontaneous outburst of grief, Barbara goes off to look for Sir Tom, who is charmed by the two men and by their life stories. Sir Tom is struck by their resemblance to Othello and to Aaron the Moor from *Titus Andronicus*, so he engages them to add a uniquely authentic, African quality to the gala. As Tonde and TJ rehearse with the rest of the company, TJ falls for Bryony Levering-Gough and threatens to tell her the truth about his status just before the gala. The gala goes ahead as planned, but is

---

[8] See also Woods 2013a and 2013b, and Massai 2017.

interrupted by an Immigration Officer, who had been tracking down Tonde and TJ. Disguised as women, Tonde and TJ seek shelter in Nunhead Cemetry in Peckham, South London. Bryony and fellow actress Amaka Fear come to the rescue and decide to marry TJ and Tonde to help them get their visas renewed, while the Immigration Officer mistakenly arrests and interrogates black British actor Clive Walton, another member of Sir Tom's company. The play ends when the Immigration Officer bursts into an impromptu wedding ceremony, officiated by Giles Hiddleston, another Globe actor, who, jealous of Tonde and TJ's popularity with Sir Tom, had reported them to Immigration in the first place.

In keeping with their trademark approach to Shakespeare, Munyevu and Lucas played Tonde and TJ, along with all the other characters in the play. Instead of using small props to signify different characters, as Chikura and Munyevu had done in *Vakomana Vaviri Ve Zimbabwe*, or different gestures, as they had done in *Kupenga kwa Hamlet*, Munyevu and Lucas switched characters by crossing their chest with their right arm and by modulating their voices accordingly. So Barbara, wittily nicknamed 'Major Barbara' and described as 'busty, nervous and Northerner', speaks in a distinctive Yorkshire accent, while Giles Hiddleston, described as 'white pink, self-assured, with a bit of a lisp' sounds like a classically trained actor, who comically lapses into Cockney when agitated or distressed.[9] Shakespearean lines and set pieces are drawn mostly from *Othello* and *Merchant of Venice*, but Shakespeare is also evoked by parallels between the fictive worlds of these plays and what happens once Tonde and TJ join Sir Tom's company. Bryony, 'tall, red head, killer cheek bones', for example, falls for TJ's exotic looks and the exciting tales he tells her about his life in Africa, mirroring Desdemona's fascination with Othello in the source play. As a result, the play wittily reproduces Shakespeare's language in a variety of accents, ranging from the StP to Tonde and TJ's natural (or mock) African inflections, and current, colloquial English, as spoken by the other characters.

The range of voices used to signify different characters exposes deeply rooted biases within the fictive world of *The Moors*, which in turn prompts critical reflection in the audience, who are later on invited to share their thoughts with Munyevu and Lucas and with each other. In Act 1, called 'Looking for Shakespeare', Tonde and TJ, for example, discuss what accent they should use, as they approach Sir Tom and try to persuade him that

[9] All quotations from the play are from the script, which is currently unpublished, and which Munyevu kindly shared with me.

they have just arrived from Africa. Tonde cannot do a Nigerian accent and TJ cannot do a Zimbabwean accent; so they settle for a generically South African accent, and decide to claim that they come from 'Balaika'. No one, except the Immigration Officer, questions the existence of this country, or how credible Tonde or TJ's South African accent sounds. Tonde in fact jokingly points out that TJ sounds like a white South African, thus exposing the other characters' inability to identify specific accents, cultures or even countries within their own simplistic and exocitized understanding of 'Africa'. In rehearsal, Munyevu and Pohlmeier must have decided to replace the original plan to have Tonde and TJ deliver their life stories to Sir Tom in Shona and Siswati, as signalled in the script, with drumming. From the drumming Sir Tom somehow catches what he wants to hear, namely a handful of key words – 'handkerchief, strangulation; handkerchief, strangulation' and 'tribal wars, mixed race baby; tribal wars, mixed race baby'. These key words remind him of the plots of *Othello* and *Titus Andronicus* and prompt him to greet them as the real-life counterparts of Shakespeare's Moors. The replacement of two African languages with drumming is a witty, strategic change, which suggests the extent of Sir Tom's stereotypical expectations of how 'authentic African men' should sound.

In Act 2, called 'Work, Work, Work', the rehearsal room at Shakespeare's Globe provides more opportunities to reflect on how voicing identity, on and off the Shakespearean stage, is a fraught process that requires careful phonetic coding and decoding. When Amaka, 'cool, boyish, mixed race', finishes delivering her lines as Nerissa to Bryony's Portia, and the latter remarks, 'Good sentences, and well pronounc'd' (1.2.10), this line acquires a very local, loaded resonance, because Sir Tom had patronizingly introduced her to Tonde and TJ as a 'lovely black actress', who is 'surprisingly adept at classical work'. Clive, the only black actor in Sir Tom's company, is a 'blacker ... muscular and very good-looking', and speaks in StP overlaid with a generic African accent. Clive is unceremoniously asked to get off the stage to let 'proper Africans' deliver his Prince of Morocco's lines, but not before Tonde and TJ are given a chance to wonder 'where that accent is from' and to decide that Clive 'doesn't sound Moroccan' at all. TJ then gets to paraphrase the Prince of Morocco's line from the 'casket scene' in his own accent. His delivery wins over Bryony *and* Sir Tom.

A short prologue warns the audience that 'similarities to persons known in the theatre world' are coincidental, and that the play is 'entirely fictional'. However, the parallels between Sir Tom's engagement of Tonde and TJ and how TwoGents got involved in G2G are hard to miss. Sir Tom's insistence on having 'proper Africans' deliver the Prince of Morroco's lines or Othello's lines is a poignant reminder of the fact that TwoGents, who normally perform in a mixture of English and Shona for diverse audiences in London, the UK, Continental Europe and Zimbabwe, were asked to perform exclusively in Shona on the Globe stage, in keeping with the ban on English that applied to all international companies who participated in G2G. When asked by Sir Tom if they can sing and dance, Tonde performs an exaggerated mock-African dance for him. Performing 'Africa' involves pandering to a reductive understanding of Africa as primitive and tribal, which is how some of the African companies who participated in G2G, and especially the ones coached by Globe practitioners, chose to represent 'their' Shakespeare on the Globe stage.[10]

In Act 3, which is called 'Oscar Night', Sir Tom explains how other theatres would have turned his two 'boys' away. 'Not us!' he adds:

> We brought these Amateurs from Africa
> Into our very own REHEARSAL ROOM!
> *Encourages applause from the audience.*
> And now ladies and gents, they're here tonight:
> I give you the real Moors from Africa.

During G2G, TwoGents were commissioned to perform 'Africa' by switching from their usual use of a blend of languages and accents to performing almost exclusively in Shona, so that G2G audiences could see them and hear them as 'real Moors from Africa'. Also in Act 3, the Lord Chairperson thanks Sir Tom for producing *Richard III* in OP:

> Only this season, Sir Tom gave us his sensational original practice production of *Richard III*. We saw twenty two (white) ENGLISH men brave the stage and speak Shakespeare's words, which of course we know speak to ALL of us, no matter who we are.

In this context, OP, evoking an established tradition discussed at length in Chapter 2, is deployed for its legitimizing function to lend authority to how Shakespeare is re-presented in its natural home, the Globe. The Englishness of Shakespeare is reasserted both by Sir Tom's OP production of *Richard III* and by Sir Tom's engagement of Tonde and TJ to perform 'Africa' as exotic and entirely 'other'.

---

[10] Representative, in this respect, was a production of *The Winter's Tale*, as staged in Juba Arabic by the South Sudan Theatre Company.

In Acts 4 and 5, which are called respectively 'The Flight of the Bumble Bees' and 'Wedding at Cana', the Shakespearean context is once again used to comment not only on the plight of illegal immigrants but also on the double standards that affect quality of living, equal opportunities and the general well-being of ethnic minorities currently living in the UK. The Immigration Officer, for example, cannot tell a black man from another – he 'just saw a black man and thought it was one of you', says Amaka to Tonde and TJ, as she catches up with them in Peckham. Clive gets into more and more trouble, as he explains that he was playing the Prince of Morocco and hilariously describes this character as a 'real African fresh off the boat'. 'So you pretended to be just fresh of the boat? / And you have been calling yourself Clive?' shouts John, the Immigration Officer. 'Well, no, I mean yes. I am Clive but I was playing an African fresh of the boat, he was fictional: The Prince of Morocco!' Identities – fictive, Shakespearean, real ones – blend into one another, encouraging the audience of *The Moors* to think about how they see and hear others. The fictive action of the play stopped between the end of Act 4 and the beginning of Act 5, and members of the audience were invited to share their thoughts about citizenship, status and national identity. This open, direct exchange between performer and spectator prompted relevant, personal and urgent interventions by members of the audience from very different backgrounds, and apparently proved popular with audiences during the show's entire London run.[11]

Right at the beginning of the show, even before Munyevu and Lucas deliver their prologue, Ebony Bones's song 'There ain't no Black in the Union Jack' sets the tone for the rest of the evening. The lyrics connect Brexit and the election of Donald Trump to the American presidency to the xenophobia and racism that prompted Enoch Powell to deliver his 'Rivers of Blood' speech at the Conservative Political Centre in Birmingham in 1968. Bones's eclectic and idiosyncratic style as a musician merges Afrobeat with Art Rock, classical with electronic sounds, creating a pregnant ideological context and soundscape for this production. It also primes the audience to spot parallels not only between the fictive world of Shakespeare's Moors and the fictive world of Munyevu's Moors but also with the real world of Munyevy and Lucas, who first arrived in this country aged twelve and five. On the two nights when I attended the show, members of the audience who identified themselves as British admitted to having applied for, or were planning to apply for, a second

---

[11] In conversation with Tonderai Munyevu and Arne Pohlmeier.

passport in order to have dual citizenship. Others who identified themselves as Europeans were in the process of becoming naturalized as a consequence of Brexit, while others explained how they were resisting naturalization. Others identified themselves as being British Ghanaian, or British Zimbabwean, or British Nigerian. The work staged by TwoGents turned the theatre into a safe space where members of the audience felt encouraged to share their own complex and hybrid identities and experiences of living as citizens or as immigrants in the same space that some identify as home, others as an elective home away from home, and others still as a haven away from a home to which they will never be able to return.

This astonishing level of interaction, of co-creation between actor and performer, is achieved through a sophisticated process of voicing, which in turn produces a range of identities and subject positions. This production, by striving to be acoustically inclusive, has managed to conjure that elusive sense of conviviality that according to Gilroy can and should replace categories like 'race' and 'nationality', because they continue to separate us.[12] More generally, this production has offered an isolated, but inspiring, example of what acoustic diversity can achieve in terms of promoting an inclusive, ethical, performative sense of belonging, of connection and fellow feeling, in the face of resurgent forms of nationalism, racism and xenophobia.

One of the main aims of this book is to provide a historically informed context for contemporary theatrical practice, in order to be able to look at the work of companies like TwoGents as the latest development of a long performance tradition, within which standard and non-standard voices have jostled for attention, reinforcing or challenging assumptions about class and nationality, about high and popular culture, about access to education and the role of the arts in society. This book was written to fulfil an intellectual curiosity of mine. I have spent my entire adult life studying and teaching, researching and watching Shakespeare, and I have become increasingly aware of the fact that my own engagement with Shakespeare has been marked by the unique combination of foreign and regional accents that inflect my own voice. But this book was also written in the hope that producers and funders of theatre in this country will start thinking more innovatively and more consistently about acoustic diversity in (Shakespearean) performance as a pre-requisite to achieve a higher standard of diversity and inclusion in the arts and in society more generally. Who knows – maybe the time has come for us to look at and listen to Shakespeare, and each other, as if 'we had eyes [and ears] again'.

---

[12] See also p. 48.

Bibliography

A. R. 1615. *The Valiant Welshman* (STC 16).

ACE (Arts Council England) 2018. 'Our National Portfolio, 2018–2022: Diversity Narrative'. www.artscouncil.org.uk/sites/default/files/download-file/Diversity.pdf. Last accessed: 8 November 2018.

Adamson, Sylvia, Lynette Hunter, Lynne Magnusson, Ann Thompson and Katie Wales eds. 2001. *Reading Shakespeare's Dramatic Language: A Guide*. London: Thomson Learning.

Agamben, Giorgio 1991. *Language and Death: The Place of Negativity*. Minneapolis: University of Minnesota Press.

Allain, Paul and Jen Harvie 2006. 'Festivals' in *The Routledge Companion to Theatre and Performance*. Abingdon, Oxon and New York: Routledge, 155–7.

Anderson, Benedict 2006. *Imagined Communities: Reflections on the Origin and Spread of Nationalism*. Revised edition. London and New York: Verso.

Anonymous c. 1550. *Wit and Science* (MS) in Arthur Brown 1951. *Wit and Science. By John Redford*. The Malone Society Reprints. Oxford: Oxford University Press.

 1596. *The Reigne of King Edward III*. STC 7501.

 1602. *The Contention between Liberality and Prodigality*. STC 5593.

 1605a. *The Life and Death of Captain Thomas Stukeley*. STC 23405.

 1605b. *The London Prodigal*. STC 22333.

 1605c. *The True Chronicle History of King Leir*. STC 15343.

 1742. 'A Clear Stage, and no Favour: Or, Tragedy and Comedy at War, Occasion'd by the Emulation of the two Theatric Heroes, David and Goliah. Left to the impartial Decision of the Town'. London.

 1751. *The Theatrical Manager: A Dramatic Satire [upon David Garrick]*. London.

 1756. *Original Prologues, Epilogues, and Other Pieces never before printed*. London.

 1756a. 'Art XVI. The Spouter, or, The Triple Revenge. A Comic Farse in Two Acts' in *The Critical Review, or, Annals of Literature*. Vol. 1, issue 2, March, 146–7.

 1758. 'The Case of the Stage in Ireland; Containing the Reasons for and against a Bill for limiting the Number of Theatres in the City of Dublin'. Dublin.

1760. *An Essay upon the present State of the Theatre in France, England and Italy.* London.

1768. *The Essence of Theatrical Wit: Being a Select Collection of the best and most admired Prologues and Epilogues, that have been delivered from the Stage.* London.

1769. *The Court of Thespis; Being A Collection Of the most admired Prologues and Epilogues That have appeared for many Years; Written by some of the most approved Wits of the Age, viz. Garrick, Coleman, Foote, Murphy, Lloyd, &c.* London.

1770?. *The Sprouter's Companion; Or, The Theatrical Remembrancer. To which is added, the Sprouter's Medley* .... London.

1772?. *The Sprouter's Companion; Or, The Theatrical Remembrancer.* ... *To which is added, the Sprouter's Medley* ... *Together with The Sprouting Club in an Uproar; Or, The Battle of Socks and Buskins.* London.

1787a. *A Review of the Present Contest between the Managers of the Winter Theatres, the Little Theatre in the Hay-Market, and the Royalty in Well-Close Square.* London.

1787b. 'The Royalty Theatre' in *The World, Fashionable Advertiser.* 27 June.

1787c. *A Letter to the Author of the Burletta called Hero and Leander, in Refutation of what he has advanced in his Dedication to Philips [sic] Glover, Esq. On the Statutes for the Regulation of Theatres, The Conduct of Mr. Palmer, of Mr. Justice Staples, and the other Justices; and also of his Observations on the Consequences that must arise to the Citizens of London and to Government from the Parliamentary Establishment of a Theatre in Wellclose Square.* London.

1787d. 'An Accurate Description of the Building, Decorations, and Convenience of the New Royalty Theatre' in *The Gentleman's Magazine* 61.

1791. *The Thespian Oracle.* London.

1810. *The Prompter, or Cursory Hints to Young Actors. A Didactic Poem, to which are prefaced Strictures on Theatrical Education.* Dublin.

1952a. 'Our London Correspondence' in *The Manchester Guardian*, April.

1952b. 'Our London Correspondence' in *The Manchester Guardian*, July.

1952c. 'Our London Correspondence' in *The Manchester Guardian*, November.

1997. 'Review' in *The Express*, 29 May.

1997a. 'Review' in *The Financial Times*, 23 May.

1997b. 'Review' in *The Evening Standard*, 2 February.

1998. 'Review' in *The Evening Standard*, 5 February.

Archer, Stephen M. 1992. *Junius, Brutus Booth: Theatrical Prometheus.* Carbondale and Edwardsville: Southern Illinois University Press.

Armin, Robert 1609. *The Two Maids of Moore-clacke.* STC 773.

Barber, Charles Laurence 1986. '"You" and "Thou" in Shakespeare's *Richard III*' in Vivian Salmon and Edwina Burness, eds. *A Reader in the Language of Shakespearean Drama*, 163–79 [273–89].

1997. *Early Modern English.* Edinburgh: Edinburgh University Press.

Barker, Clive 1971. 'A Theatre for the People' in Kenneth Richards and Peter Thomson, eds. *Essays on Nineteenth-Century British Theatre*, 3–24.

Barker, Felix 1972. 'Review' in *Evening News*, 4 April.

Barthes, Roland 1982 [1977]. *Image / Music / Text*. Third edition. London: Fontana.

Bassett, Kate 2011. 'Review' in *The Independent*, 4 December.

Bate, Jonathan and Eric Rasmussen, eds. 2007. *William Shakespeare: Complete Works*. Basingstoke: Palgrave Macmillan.

    eds. 2013. *William Shakespeare and Others*. Basingstoke: Palgrave Macmillan.

Beaumont, Francis, John Fletcher and Philip Massinger 1621. *Thierry and Theodoret*. STC 11074.

Benedetti, Jean 2001. *David Garrick and the Birth of Modern Theatre*. London: Methuen.

Bennett, Susan 1997. *Theatre Audiences: A Theory of Production and Reception*. Second edition. New York and London: Routledge.

Berg, James E. 2012. 'Moral Agency as Readerly Subjectivity: Shakespeare's Parolles and the Theophrastan Character Sketch' in *Shakespeare Studies* 40, 36–43.

Bevington, David, Martin Butler and Ian Donaldson, eds. 2012. *The Cambridge Edition of the Works of Ben Jonson*. Seven vols. Cambridge: Cambridge University Press.

Bharucha, Rustom 1993. *Theatre and the World: Performance and the Politics of Culture*. London and New York: Routledge.

    2004. 'Foreign Asia / Foreign Shakespeare: Dissenting Notes on New Asian Interculturality, Postcoloniality, and Recolonization', in *Theatre Journal* 56, 1–28.

Billington, Michael 1980. 'Review' in *The Guardian*, 21 March.

    1997. 'Review' in *The Guardian*, 20 August.

    2005. 'Review' in *The Guardian*, 5 May.

    2008. 'Review' in *The Guardian*, 9 October.

    2011. 'Review' in *The Guardian*, 30 November.

    2012. 'Review' in *The Guardian*, 9 August.

    2013a. 'Review' in *The Guardian*, 26 July.

    2013b. 'The National Theatre at 50: Michael Billington's View from the Stalls' in *The Guardian*, 18 October.

    2018a. 'Ecclestone Is Every Inch the Rugged Soldier' in *The Guardian*, 21 March. www.theguardian.com/stage/2018/mar/21/macbeth-review-christopher-eccleston-royal-shakespeare-theatre. Last accessed: 8 November 2018.

    2018b. '*Twelfth Night*, Review: Kwame Kwei-Armah Brings Carnival Spirit to Young Vic' in *The Guardian*, 9 October. www.theguardian.com/stage/2018/oct/09/twelfth-night-review-kwame-kwei-armah-young-vic. Last accessed: 8 November 2018.

Blackwell, Michael and Carole Blackwell 2007. *Norwich Theatre Royal*. Norwich: Connaught Books.

Blank, Paula 1996. *Broken English: Dialects and the Politics of Language in Renaissance Writings*. London: Routledge.

2006. 'The Babel of Renaissance English', in Lynda Mugglestone, ed. *The Oxford History of English*, 212–39.

Bloom, Arthur 2013. *Edwin Booth: A Biography and Performance History*. Jefferson, NC: McFarland & Company.

Bloom, Gina 2007. *Voice in Motion: Staging Gender, Shaping Sound in Early Modern England*. Philadelphia: University of Pennsylvania Press.

Blount, Thomas 1656. *Glossographia*. B3334.

Boaden, James 1831–32. *The private Correspondence of David Garrick, with the most celebrated persons of his times, now first published from the originals ... with notes, and a new biographical memoir of Garrick*. London.

Bolton, Betsy 2014. 'Theorizing Audience and Spectatorial Agency' in Julia Swindells and David Francis Taylor, eds. *The Oxford Handbook to Georgian Theatre, 1737–1832*, 31–52.

Bragg, Melvyn 1989. *Rich: The Life of Richard Burton*. London: Hodder and Stoughton.

Brantley, Ben 1998. 'Theater Review: A Down-to-Earth Iago: Evil Made Ordinary' in *The New York Times*, 11 April.

Brayne, Charles 2004. 'James Lacy' in *ODNB*. www.oxforddnb.com/view/10.1093/ref:odnb/9780198614128.001.0001/odnb-9780198614128-e-39770?rskey=kJ3AYH&result=1. Last accessed: 1 December 2017.

Britton, Derek 1993. 'The Meaning of Geances in Jonson's *A Tale of a Tub*' in *Notes & Queries* 40(1), 26–9.

Brome, Richard. *Richard Brome Online*. www.hrionline.ac.uk/brome. Last accessed: 18 December 2018.

1659. *The English Moor*, in Richard Brome. *Five New Plays*.

1659. *Five Plays*. B4872.

Brown, Ivor 1952. 'A Throne for Two' in *The Observer*, 14 September.

Bryden, Ronald 1969. 'The Comedy of Blasphemy' in Gerald Frow, ed. *The Mermaid 10: A Review of the Theatre 1959–1969, Published to Mark the Anniversary of the Opening of the Mermaid Theatre, Puddle Dock*, 6–52.

Buchanan, Brenda J. 2004. 'John Palmer, 1742–1818' in *ODNB*. *www.oxforddnb.com/view/10.1093/ref:odnb/9780198614128.001.0001/odnb-9780198614128-e-21199?rskey=btr7Ez&result=1*. Last accessed: 5 December 2017.

Buchanan, James 1766. 'An Essay towards Establishing a Standard for an Elegant and Uniform Pronunciation of the English Language throughout the British Dominions, as practised by the Most Learned and Polite Speakers'. London.

Buchanan-Brown, John ed. 2000. *John Aubrey: Brief Lives*. London, Penguin.

Bull, John 2004. 'John Palmer, 1744–1798' in *ODNB*. *www.oxforddnb.com/view/10.1093/ref:odnb/9780198614128.001.0001/odnb-9780198614128-e-21198?rskey=RCXA26&result=1*. Last accessed: 5 December 2017.

Bullokar, John 1616. *An English Expositor*. STC 4083.

Bulman, James C. 2008. *Shakespeare Re-dressed: Cross-gender Casting in Contemporary Performance*. Madison: Fairleigh Dickinson University Press.

2017. *The Oxford Companion to Shakespeare and Performance*. Oxford: Oxford University Press.

Burgess, Sarah K. and Stuart J. Murray 2006. 'Review' in *Philosophy and Rhetoric* 39(2), 166–69.

Burke, Helen 2011. 'Integrated as Outsiders: Teague's Blanket and the Irish Immigrant "Problem"' in *Éire-Ireland: A Journal of Irish Studies* 46(1–2), 20–42.

Burke, Jim 2006. 'Interview with Finbar Lynch' in *Metro West Midlands*, 3 July.

Burnett, Mark Thornton, Adrian Streete and Ramona Wray, eds. 2011. *The Edinburgh Companion to Shakespeare and the Arts*. Edinburgh: Edinburgh University Press.

Caines, Michael 2008. *Lives of Shakespearian Actors, Volume I: David Garrick, Charles Macklin and Margaret Woffington*. Gail Marshall, ed. London: Pickering and Chatto.

Calder, John 2012. 'Nicol Williamson's Obituary' in *The Independent*, 26 January.

Calvin, Jean 1561. *The Institution of the Christian Religion*. Thomas Norton, trans. STC 4415.

Carew, Richard 1602. *The Survey of Cornwall*. STC 4615.

Carey, David 2007. 'Review of Troilus and Cressida by William Shakespeare, in Original Pronunciation; Directed by Giles Block, Shakespeare's Globe, London, 2005 Season' in *Voice and Speech Review*, 5(1), 403–6.

Cartelli, Thomas 2008. 'Channeling the Ghosts: The Wooster Group's Remediation of the 1964 Electronovision *Hamlet*' in *Shakespeare Survey* 61, 147–60.

Cavarero, Adriana 2005. *For More Than One Voice: Toward a Philosophy of Voice Expression*. Paul A. Kottman, trans. Stanford: Stanford University Press.

Cavendish, Dominic 2001. 'Review' in *The Telegraph*, 30 June.

2003. 'Review' in *The Telegraph*, 17 May.

2015. 'Review' in *The Telegraph*, 12 June.

2016. '*Hamlet* at the RSC: A New Star Is Born' in *The Telegraph*, 22 March. www.telegraph.co.uk/theatre/what-to-see/hamlet-at-the-rsc-a-new-star-is-born. Last accessed: 11 December 2018.

2018a. 'Paapa Essiedu Is a Prince of Sweetness and Wonder in This West African *Hamlet* from the RSC' in *The Telegraph*, 1 February. www.telegraph.co.uk/theatre/what-to-see/paapa-essiedu-prince-sweetness-wonder-west-african-hamlet-rsc. Last accessed: 11 December 2018.

2018b. '*Macbeth* Review, RSC, Stratford-upon-Avon: A Case of Theatrical Overkill' in *The Telegraph*, 21 March. www.telegraph.co.uk/theatre/what-to-see/macbeth-review-rsc-stratford-upon-avon-christopher-eccleston/. Last accessed: 8 November 2018.

2018c. '*Twelfth Night*, Review, Young Vic: Kwame Makes Mark by Reinventing Shakespeare's Tale of Reinvention' in *The Telegraph*, 8 October.

www.telegraph.co.uk/theatre/what-to-see/twelfth-night-review-young-vic-kwame-makes-mark-reinventing/. Last accessed: 8 November 2018.

Cawdry, Robert 1604. *Table Alphabeticall ... of hard vsuall English wordes, borrowed from the Hebrew, Greeke, Latine, or French &c.* STC 4884.

Cercignani, Fausto 1981. *Shakespeare's Works and Elizabethan Pronunciation.* Oxford: Clarendon Press.

Chapman, George, Ben Jonson and John Marston 1605. *Eastward Ho!* STC 4970.

Chettle, Henry and William Haughton 1603. *Patient Grissel* STC 6518.

Christopher, James 1994. 'Review' in *Time Out,* 26 January.

Cibber, Theophilus 1755. 'An Epistle from Mr. Theophilus Cibber, to David Garrick, Esq.' London.

Collins, Beverly and Inger M. Mees 1998. *The Real Professor Higgins: The Life and Career of Daniel Jones.* Berlin: Mouton de Gruyter.

Conekin, Becky 2003. *The Autobiography of a Nation: The 1951 Festival of Britain.* Manchester: Manchester University Press.

Connolly, Annaliese and Lisa Hopkins, eds. 2013. *Essex: The Cultural Impact of an Elizabethan Courtier.* Manchester: Manchester University Press.

Cooke, Jo. 1614. *Greenes Tu Quoque.* STC 5673.

Cordner, Michael and Peter Holland, eds. 2007. *Players, Playwrights, Playhouses: Investigating Performance, 1660–1800.* Basingstoke: Palgrave Macmillan.

Coupland, Nikolas 2000. 'Sociolinguistic Prevarication about "Standard English"' in *The Journal of Sociolinguistics* 4, 622–34.

Coveney, Michael 1983. 'Review' in *The Financial Times,* reproduced in *The Theatre Record* 3(17) July–December 1983, 8–11 August, 639.

Craik, George L. 1857. *The English of Shakespeare, Illustrated in a Philological Commentary on his 'Julius Caesar'.* London.

Craik, T. W. ed. 1990. *William Shakespeare: The Merry Wives of Windsor.* The Oxford Shakespeare Series. Oxford: Oxford University Press.

Crompton, Sarah 2012. 'Michael Boyd: The Modest Man Who Saved the RSC' in *The Telegraph,* 14 September.

Crowl, Samuel 2014. *Screen Adaptations: Shakespeare's 'Hamlet': The Relationship between Text and Film.* London: Bloomsbury.

Crowley, Tony 1988. *The Politics of Discourse: The Standard Language Question in British Cultural Debates.* Basingstoke: Macmillan.

Crystal, David 1995. *The Cambridge Encyclopedia of the English Language.* Cambridge: Cambridge University Press.

    2005. *Pronouncing Shakespeare: The Globe Experiment.* Cambridge: Cambridge University Press.

    2012. 'Interview' in *Shakespeare's Original Pronunciation (CD).* London: British Library.

    2013. 'Early Interest in Shakespearean Original Pronunciation' in *Language & History* 56, 5–17.

Crystal, David 2016a. *The Oxford Dictionary of Original Shakespearean Pronunciation.* Oxford: Oxford University Press.

2016b. 'In Original Pronunciation the Plays Become Easier to Understand' in *Exeunt Magazine*, 5 May. http://exeuntmagazine.com/features/34086/. Last accessed: 15 November 2018.

Culpeper, Jonathan 2001. *Language and Characterization: People in Plays and Other Texts*. Harlow: Longman.

Curtis, Nick 1994. 'Review' in *The Evening Standard*, 19 January.

Cushman, Robert 1983. 'Review' reproduced in *The Theatre Record* 3(17) July–December 1983, 18–21 August, 640.

Daniel, Samuel 1599. *Poeticall Essayes*. STC 6261.

Davies, John 1603. *Microcosmos: The Discovery of the Little World, with the Government thereof*. STC 6333.

Davies, Robertson 2008. 'Irving, Sir Henry' in *ODNB*. www.oxforddnb.com/view/10.1093/ref:odnb/9780198614128.001.0001/odnb-9780198614128-e-34116?rskey=ITejev&result=1. Last accessed: 4 October 2018.

Davies, Serena 2016. 'A Chilling End to *The Hollow Crown*' in *The Telegraph*, 21 May.

Dean, William 1977. 'The Law of Criminal Procedure in the Contention between Liberality and Prodigality' in *Renaissance and Reformation / Renaissance et Réforme*. New series. 1, 59–71.

de Francisci, Enza and Chris Stamatakis, eds. 2017. *Transnational Exchange between Shakespeare and Italy*. London and New York: Routledge.

Dekker, Thomas [and John Ford?], 1920 [1921]. *The Welsh Embassador*. The Malone Society Reprints. H. Littledale, ed. Oxford: Oxford University Press.

1600. *Old Fortunatus*. STC 6517.

Dickson, Andrew 2012. 'A Life in the Theatre: Barrie Rutter' in *The Guardian*, 9 March.

Dillon, Janette 1994. 'Is There a Performance in This Text' in *Shakespeare Quarterly* 45, 74–86.

Dobson, E. J. 1968. *English Pronunciation 1500–1700*. Oxford: Clarendon Press.

Dobson, Michael 1992. *The Making of the National Poet: Shakespeare, Adaptation, and Authorship, 1660–1769*. Oxford: Clarendon Press.

2011. *Shakespeare and Amateur Performance: A Cultural History*. Cambridge: Cambridge University Press.

Dollimore, Jonathan and Alan Sinfield, eds. 1994. *Political Shakespeare: Essays in Cultural Materialism*. Second edition. Manchester: Manchester University Press.

Donald, Caroline 1991. 'Never Mind the Meaning, Just Enjoy the Show' in *The Independent*, 21 August.

Donohue, Joseph 2004. 'Introduction: The Theatre from 1660 to 1800' in Joseph Donohue, ed. *The Cambridge History of British Theatre, 1660–1895*, 2, 3–52.

2004. *The Cambridge History of British Theatre, 1660–1895*, vol. 2. Cambridge: Cambridge University Press.

Duncan-Jones, Katherine 2007. 'Complete Works: Essential Year? (All of) Shakespeare Performed' in *Shakespeare Quarterly* 58, 353–66.

Dymkowski, Christine and Christie Carson, eds. 2010. *Shakespeare in Stages: New Theatre Histories*. Cambridge: Cambridge University Press.

Edmondson, Paul, Paul Prescott and Erin Sullivan, eds. 2013. *A Year of Shakespeare: Re-living the World Shakespeare Festival*. London: Bloomsbury.

Edwards, Christopher 1987. 'Review' in *The Spectator*, 2 October.

Eklund, Hillary, ed. 2017. *Ground-Work: English Renaissance Literature and Soil Science*. Pittsburgh, Pennsylvania: Duquesne University Press.

Ellis, Alexander John 1869–1889. *On Early English Pronunciation*. 5 vols. London.

Eschenbaum, Natalie K. and Barbara Correll, eds. 2016. *Disgust in Early Modern English Literature*. London: Routledge.

Escolme, Bridget 2005. *Talking to the Audience: Shakespeare, Performance, Self*. London and New York: Routledge.

Fabricius, Anne 2006. 'The "vivid sociolinguistic profiling" of Received Pronunciation: Responses to gendered dialect in discourse' in *Journal of Sociolinguistics* 10, 111–22.

Falocco, Joe 2010. *Reimagining Shakespeare's Playhouse: Early Modern Staging Conventions in the Twentieth Century*. Cambridge: D. S. Brewer.

Farnsworth Smith, Dane 1936. *Plays about the Theatre in England from 'The Rehearsal' in 1671 to the Licensing Act in 1737; or, the Self-Conscious Stage and Its Burlesque and Satirical Reflections in the Age of Criticism*. London and New York: Oxford University Press.

Fenton, Rose de Wend 1991. 'End of Festival Report' in the LIFT Living Archive (LLA), LIFT/1991, held in the Special Collections Library at Goldsmiths, University of London.

Fenton, Rose de Wend and Lucy Neal, eds. 2005. *The Turning World: Stories from the London International Festival*. London: Calouste Gulbenkian Foundation.

Fitzmaurice, Susan and Jeremy Smith 2012. 'Evidence for the History of English: Introduction' in Terttu Nevalainen and Elizabeth Closs Traugott, eds. *The Oxford Handbook of the History of English*, 19–36.

Fitzpatrick, Thaddeus 1760. 'An Enquiry into the Real Merit of a Certain Popular Performer'. London.

Folkerth, Wes 2002. *The Sound of Shakespeare*. New York and London: Routledge.

Foster, Peter 2006. 'An Indian Dream' in *The Daily Telegraph*, 3 June.

Foulkes, Paul and Gerard Docherty, eds. 1999. *Urban Voices: Accent Studies in the British Isles*. London: Arnold.

Foulkes, Richard 2008. *Henry Irving: A Re-evaluation of the Pre-eminent Victorian Actor Manager*. Aldershot: Ashgate.

    2012. 'Shakespeare in the Provinces' in Gail Marshall ed. *Shakespeare in the Nineteenth Century*, 169–86.

Fox, Adam 2000. *Oral and Literate Culture in England, 1500–1700*. Oxford: Oxford University Press.

Fox, Sue 2007. 'The Demise of Cockneys? Language Change among Adolescents in the "Traditional" East End of London'. PhD Dissertation, University of Essex.

Frow, Gerald ed. 1969. *The Mermaid 10: A Review of the Theatre 1959–1969, Published to Mark the Anniversary of the Opening of the Mermaid Theatre, Puddle Dock*. London: The Mermaid Theatre.

Fullard, Joyce 2004. 'William Woty' in *ODNB*. www.oxforddnb.com/view/ 10.1093/ref:odnb/9780198614128.001.0001/odnb-9780198614128-e-30006?rskey=ZZQVEp. Last accessed: 7 December 2017.

G. I. 1615. *A Refutation of the Apology for Actors*. STC 12214.

Garrick, David 1785. *The Poetical Works of David Garrick, Esq*. London.

Gielgud, Val 1957. *British Radio Drama, 1922–1956: A Survey*. London: George G. Harrap.

Gil, Alexander 1619. *Logonomia Anglicana*. STC 11873.

Giles, Howard 1970. 'Evaluative Reactions to Accents', in *Educational Review* 22, 211–27.

Gilroy, Paul 1987. *There Ain't No Black in the Union Jack: The Cultural Politics of Race and Nation*. London: Hutchinson.

  1993. *The Black Atlantic: Modernity and Double Consciousness*. London: Verso.

Gimson, Alfred Charles 1970. *An Introduction to the Pronunciation of English*. Second edition. London: Edward Arnold.

Goddard, Lynette 2010. '"Haply for I am black": Shifting Race and Gender Dynamics in Talawa's Othello' in Christine Dymkowski and Christie Carson, eds. *Shakespeare in Stages: New Theatre Histories*, 248–63.

Görlach, Manfred 1999. 'Regional and Social Variation' in Roger Lass, ed. *The Cambridge History of the English Language*, 459–538.

Gosling, Nigel 1952. 'Table Talk' in *The Observer*, 27 July.

Gossett, Suzanne ed. 2000. *Ben Jonson: Bartholomew Fair*. Manchester: Manchester University Press.

Gosson, Stephen 1579. *The Schoole of Abuse*. STC 12097.5.

  1582. *Playes Confuted in Fiue Actions*. STC 12095.

Greene, Robert 1592. *Greene's Groats-Worth of Wit*. STC 12245.

  1598. *The Scottish History of James the Fourth*. STC 12308.

Greenhalgh, Susanne 2011. 'Shakespeare and Radio' in Mark Thornton Burnett, Adrian Streete and Ramona Wray, eds. *The Edinburgh Companion to Shakespeare and the Arts*, 541–57

Greenslade, William 2012. 'Shakespeare and Politics' in Gail Marshall, ed. *Shakespeare in the Nineteenth Century*, 229–50.

Griffiths, Huw 2010. '"O, I am ignorance itself in this!": Listening to Welsh in Shakespeare and Armin' in Maley and Schwyzer, eds. *Shakespeare and Wales: From the Marches to the Assembly*, 111–26.

Grimley, Terry 2006. 'Review' in *The Birmingham Post*, 22 June.

Guidi, Chiara and Sonia Massai 2017. 'Shakespeare, Tradition, and the Avant-garde in Chiara Guidi's Macbeth su Macbeth su Macbeth' in Enza de Francisci and Chris Stamatakis, eds. *Transnational Exchange between Shakespeare and Italy*, 277–92.

Gurr, Andrew 2009. *Shakespeare's Opposites: The Admiral's Company*. Cambridge: Cambridge University Press.

Halliburton, Rachel 1999. 'Review' in *The Independent*, 16 June.

Hallmark, Stephen 2006. 'Review' in *The Coventry Evening Telegraph*, 12 June.

Hammer, Paul E. J. 2008. 'Devereux, Robert, Second Early of Essex', in *ODNB*. www.oxforddnb.com/view/10.1093/ref:odnb/9780198614128.001.0001/odnb-9780198614128-e-7565?rskey=8DnGHh&result=9. Last accessed: 9 December 2018.

Hansen, Adam and Monika Smialkowska 2014. 'Shakespeare in the North: Regionalism, Culture and Power' in Paul Prescott and Erin Sullivan, eds. *Shakespeare on the Global Stage: Performance and Festivity in the Olympic Year*, 101–32.

Happé, Peter, ed. 2012. *Ben Jonson: A Tale of a Tub*, in David Bevington, Martin Butler and Ian Donaldson, eds. *The Cambridge Edition of the Works of Ben Jonson, vol. 6*.

Hart, Christopher 2011. 'Review' in *The Sunday Times*, 4 December.

Hart, John 1569. *An Orthographie*. STC 12890.

Hassell, Graham 1993. 'Review' in *What's On*, 27 January.

Hastings, Ronald 1969. 'Waiting for the Bang', in Gerald Frow, ed. *The Mermaid 10: A Review of the Theatre 1959–1969, Published to Mark the Anniversary of the Opening of the Mermaid Theatre, Puddle Dock*, 4–5.

Hazlitt, William 1817. *Characters of Shakespeare's Plays*. London.
  1818. *A View of the English Stage*. London.

Heywood, Thomas 1599. *1 and 2 Edward IV*. STC 13341.
  1612. *An Apology for actors*. STC 13309.

Hill, John 1759. *To David Garrick, Esq; The Petition of I*. London.

Hillman, David 1996. 'Puttenham, Shakespeare, and the Abuse of Rhetoric' in *Studies in English Literature*, 36, 70–93.

Holland, Peter 2007. 'Hearing the Dead: the Sound of David Garrick' in Michael Cordner and Peter Holland, eds. *Players, Playwrights, Playhouses: Investigating Performance, 1660–1800*, 248–70.

Holland, Peter and Stephen Orgel, eds. 2006. *From Performance to Print in Shakespeare's England*. Basingstoke: Palgrave Macmillan.

Holland, Peter and Adrian Poole, eds. 2013. *Poel, Granville Barker, Guthrie, Wanamaker: Great Shakespeareans Series*. Vol. 15. London: Bloomsbury.

Holmberg, Börje 1964. *On the Concept of Standard English and the History of Modern English*. Lund: C. W. K. Gleerup.

Hope, Jonathan 1999. 'Shakespeare's "Native English"' in David Scott Kastan, ed. *A Companion to Shakespeare*, 237–55.

Hope, Jonathan 2008. 'Varieties of Early Modern English' in Haruko Momma and Michael Matto, eds. *A Companion to the History of the English Language*, 216–23.

2010. *Shakespeare and Language: Reason, Eloquence and Artifice in the Renaissance*. London: Bloomsbury.

Hotson, Leslie 1928. *The Commonwealth and Restoration Stage*. Cambridge, MA: Harvard University Press.

Huston, J. Dennis 1970. '"Some Stain of Soldier": The Functions of Parolles in *All's Well That Ends Well*' in *Shakespeare Quarterly* 21, 431–8.

Hytner, Nicholas 2011. 'Director's Notes' in Theatre Programme, deposited at the National Theatre Archive, London.

Jackman, Isaac 1787. *Royal and Royalty Theatres. Letter to Phillips Glover, Esq. of Wispington, in Lincolnshire; In a Dedication to the Burletta of 'Hero and Leander', now performing, with the most distinguished applause at the Royalty Theatre in Goodman's Fields*. London.

Jensen, Michael P. 2008. '"Lend Me Your Ears": Sampling BBC Radio Shakespeare' in *Shakespeare Survey* 61, 170–80.

Johnson-Haddad, Miranda 1991. 'The Shakespeare Theatre at the Folger, 1990–91' in *Shakespeare Quarterly* 42, 472–84.

Jones, Daniel 1909. *The Pronunciation of English: Phonetics and Phonetic Transcriptions*. Cambridge: Cambridge University Press.

1917. *An English Pronouncing Dictionary*. London: Dent.

1949. 'The Tongue That Shakespeare Spake …' in *The Radio Times*, 16 December.

Jones, Rebecca 2018. 'Christopher Ecclestone: Northern Accent "Held Me Back"'. *BBC News*. www.bbc.co.uk/news/entertainment-arts-43139805. Last accessed: 8 November 2018.

Jonson, Ben 1607. *Volpone*. STC 14783.

1612. *The Alchemist*. STC 14755.

1616a. *Masque at Court*, in Ben Jonson. *The Workes*.

1616b. *The Workes*. STC 14751.

1631. *Bartholomew Fair* (STC 14753.5).

1641a. *A Tale of a Tub*, in Ben Jonson. *The Workes*.

1641b. *The Sad Shepherd*, in Ben Jonson, *The Workes*.

1641c. *The Workes*. STC 14754.

Kastan, David Scott, ed. 1999. *A Companion to Shakespeare*. Oxford: Wiley Blackwell.

Kenrick, William 1765. *A Review of Doctor Johnson's New Edition of Shakespeare: In Which the Ignorance, or Inattention, of That Editor is Exposed, and the Poet Defended from the Persecution of his Commentators*. London.

1784. 'Introduction' in William Kenrick. *A New Dictionary of the English Language*, prefaced to *A Rhetorical Grammar of the English Language*.

Kerrigan, John 2008. *Archipelagic English: Literature, History, and Politics, 1603–1707*. Oxford: Oxford University Press.

Khan, Naseem 2005. 'Building from Below' in Rose de Wend Fenton and Lucy Neal, eds. *The Turning World: Stories from the London International Festival*, 61–72.

Kidnie, Margaret Jane 2006. *The Shakespeare Handbooks: The Taming of the Shrew* (Basingstoke: Palgrave Macmillan).

   2009. *Shakespeare and the Problem of Adaptation*. London and New York: Routledge.

Kimbrough, Andrew 2010. *Dramatic Theories of Voice in the Twentieth Century*. Amherst, NY: Cambria Press.

Kingston, Jeremy 1997. 'Review' in *The Times*, 13 August.

Kinney, Arthur ed. 2012. *The Oxford Companion to Shakespeare*. Oxford: Oxford University Press.

Kirwan, Peter 2007. '"Eke Out Our Imperfections with Your Minds": The Festival's Impact on Audience Expectations and Involvement', in *Cahiers Élisabéthains* 71, 99–102.

Knight, Joseph, rev. by Katharine Cockin 2004. 'Thomas Cobham', in *ODNB*. www.oxforddnb.com/view/10.1093/ref:odnb/9780198614128.001.0001/ odnb-9780198614128-e-5746?rskey=tk2OsB&result=1. Last accessed: 14 December 2017.

Knowles, James 2015. *Politics and Political Culture in the Court Masque*. Basingstoke: Palgrave Macmillan.

Koenig, Rhoda 1995. 'Review' in *The Independent*, 2 June.

Kökeritz, H. 1953. *Shakespeare's Pronunciation*. New Haven, CT: Yale University Press.

Kortmann, Bernd and Clive Upton, eds. 2008. *Varieties of English 1: The British Isles*. Berlin and New York: Mouton de Gruyter.

Lahr, John 2005. 'Talking the Talk: The Globe Goes Elizabethan', in *The New Yorker*, 19 September. www.newyorker.com/magazine/2005/09/19/talking-the-talk. Last accessed: 15 November 2018.

Lass, Roger 1997. *Historical Linguistics and Language Change*. Cambridge: Cambridge University Press.

   1999. *The Cambridge History of the English Language, 1476–1776*. Vol. 3. Cambridge: Cambridge University Press.

Lawrence, William Witherle 1922. 'The Meaning of *All's Well That Ends Well*', in *PMLA* 37, 418–69.

Le Page, Robert Brock and Andrée Tabouret-Keller 1985. *Acts of Identity: Creole-Based Approaches to Language and Ethnicity*. Cambridge: Cambridge University Press.

Le Roy, Louis 1594. *Of the Interchangeable Course, or Variety of Things in the whole World*. Robert Ashley, trans. STC 15488.

LeCompte, Elizabeth, Kate Valk, Ari Fliakos, and Maria Shevtsova 2013. 'A Conversation on the Wooster Group's *Hamlet*' in *The New Theatre Quarterly* 29. 121–31.

Lester, Adrian 2013. 'Interview' in *The Telegraph*, 16 April.

Letts, Quentin 2010. 'Review' in *The Daily Mail*, 8 October.

Levine, Laura 1994. *Men in Women's Clothing: Anti-theatricality and Effeminaza-tion, 1579–1642*. Cambridge: Cambridge University Press.

Lindley, David 1986. 'Embarrassing Ben: The Masques of Frances Howard', in *English Literary Renaissance* 16, 343–59.

Little, David M. and George M. Kahrl, eds. 1963. *The Letters of David Garrick*. Oxford: Oxford University Press.

Lloyd, Megan 2010. 'Rhymer, Minstrel Lady Mortimer and the Power of Welsh Words', in Maley and Schwyzer, eds. *Shakespeare and Wales: From the Marches to the Assembly*, 59–74.

Logaldo, Mara 2010. '"Only the immigrants can speak the Queen's English these days" but All the Kids Have a Jamaican Accent: Overcompensation vs. Urban Slang in Multiethnic London' in *Linguistic Insights* 95, 115–46.

Loveridge, Charlotte 2004. '*The Winter's Tale* in the Spiegeltent' in *Curtain Up*. www.curtainup.com/winterstalespiegel.html. Last accessed: 15 December 2018.

Macaulay, Alastair 1997. 'Review' in *The Financial Times*, 18 September.

2006. 'Review' in *The Financial Times*, 23 June.

MacMahon, M. K. C. 2004. 'Alexander John Ellis', in *ODNB*. www.oxforddnb.com/view/10.1093/ref:odnb/9780198614128.001.0001/odnb-9780198614128-e-8683?rskey=ZK7RD2&result=1. Last accessed: 25 September 2018.

Mahon, M. Wade 2001. 'The Rhetorical Value of Reading Aloud in Thomas Sheridan's Theory of Elocution', in *Rhetoric Society Quarterly* 31(4), 67–88.

Maley, Willy and Margaret Tudeau-Clayton, eds. 2010. *This England, That Shakespeare: New Angles on Englishness and the Bard*. Farnham: Ashgate.

Maley, Willy and Philip Schwyzer, eds. 2010. *Shakespeare and Wales: From the Marches to the Assembly*. Farnham and Burlington, VT: Ashgate.

Marlowe, Christopher 1590. *Tamburlaine*. STC 17425.

Marshall, Gail 2012. *Shakespeare in the Nineteenth Century*. Cambridge: Cambridge University Press.

Marshall, Tristan 2000. *Theatre and Empire: Great Britain on the London Stages under James VI and I*. Manchester: Manchester University Press.

Marston, John 1604. *The Malcontent*. STC 17479.

Massai, Sonia 2007. *Shakespeare and the Rise of the Editor*. Cambridge: Cambridge University Press.

2017. 'Shakespeare With and Without Its Language', in James C. Bulman, ed. *The Oxford Companion to Shakespeare and Performance*, 475–94.

McDonald, Russ 2001. *Shakespeare and the Arts of Language*. Oxford: Oxford University Press.

McLuskie, Kate 1999. '*Macbeth/uMabatha*: Global Shakespeare in a Post-Colonial Market' in *Shakespeare Survey* 52, 154–65.

McMurtry, Marvyn 1999. 'Doing Their Own Thane: The Critical Reception of *Umabatha*, Welcome Msomi's Zulu *Macbeth*' in *Ilha Do Desterro: A Journal of English Language, Literatures in English and Cultural Studies* 36, 309–35.

Melchiori, Giorgio ed. 1999. *William Shakespeare: The Merry Wives of Windsor*. The Arden Shakespeare. Third Series. London: Thomson Learning.

Mendes, Sam 1997. 'Programme Note', copy deposited at the National Theatre Archive.

Middleton, Thomas 1607. *The Phoenix*. STC 17892.

Middleton, Thomas c. 1616. *The Witch*. Malone MS 12. Bodleian Library, Oxford.

Miles, Bernard and Josephine Wilson 1951. *The Mermaid Theatre*. London: The Mermaid Theatre Trust.

Milhous, Judith 2004. 'Theatre Companies and Regulation' in Joseph Donohue, ed., *The Cambridge History of British Theatre, 1660–1895*, 108–25.

Minamore, Bridget 2018. 'Paapa Essiedu on BBC's "Press" and Identity: "The word diversity doesn't mean anything"' in *The Guardian*, 8 September.

Momma, Haruko and Michael Matto, eds. 2008. *A Companion to the History of the English Language*. Oxford: Wiley-Blackwell.

Moody, Jane 2000. *Illegitimate Theatre in London, 1770–1840*. Cambridge: Cambridge University Press.

Morgan, Fergus 2018. 'Review Round-Up of *Macbeth* ... at the National Theatre' in *The Stage*. 8 March. www.thestage.co.uk/opinion/2018/macbeth-national-theatre-london-review-round/. Last accessed: 11 December 2018.

Morley, Sheridan 1983. 'Review' in *Punch*, reproduced in *The Theatre Record* 3 (17) July–December 1983, 8–11 August, 640.

 1993. *The Spectator*, 30 January.

 2001. *John G: The Authorized Biography of John Gielgud*. London: Hodder and Stoughton.

 2004. 'Bernard Miles', in *ODNB*. www.oxforddnb.com.libproxy.kcl.ac.uk/view/10.1093/ref:odnb/9780198614128.001.0001/odnb-9780198614128-e-49899. Last accessed: 23 April 2018.

 2005. 'Review' in *The Express*, 5 May.

Mountford, Fiona 2015. 'Review' in *The Evening Standard*, 12 June.

Mugglestone, Lynda 2007 [1995]. *'Talking Proper': The Rise and Fall of the English Accent as a Social Symbol*. Second Edition. Oxford: Oxford University Press.

Mugglestone, Lynda ed. 2006. *The Oxford History of English*. Oxford: Oxford University Press.

Murphy, Andrew 2008. *Shakespeare for the People: Working-Class Readers, 1800–1900*. Cambridge: Cambridge University Press.

Murphy, Arthur 1756. *The Apprentice: A Farce in Two Acts*. London.

 1801. *A Life of David Garrick, Esq*. London.

Murphy, Kate 2016. *Behind the Wireless: A History of Early Women at the BBC*. Basingstoke: Palgrave Macmillan.

Naunton, Robert 1870. *Fragmenta Regalia, or Observations of the late Queen Elizabeth, Her Times, and Favourites. Reprinted from the Third Posthumous Edition of 1653*. Edward Arber, ed. London.

Nevalainen, Terttu and Elizabeth Closs Traugott, eds. 2012. *The Oxford Handbook of the History of English*. Oxford: Oxford University Press.

Nightingale, Benedict 2006. 'Review' in *The Times*, 21 August.

Noël-Armfield, G. 1910. 'Scenes from Shakespeare in the Original Pronunciation' in *Le Maître phonétique* 24, 117–19.

O'Connor, Marion 2002. 'Reconstructive Shakespeare; Reproducing Elizabethan and Jacobean Stages' in Stanley Wells and Sarah Stanton, eds. *The Cambridge Companion to Shakespeare on Stage*, 76–97.

   2013. *Poel, Granville Barker, Guthrie, Wanamaker*, in Peter Holland and Adrian Poole, eds. *Great Shakespeareans Series*, 15: 7–54.

Orgel, Stephen 2006. 'The Book of the Play', in Peter Holland and Stephen Orgel, eds. *From Performance to Print in Shakespeare's England*, 13–54.

Ormsby, Robert 2011. 'Québécois Shakespeare goes Global: Robert Lepage's *Coriolan*' in *Shakespeare Survey* 64, 317–27.

Palmer, John 1781. *The New and Complete English Sprouter; Or, An [sic] Universal Key to Theatrical Knowledge. Containing a Complete Collection of all Favourite and most esteemed Prologues and Epilogues*. London.

   1790?. *The New Sprouter's Companion; Or, A Choice Collection of Prologues and Epilogues: Being a Complete Theatrical Remembrancer, and Universal Key to Theatrical Knowledge ... A New Edition, Carefully Revised and Corrected by Mr. Palmer*. London.

Palmer, Patricia 2001. *Language and Conquest in Early Modern Ireland: English Renaissance Literature and Elizabethan Imperial Expansion*. Cambridge: Cambridge University Press.

Pao, Angela C. 2006. 'Ocular Revisions: Re-casting Othello in Text and Performance', in Ayanna Thompson, ed. *Color-Blind Shakespeare: New Perspectives on Race and Performance*, 27–46.

Parsons, Elinor 2007. '"This Wide and Universal Theatre": Shakespeare in Different Voices' in *Cahiers Élisabéthains* 71, 7–12.

Parsons, Gordon 2006. 'Review' in *The Morning Star*, 13 June.

Partridge, Mary 2013. 'Prodigality and the Earl of Essex', in Annaliese Connolly and Lisa Hopkins, eds. *Essex: The Cultural Impact of an Elizabethan Courtier*, 263–78.

Paster, Gail Kern 2004. *Humoring the Body: Emotions and the Shakespearean Stage*. Chicago and London: Chicago University Press.

Patterson, Christina 2009. 'Review' in *The Independent*, 6 January.

Peele, George 1593. *Edward I*. STC 19535.

Penlington, Amanda 2010. '"Not a Man from England": Assimilating the Exotic "Other" through Performance, from Henry IV to Henry V', in Maley and Tudeau-Clayton, eds. *This England, That Shakespeare: New Angles on Englishness and the Bard*, 234–62.

Petcher, Edward 1999. *Othello and Interpretative Traditions*. Iowa City: University of Iowa Press.

Peters, John 1993. 'Review' in *The Sunday Times*, 30 January.

Pickering, D. 1761. *The Statutes at Large, from Magna Charta to ... 1761. Carefully collated and revised, with references, a preface, and a new and accurate index ...* 24 vols, vol. 17. London.

Plastow, Jane 2013. *African Theatre 12: Shakespeare in & out of Africa.* Woodbridge: Boydell and Brewer.

Plutarch 1603. *Moralia.* Philemon Holland, trans. STC 20063.

Poel, William 1913. *Shakespeare in the Theatre.* London and Toronto: Sidwick and Jackson.

Pons-Sanz, Sara M. 2014. *The Language of Early English Literature: From Cædmon to Milton.* Basingstoke: Palgrave Macmillan.

Prescott, Paul 2013. 'Review of *Troilus and Cressida*, Directed by Elizabeth LeCompte for the Wooster Group ... and Mark Ravenhill for the Royal Shakespeare Company ...', in Edmondson, Prescott and Sullivan, eds. *A Year of Shakespeare: Re-living the World Shakespeare Festival,* 213–16.

Prescott, Paul and Erin Sullivan, eds. 2014. *Shakespeare on the Global Stage: Performance and Festivity in the Olympic Year.* London: Bloomsbury.

Proudfoot, Richard and Nicola Bennett, eds. 2017. *Edward III. The Arden Shakespeare, third series.* London: Bloomsbury.

Proudfoot, Richard, Ann Thompson and David Scott Kastan, eds. 2011. *The Arden Shakespeare: The Complete Works.* Revised Edition. London: Bloomsbury.

Prynne, William 1633. *Histrio-Mastix.* STC20464a.

Purchas, Samuel 1613. *Purchas his pilgrimage.* STC 20505.

Purves, Libby 2011. 'Review' in *The Times,* 30 November.

Puttenham, George 1589. *The Arte of English Poesie.* STC 20519.

Quarmby, Kevin 2016. 'Review', in *The British Theatre Guide.* www.britishtheatreguide.info/reviews/much-ado-about-rsc-courtyard-t-7732. Last accessed: 20 December 2016.

Radio Times, The 1936. 'London Calling 1600', Wednesday, 15 April 1936, issue 654, 42. http://genome.ch.bbc.co.uk/page/b141784e722f43b2823fd219b2226a70. Last accessed: 11 December 2018.

   The 1937. 'Take Your Choice', Monday, 6 December 1937, issue 740, 31. http://genome.ch.bbc.co.uk/page/ae3cd719fb494fd9bbc1955e4591c7c5. Last accessed: 11 December 2018.

Rancière, Jacques 2011. *The Emancipated Spectator.* London: Verso.

Rees, Jasper 2013. 'Adrian Lester Interview: Othello, 'It's not Just About His Colour' in *The Telegraph,* 16 April 2013.

Refskou, Anne Sophie 2019. '"Not Where He Eats, but Where He Is Eaten: Rethinking Otherness in (British) Global Shakespeare' in Anne Sophie Refskou, Marcel Alvaro de Amorim and Vinicius Mariano de Carvalho, eds. *Eating Shakespeare: Cultural Anthropophagy as Global Methodology.* London: Bloomsbury.

Richard, Jeremy 1986. '"The Thing I am": Parolles, the Comedic Villain, and Tragic Consciousness' in *Shakespeare Studies* 18, 145–59.

Richards, Jeffrey 2005. *Sir Henry Irving: Victorian Actor and His World*. London and Hambledon: Continuum.

Richards, Kenneth and Peter Thomson, eds. 1971. *Essays on Nineteenth-Century British Theatre*. London: Methuen.

Rickson, Graham 2017. 'Review of *Romeo and Juliet*, West Yorkshire Playhouse' in *The Arts Desk*. www.theartsdesk.com/theatre/romeo-and-juliet-west-york shire-playhouse. Last accessed: 8 November 2018.

Ridout, Nicholas 2009. *Theatre & Ethics*. Basingstoke: Palgrave Macmillan.

Ritchie, Fiona and Peter Sabor, eds. 2012. *Shakespeare in the Eighteenth Century*. Cambridge: Cambridge University Press.

Ritchie, Leslie 2012. 'The Spouters' Revenge: Apprentice Actors and the Imitation of London's Theatrical Celebrities' in *The Eighteenth Century* 53(1), 41–71.

Rogers, Richard 1615. *A Commentary vpon the vvhole booke of Iudges*. STC 21204.

Rolt, Richard 1752. 'A Poetical Epistle from Shakespear in Elysium to Mr Garrick, at Drury Lane Theatre. To which is added, a view from Heymon-Hill, near Shrewsbury; a solitudinarian ode'. London.

Rosewarne, David 1984. 'Estuary English' in *Times Educational Supplement*, 19 October.

Rothman, Jules 1972. 'A vindication of Parolles' in *Shakespeare Quarterly* 23, 183–96.

Rumbold, Kate 2013. 'Review of *Much Ado About Nothing*, Directed by Iqbal Kahn for the Royal Shakespeare Company', in Edmondson, Prescott and Sullivan (eds), *A Year of Shakespeare: Re-living the World Shakespeare Festival*, 149–52.

Rutherford, Malcolm 1993. 'Review' in *The Financial Times*, 23 January.

Rutter, Carol 2003. 'Rough Magic: Northern Broadsides at Work at Play' in *Shakespeare Survey* 56, 236–55.

Salmon, Eric 2004. 'Colley Cibber' in *ODNB*. www.oxforddnb.com/view/ 10.1093/ref:odnb/9780198614128.001.0001/odnb-9780198614128-e-5416?rskey=BvNqm1&result=1. Last accessed: 1 December 2017.

Salmon, Vivian and Edwina Burness, eds. 1987. *A Reader in the Language of Shakespearean Drama*. Amsterdam and Philadelphia: John Benjamins.

Sandhu, Angie 2014. 'Enlightenment, Exclusion, and the Theatre' in Julia Swindells and David Francis Taylor, eds. *The Oxford Handbook to Georgian Theatre, 1737–1832*, 11–30.

Santor, Bar-On Gefen 2014. 'Shakespeare in the Georgian Theatre' in Julia Swindells and David Francis Taylor, eds. *The Oxford Handbook to Georgian Theatre, 1737–1832*, 213–28.

Shakespeare, William 1597. *Richard II*. STC 22307.

   1600. *A Midsummer Night's Dream*. STC 22302.

   1602. *The Merry Wives of Windsor*. STC 22299.

   1608. *The Historie of King Lear*. STC 22292.

   1623a. *Comedies, Histories and Tragedies*. STC 22273.

   1623b. *Cymbeline*. In William Shakespeare. *Comedies, Histories and Tragedies*.

1623c. *Measure for Measure*. In William Shakespeare. *Comedies, Histories and Tragedies*.

1623d. *The Merry Wives of Windsor*. In William Shakespeare. *Comedies, Histories and Tragedies*.

1623e. *The Taming of the Shrew*. In William Shakespeare. *Comedies, Histories and Tragedies*.

1623f. *The Tempest*. In William Shakespeare. *Comedies, Histories and Tragedies*.

Sharpam, Edward 1606. *The Fawn*. STC 17483.

Shaughnessy, Robert 2009. 'Accents yet unknown', paper delivered at the Barbican Centre, 21 November.

Shaw, George Bernard 1920. 'The Dying Tongue of Great Elizabeth', reprinted from *The Saturday Review*, February 1905. London: the London Shakespeare League.

Shaw, Jonathan 2014. 'Programme Note', deposited at the National Theatre Archive.

Sheldon, Esther Keck 1967. *Thomas Sheridan of Smock-Alley, recording his life as actor and theater manager in both Dublin and London; and including a Smock-Alley calendar for the years of his management*. Princeton: Princeton University.

Shellard, Dominic 1999. *British Theatre since the War*. New Haven, CT, and London: Yale University Press.

Shepherd, Simon 2006. *Theatre, Body and Pleasure*. London and New York: Routledge.

Sheridan, Thomas 1786, *Elements of English: Being a New Method of Teaching the Whole Art of Reading, both with Regard to Pronunciation and Spelling, Part the First*. London.

Shevtsova, Maria 2010. 'BITE at the Barbican' in *Theatre Quarterly* 26(3), 293–6.

Shilling, Jane 2012. 'Review' in *The Telegraph*, 9 August.

Shrank, Cathy 2012. 'The Formation of Nationhood' in Arthur Kinney ed. *The Oxford Companion to Shakespeare*, 571–86.

Shuttleworth, Ian 1993. 'Review' in *City Limits*, 28 January.

2006. 'Review' in *The Financial Times*, 13 June.

2011a. 'Review' in *The Financial Times*, 29 November.

2011b. 'Review' in *The Financial Times*, 1 December.

Siegmund, Gerald 2005. 'Voice Masks: Subjectivity, America, and the Voice in the Theatre of the Wooster Group' in Johan Callens, ed. *The Wooster Group and Its Traditions*, 167–78.

Simon, John 1969. 'My Throat Is in the Midlands' in *The New York Magazine*, 19 May.

Sinfield, Alan 1994. 'Royal Shakespeare: Theatre and the Making of Ideology' in Jonathan Dollimore and Alan Sinfield, eds. *Political Shakespeare: Essays in Cultural Materialism*, 182–205.

Smialkowska, Monika 2013. 'Review of *Julius Caesar*, Directed by Gregory Doran for the Royal Shakespeare Company' in Edmondson, Prescott and Sullivan eds. *A Year of Shakespeare: Re-living the World Shakespeare Festival*, 91–4.

Smith, Bruce R. 1999. *The Acoustic World of Early Modern England*. Chicago: Chicago University Press.

Smith, James M. 1998. 'Effaced History: Facing the Colonial Context of Ben Jonson's Irish Masque at Court' in *English Literary History* 65, 297–321.

Smith, Peter J. 2007. 'Michael Boyd Speaks to Peter J. Smith' *in Cahiers Élisabéthains* 71, 13–18.

2004. '*Romeo and Juliet*: Presented by the Globe Theatre' in *Shakespeare Bulletin* 22, 145–7.

Snyder, Susan, ed. 1998. *William Shakespeare: All's Well That Ends Well*. The Oxford Shakespeare. Oxford: Oxford University Press.

Spencer, Charles 1993. 'Review' in *The Daily Telegraph*, 25 January.

2006. 'Review' in *The Daily Telegraph*, 22 June.

2006a. 'Review' in *The Daily Telegraph*, 21 August.

2006b. 'Review' in *The Daily Telegraph*, 13 July.

2007. 'How to Massacre a Tragedy' in *The Telegraph*, 19 April.

2008. 'Review' in *The Telegraph*, 10 October.

Spoel, Philippa M. 2001, 'Rereading the Elocutionists: The Rhetoric of Thomas Sheridan's *A Course of Lectures in Elocution* and John Walker's *Elements of Elocution*' in *Rhetorica* 19(1), 49–91.

Sprague, Arthur Colby 1947. 'Shakespeare and William Poel' in *The University of Toronto Quarterly* 17, 1–37.

Steggle, Matthew 2004. *Richard Brome: Place and Politics on the Caroline Stage*. Manchester: Manchester University Press.

2016. 'Introduction', in *Richard Brome Online*. www.hrionline.ac.uk/brome/viewOriginal.jsp?play=EM&type=CRIT. Last accessed: 4 May 2016.

Stewart, Lauren Mary 2011. *The Representation of Northern English and Scots in Seventeenth Century Drama*. Ph.D. Dissertation, unpublished: University of Edinburgh.

Stow, John 1580. *The Chronicles of England from Brute vnto this present yeare of Christ. 1580*. STC 23333.

Sullivan, Erin 2014. 'Olympic Shakespeare and the Idea of Legacy: Culture, Capital and the Global Future', in Prescott and Sullivan, eds. *Shakespeare on the Global Stage: Performance and Festivity in the Olympic Year*, 283–320.

Supple, Tim 2006. 'Making the Dream: A Director's Story', Programme Note.

Swindells, Julia 2001. *Glorious Causes: The Grand Theatre of Political Change, 1789–1833*. Oxford: Oxford University Press.

Swindells, Julia and David Francis Taylor, eds. 2014. *The Oxford Handbook to Georgian Theatre, 1737–1832*. Oxford: Oxford University Press.

Szalwinska, Maxie 2018. 'Theatre Review: *Twelfth Night*, Young Vic' in *The Sunday Times*, 14 October. www.thetimes.co.uk/article/theatre-review-twelfth-night-young-vic-london-se1-27bwm2lh5. Last accessed: 8 November 2018.

T. D. 1608. *Essaies Politicke, and Morall*. STC 24396.

Taylor, Antony 2002. 'Shakespeare and Radicalism: The Uses and Abuses of Shakespeare in Nineteenth-Century Popular Politics' in *Historical Journal* 45, 357–79.

Taylor, Paul 1996. 'Review' in *The Independent*, 6 September.

  1997. 'Review' in *The Independent*. 20 August.

  1998. 'Review' in *The Independent*,.9 February.

  2006. 'Review' in *The Independent*, 12 July.

  2008. 'Review' in *The Independent*, 5 August.

  2013. 'Review' in *The Independent*, 26 July.

  2015. 'Review' in *The Independent*, 15 June.

Thieme, John A. 1975. 'Spouting, Spouting-Clubs and Spouting Companions' in *Theatre Notebook* 29, 9–18.

Thomaidis, Konstantinos 2017. *Theatre & Voice*. Basingstoke: Palgrave Macmillan.

Thompson, Ann 1987. *Shakespeare's Chaucer: A Study in Literary Origins*. Liverpool: University of Liverpool Press.

Thompson, Ayanna ed. 2006. 'Introduction', in *Color-Blind Shakespeare: New Perspectives on Race and Performance*. New York and London: Routledge, 1–26.

Thomson, Peter 2004a. 'David Garrick' in *ODNB*. www.oxforddnb.com/view/ 10.1093/ref:odnb/9780198614128.001.0001/odnb-9780198614128-e-10408?rskey=xvsvZH&result=1. Last accessed: 29 November 2017.

  2004b. 'Thomas Sheridan' in *The Oxford Dictionary of National Biography*. www.oxforddnb.com/view/10.1093/ref:odnb/9780198614128.001.0001/ odnb-9780198614128-e-25371?rskey=TAXg58&result=1. Last accessed: 27 November 2017.

Tilley, M. P. 1950. *A Dictionary of the Proverbs of England in the Sixteenth and Seventeenth Centuries: A Collection of the Proverbs found in English Literature and the Dictionaries of the Period*. Ann Arbor: University of Michigan Press.

Trewin, Ion 1973. 'Peter Daubeny; World Theatre's Inspiration' in *The Times*, 3 March.

Trudgill, Peter 2002. *Sociolinguistic Variation and Change*. Edinburgh: Edinburgh University Press.

Tudeau-Clayton, Margaret 2010. 'Shakespeare's "Welsch Men" and the "King's English"', in Maley and Schwyzer. *Shakespeare and Wales: From the Marches to the Assembly*, 91–110.

Upton, Clive 2008. 'Received Pronunciation' in Bernd Kortmann and Clive Upton, eds. *Varieties of English 1: The British Isles*. Berlin and New York: Mouton de Gruyter.

Various Artists 2000. *Great Historical Shakespeare Recordings*. Naxos Audio Books.

Verma, Jatinder 2008. 'What the Migrant Saw' in *The Guardian*, 10 January.

Wainwright, Jeffrey 1993. 'Review' in *The Independent*, 4 October.

Wales, Katie 2001. 'Varieties and Variation', in Sylvia Adamson, Lynette Hunter, Lynne Magnusson, Ann Thompson and Katie Wales, eds. *Reading Shakespeare's Dramatic Language: A Guide*, 192–209.

Walker, John 1791. *A Critical Pronouncing Dictionary and Expositor of the English Language*. London.

Wardle, Irving 1994. 'Review' in *The Independent*, 14 May.

Wells, J. C. 1999. 'British English Pronunciation Preferences: A Changing Scene' in *Journal of the International Phonetic Association* 29, 33–50.

Wells, Stanley and Gary Taylor 1987. *William Shakespeare: A Textual Companion*. Oxford: Clarendon Press.

Wells, Stanley and Sarah Stanton, eds. 2002. *The Cambridge Companion to Shakespeare on Stage*. Cambridge: Cambridge University Press.

Whitfield White, Paul and Suzanne Westfall, eds. 2002. *Shakespeare and Theatrical Patronage in Early Modern England*. Cambridge: Cambridge University Press.

Wilkinson, Robert 1602. *The Ievvell for the Eare*. STC 25652.7.

Wilson, Richard 2010. 'Cackling Home to Camelot: Shakespeare's Welsh Roots', in Maley and Schwyzer. *Shakespeare and Wales: From the Marches to the Assembly*, 191–210.

Wilson, Robert, Michael Drayton, Anthony Munday and Richard Hathaway 1600. *Sir John Oldcastle*. STC 18795.

Wilson, Thomas 1553. *The Arte of Rhetorique*. STC 25799.

Wolf, Matt 2018. 'Double, Double: Two Troublesome Takes on *Macbeth*' in *The New York Times*, 22 March. www.nytimes.com/2018/03/22/theater/macbeth-national-theater-royal-shakespeare-company.html. Last accessed: 8 November 2018.

Wood, Andy 1991. 'International theatre does not always turn out to be theatre of the world' in *The Guardian*, 6 August.

Woods, Leigh 1984. *Garrick Claims the Stage: Acting as Social Emblem in Eighteenth-Century England*. Westport, CT, and London: Greenwood Press.

Woods, Penelope 2013a. '*The Two Gentlemen of Verona*: Directed by Arne Pohlmeier for the Two Gents Theatre Company (Harare, Zimbabwe and London, UK)' in Edmondson, Prescott and Sullivan (eds), *One Year of Shakespeare: Re-living the World Shakespeare Festival*, 223–6.

Woods, Penelope 2013b. 'Two Gentlemen of Zimbabwe and Their Diaspora Audience', in Plastow ed. *African Theatre 12: Shakespeare in & out of Africa*, 13–27.

Worrall, David 2006. *Theatric Revolution: Drama, Censorship and Romantic Period Subcultures*. Oxford: Oxford University Press.

2007. *The Politics of Romantic Theatricality: The Road to the Stage*. Basingstoke: Palgrave Macmillan.

Worthen, William B. 2003. *Shakespeare and the Force of Modern Performance*. Cambridge: Cambridge University Press.

Woty, William 1760. 'The Spouting Club' in *The Shrubs of Parnassus*, 91–8.

1780?. *The Stage: A Poetical Epistle, to a Friend*. London.

Wright, Thomas 1604. *The Passions of the Minde*. STC 26040.

Index